THE HEEBIE-JEEBIES AT CBGB'S

A Secret History of Jewish Punk

Steven Lee Beeber

CHICAGO
REVIEW
PRESS

An A Cappella book

Library of Congress Cataloging-in-Publication Data
Beeber, Steven Lee.
    The heebie-jeebies at CBGB's : a secret history of Jewish punk / Steven Lee Beeber.
        p. cm.
    ISBN-13: 978-1-55652-613-8
    ISBN-10: 1-55652-613-X
    1. Punk rock music—New York (State)—New York—History and criticism. 2.
Jews—New York (State)—New York—Music—History and criticism. 3. CBGB
OMFUG (Nightclub) I. Title.
    ML3534.3.B44 2006
    781.66—dc22

                                                                        2006006259

Cover and interior design: Rattray Design
Cover photo: © Denis O'Regan/CORBIS

Published by Chicago Review Press, Incorporated
814 North Franklin Street
Chicago, Illinois 60610
ISBN-13: 978-1-55652-613-8
ISBN-10: 1-55652-613-X
Printed in the United States of America
5 4 3 2 1

For my parents, who made me a Jew
And for Dany, who kept me a punk

hee·bie·jee·bies pl.n. *Slang*
a feeling of uneasiness or nervousness; the jitters.

—*The American Heritage Dictionary of
the English Language,* 4th edition

Many people have wondered whence come the waves upon waves of musical slush that invade decent homes and set the young people of this generation imitating the drivel of morons. Popular music is a Jewish monopoly . . . a Jewish creation. The mush, slush, the sly suggestion, the abandoned sensuousness of sliding notes, are of Jewish origin.

—Henry Ford, *The International Jew,*
chapter 11, "Jewish Jazz Becomes Our
National Music"

You can't fully understand [Isaac] Babel unless you grasp the special strategy of Odessan-Jewish humor, the way it achieves its revenge on the world by proclaiming an ideal and then bringing down the roof both on the ideal and the joke teller . . . The more accurate comparison is with the German-Jewish poet Heinrich Heine, who loved to floridly express a romantic or heroic sentiment and then violently pull the rug out from underneath it. Heine, however, remained standing. The Odessan comedian tumbles along with the high sentiment, as if the only honest and convincing criticism of life were one that left nobody standing, including the critic.

—Lee Siegel, "The Tower of Babel,"
The Nation, December 5, 2005

As we survey Jewish history as a whole from the vantage point of the late twentieth century, Judah Halevi's phrase "prisoner of hope" seems entirely apposite. The prisoner of hope is sustained and encouraged by his hope, even as he is confined by it.

—*The Illustrated History of the Jewish People,*
Introduction, by Nicholas de Lange

ACKNOWLEDGMENTS

Completing this book was a bit like putting on a music festival: there was the idea, the booking, and then the show. Or, to put that otherwise: I had to figure out who to talk to, how to contact them, then hope that they would provide me with what I needed. All of this before the writing even began. Yet without this, I know I couldn't have written a damn thing.

On that note, I'd like to thank the following individuals who were invaluable performers, managers, and, in some cases, roadies. They include, in no particular order: Danny Fields, still the coolest guy in the room; Tommy Ramone, by far one of the most important; Chris Stein and Debbie Harry, both inspiring and entertaining in so many ways; Tish and Snooky Bellomo, the truest punks ever—and still; Lenny Kaye, the sage, the artist, and all-around very good guy; Andy Shernoff, Richard Blum, Scott Kempner, and J. P. Pattersen, the most benevolent of Dictators; John Felice, Jerry Harrison, Ernie Brooks, Asa Brebner, and Joe Harvard, the men who made Jonathan Richman come to life by proxy; Alan Vega, a true artist committed from the beginning; Hilly Kristal, the front door, backstage, and behind the bar of punk; Joey Ramone's mother, Charlotte, and brother, Mickey, both far more understanding and helpful than I deserved at times; John Holmstrom, the punk who put the PUNK in Punk; Malcolm McLaren, the master storyteller (and revealer of the *Cinq à Sept*); John Zorn, Marc Ribot, Anthony Coleman, and Gary Lucas, all "downtown" geniuses; Yuval Taylor, editor extraordinaire; David Dunton, agent to the stars; and, in too many ways to list here individually: Seth Abrams, Mariah Aguiar, Michael Alago, Odile Allard, Jonathan Ames, Johnny Angel, Nina Antonia, Al Aronowitz, Annalee Baker, Mike Barnes, Roberta Bayley, Priscilla Becker, Janette Beckman, Scott Beibin, Ishay Berger, David Berman, Jennifer Bleyer, Thelma Blitz, Steven Blush, Victor Bockris, Albert Bouchard, Joe Bouchard, Cory Brown, Daniel Brown,

Kitty Bruce, Bebe Buell, Paul Buhle, Lisa Burns, Curtis Cates, Stephanie Chernikowski, David Chevan, Robert Christgau, Douglas Clubok, Ira Cohen, Rich Cohen, Eli Consilvio, N. C. Christopher Couch, Stuart Cudlitz, David Dalton, Jed Davis, deerfrance, Hector DeJean, Carola Dibbell, Michael Dorf, Mike Edison, Stewart Edwards, Melanie Einzig, Will Eisner, Jon Espinosa, Rachel Felder, Billy Ficca, Eddi Fiegel, Jim Fields, Nat Finkelstein, Rami Fortis, Josh Frank, Nat Friedburg, Myra Friedman, Deborah Frost, Neil Gaiman, Elda Gentile, Gordon Gerbert, David Godlis, Annie Golden, Vivien Goldman, Toby Goldstein, Richard Gottehrer, Richard Grabel, Michael Gramalgia, Rina Gribovsky, Bob Gruen, Ruben Guzman, John Hagelston, Clinton Heylin, Craig Inciardi, Regina Joskow, Ivan Julian, Theresa Kereakes, Denis Kitchen, Young Kim, Howie Klein, Leah Kowalski, Tuli Kupferberg, Gary Kurfirst, Seth Kushner, Gary "Valentine" Lachman, Elizabeth Lamere, Nomy Lamm, Robin Lane, Ida Langsam, Lisa Law, Aaron Lefkove, Jenny Lens, Jonathan Lethem, Don Letts, William Levay, Alan Light, Lydia Lunch, Rhonda Markowitz, Jim Marshall, Bill May, Gillian McCain, Dennis McGuire, Claire Moed, Monte Melnick, Richard Meltzer, Allan Metz, Rebecca Metzger, Sylvia Miles, Steve Miller, Tim Mitchell, Amir Neubach, Molly Neuman, David Nobakht, Liz Nord, Glenn O'Brien, Joshua Olesker, Kevin Patrick, Bart Plantenga, Amos Po, Yonatan Pollack, Martin Popoff, Ron Pownall, Jack Rabid, Maria Raha, Marky Ramone, J. J. Rassler, Genya Ravan, Marcia Resnick, Daniel Rey, Ira Robbins, Peter Robbins, Joel Rose, Charlie Roth, Robin Rothman, Alan Sacks, Camilla Saly, Eve Schlapik, Andy Schwartz, Frank Secich, George Seminara, Sylvie Simmons, James Sliman, Larry "Ratso" Sloman, Leif Sorensen, Rav Shmuel, Kate Simon, Linda Stein, Phil Strongman, Studio Stu, Mark Suall, Allan Tannenbaum, Rob Tannenbaum, Marvin Taylor, Seth Tobocman, Lynne Tillman, Everett True, Steven Tyler, Arturo Vega, Arjen Veldt, Holly Vincent, Susan Wegzyn, David Wheeler, Lee Wolfberg, Allison Wolfe, Russell Wolinsky, Jimmy Wynbrandt, Tommy Wynbrandt, Ayelet Yagil, and anyone else whom I may have neglected to mention here, though you know who you are and how much you meant every step of the way. Thanks, I say to you, thanks, thanks, and thanks.

I would like to add that there are a number of people whom I never actually got to meet for this book, but whose stories, in the minds of their friends and families, made me only want to know them all the more. So, my final acknowledgments go to Robert Quine and Joey Ramone. I can only hope the world speaks as well of me when I'm gone as it does of you.

CONTENTS

INTRODUCTION

The punks were *Jewish*?!

*—answering the question I've been asked
repeatedly while writing this book*

Punk is Jewish. Not Judaic. Jewish, the reflection of a culture that's three millennia old now. It reeks of humor and irony and preoccupations with Nazism. It's all about outsiders who are "one of us" in the shtetl of New York. It's about nervous energy, the same nervous energy that has characterized Jews from Abraham, Isaac, and Jacob through the Hasids to the plays of David Mamet. Punks, like Jews, self-consciously identify with the sick and twisted, what Hitler referred to as "the decadent." Punk's home is the home of the Jews—New York, especially downtown Lower East Side/East Village New York, the birthplace of this new music known for its populist vibe, its revolutionary attitudes, its promotion of do-it-yourself like some sort of anarchist mantra.

It's not just that so many in the music, as well as so many in the audience, happen to be Jewish, among them Lou Reed, Joey and Tommy Ramone, the Dictators, Richard Hell, Malcolm McLaren, Lenny Kaye, Genya Ravan, Chris Stein, Jonathan Richman, and Helen Wheels. Punk reflects the whole Jewish history of oppression and uncertainty, flight and wandering, belonging and not belonging, always being divided, being both in and out, good and bad, part and apart. The shpilkes, the nervous energy, of punk is Jewish. That shpilkes, the "Heebie Jeebies" of Little Richard's song, captures exactly what was happening in the Bowery as the first generation to come of age after the Holocaust made its mark on popular music at a little Jewish-owned and -run club called CBGB.

There, along with their non-Jewish brethren, the children of Hitler's genocide formed a Jewish American tradition that mixed optimism with cynicism. Like their forebears, George Gershwin, Aaron Copland, Leonard Bernstein, and Philip Glass (not to mention Irving Berlin, Jerome Kern, Carole King, and Bob Dylan), they merged the high and low cultures of America's elite and street life, creating a hybrid rock art, a conceptual music played by amateurs who could barely figure out chord changes—or if they could, tried their best not to show it.

This dance between proficiency and authenticity, gloom and hope, Jewish and Gentile is essential to punk, just as it has been essential to the Jewish experience. In this middle ground where humor helps to ease the divide, the Jewishness of punk was hidden only to those who couldn't read the script. The punks were sarcastic, cutting to the bone. Their smartass humor made you think—and perhaps change your views—when you least expected to. Ironically, they were barely conscious of this at the time, yet their personal "politics" became a part of their message. Their embrace of "freaks" and outcasts raised those figures to the heights of rock royalty in the public mind. The sexy stud reeking of cool was no longer the king of the hipster heap. The loser became the winner. The last became the first. Women swooned for the consummate New York Jew, Woody Allen, while men pondered what it meant to be a man in the wake of the neurotic comic's success.

Their parents had escaped New York, and the punks returned, bringing a pulse beat back to the long-dead tenements and shotgun shacks of the Lower East Side, hot music to the down-and-out Bowery, all of them flocking to CBGB, where the workers of a musical revolution shouted out their message:

"We are the blank generation, and we can take or leave it each time . . ."
"We're a happy family, we're a happy family, we're a happy family . . ."
"Gabba gabba hey, gabba gabba hey . . ."
"Jesus died for somebody's sins, but not mine . . ."
"Cause you know baby / I'm the next big thing."

And they were, and are, the next big thing. Yes, they were the blank generation, but as Richard Hell explained, that didn't mean they didn't care. They were looking for a way to fill in the emptiness, create new identities, and make new worlds for themselves. In that no-man's-land between the old Yiddish theater district and the ground zero of the Jewish American experience, they invented the punk sound that continues to be heard to this day. This book shows how that sound cannot be separated from their Jewishness.

1

THE PROTOCOLS OF THE ELDERS OF PUNK

Lenny Bruce: The Patron Saint of Jewish New York

There is a real common ground with the punk sensibility and the basic Jewish, Lenny Bruce, show-biz culture. There is something just generally punkish about the whole [thing]—I mean, what we see as punk, if you really break it down, I mean, what is it? It's sort of anti-establishment, and all that. Elements of it sort of remind me of the standard Jewish comedian thing. Maybe that's part of why it came out of New York. It's a smartass town. To me, it seems related.

—Chris Stein, 2004

In the beginning was the word, and the word was *fuck*.

No, wait, it was *nigger*.

No, *niggerlover*.

Motherfucker!

Cocksucker!!

Chickenfucker!!!

We'll begin again.

In the beginning was Lenny Bruce, the comedian of dirty words, the taboo-breaking social critic who died like a martyr in his own land. A quintessential New Yorker, a quintessential Jew, he raised street smarts to a searing

1

art. Punk musicians regard him as their patron saint. Many of the nearly 150 people interviewed for this book spoke of Bruce as the most important influence in their lives before the Beatles. Bruce showed Joey Ramone, Chris Stein, and Handsome Dick Manitoba how to behave like cool kids. He was the only adult they respected. Like them, Bruce was first and foremost a smartass.

Born in 1925 as Leonard Alfred Schneider to a stage mother who was a smalltime performer, Bruce epitomizes showbiz tradition in American Jewish culture, particularly New York Jewish culture. Jews predominated in Tin Pan Alley, Broadway, early nickelodeons (the precursors to Hollywood studios), comic books, radio, television, the Brill Building, The Velvet Underground, and punk. Bruce honed his craft as a truth-telling badass in strip clubs, gin joints, and broken-down burlesque houses where the comic was a filler between the acts, a dirty-joke teller who kept the audience in their seats while the girls went out for a cigarette and a shot. He was ready to move into the higher leagues by the 1950s, but like the punk rockers who followed him, he found that to succeed he had to bring the crassness of the streets along with him. In the end, he brought smartass aboveground, where it was uneasily tolerated by society.

"He was just so sarcastic," as Chris Stein puts it. "He was cool and uncompromising and he had street smarts." Stein comments that it wasn't until he was in his forties and listening again to Bruce's Carnegie Hall concert bit about his "Shiksa Goddess" wife, Honey, that he realized "how much that was like me and Debbie [Harry]."

It's not too surprising that early punk rockers worshipped Bruce. They came of age when Bruce was in his prime, a time when a new dark manifestation of the city's largest immigrant group was emerging, one that grew in the shadows of the Holocaust and burst out in *shpilkes*-like heebie-jeebies ready to exorcise those things that went bump in Elie Wiesel's night. Jewish stars like Dustin Hoffman, Elliott Gould, and George Segal ruled the screen. Philip Roth, Norman Mailer, and Bernard Malamud claimed the bestseller list. Jewish musicians like Philip Glass led the avant-garde in such a way that the classical establishment attacked him for bringing the music perilously close to pop, while Jewish artists like Diane Arbus photographed freaks; "A Jewish Giant at Home with His Parents" seems to foretell the emergence of Israel as an occupying oppressor—not to mention the emergence of Jeffry Hyman/Joey Ramone as a star.

"There is a real common ground with the punk sensibility and the basic Jewish, Lenny Bruce, show-biz culture," says Chris Stein. "There is something just generally punkish about the whole [thing]—I mean, what we see as punk, if you really break it down, I mean, what is it? It's sort of anti-establishment, and all that. Elements of it sort of remind me of the standard Jewish comedian thing. Maybe that's part of why it came out of New York. It's a smartass town. To me, it seems related."

And, indeed, it is. From the moment in 1654 when a group of twenty-three Sephardic *judíos* landed at New Amsterdam, seeking asylum from the Brazilian Inquisition (they were only saved from incarceration by the protests of Jewish shareholders on the board of the Dutch West India Company), to the point nearly two hundred years later when a larger influx of Enlightenment-liberated *Juden* from Germany began arriving, to the period less than fifty years after that when a much larger and more culturally significant influx of *Yidn* from Eastern Europe began coming (and coming and coming, close to three million by the 1920s, two-thirds of these staying in New York), there was a tug between Nice Jewish Boys, who sought respectability and acceptance, and Bad Ass Heebs, who wanted nothing more than to shock you with sick jokes.

For every Haym Solomon, financier of the American Revolution, Solomon Schechter, Jewish educator, and Louis Brandeis, Supreme Court justice, there was an entertainer, gangster, or political rabble-rouser with a name like Eddie Iskowitz (Eddie Cantor), Samuel Gompers (who founded the American Federation of Labor), and Benjamin "Bugsy" Siegel. Working outside polite society, these men created cool as we know it. Eddie Cantor led directly to Woody Allen and Ali G; Samuel Gompers set the stage for Abbie Hoffman and Jerry Rubin; and Bugsy Siegel, not to mention his original boss and inspiration, Arnold Rothstein, helped to create the fashionably attired sex symbol oozing menace. Lucky Luciano said of Rothstein, "He taught me how to dress. He taught me how to not wear loud things, how to have good taste . . . he was . . . real smooth." Lucky could just as well have been describing Richard Meyers Hell's influence on Malcolm McLaren and the Sex Pistols. He could have been talking about any rock star.

Most prominent Jewish Americans, of course, fell somewhere in the middle. Among them were Hollywood moguls Samuel Goldwyn (Samuel Goldfish), Jack Warner (John Leonard Eichelbaum), and Louis B. Mayer (Eliezer Meir). Al Jolson (Asa Yoelson) was a first-generation New Yorker who, like the character he portrayed in the first talkie, *The Jazz Singer* (1927), epitomized the tug between the old world and new. Defying his cantor father to pursue popular music, Jolson paved the way for numerous others, such as Fanny Brice (Fanny Borach), John Garfield (Julius Garfinkle), Molly Picon (Margaret Pyekoon), and the Borscht Belt comics, all of whom embodied the cultural conflict at the heart of Jolson's largely autobiographical film.

Fanny Brice, the darling of vaudeville-bred Tin Pan Alley, joked about the old ways while spicing up her act with a sexuality that played on the public's perception of "Jewesses" as exotic, sensual "others." John Garfield, on the other hand, took an angry, almost punkish stance toward attempts to exclude him, repeatedly playing a character who was attached to his "East Side" (code for ethnic/Jewish) origins, yet was ready to use his fists to punish any slights. Molly Picon withdrew into a sentimental world that disappeared along with the East Side's many Yiddish theaters, while the comics of the Borscht Belt, among them Henny Youngman, Buddy Hackett (Leonard Hacker), and Jerry Lewis (Jerome Levitch), created a new, cutting, self-deprecating Jewish identity that could clearly mock power but instead chose to direct its anger at itself.

Beginning as a *tumler* (master of ceremonies) in the Catskills, Lewis morphed into a personification of impotent anger and self-hatred. As B. Kite writes, Lewis was in the main a physical comic, but unlike Chaplin, he exhibited alienation from his body rather than grace. As a result, Kite says, critics often attacked him for being "too 'ethnic' (read: Jewish), and [having] an unhealthy tendency to go 'nantz.'" Kite added, "Jewishness and sissiness were often seen as equivalents." Eventually, Lewis shirked this eternal child as jerk mode, playing the Rat Pack–like punk Buddy Love opposite the bucktoothed scientist Julius Kelp in the Jekyll-and-Hyde spoof *The Nutty Professor* (1963)—a transformation from schlemiel to hipster that Mickey Leigh (Mitchell Hyman) referred to when he said that his brother, Joey Ramone, had "changed when he'd gotten onstage, almost like Jerry Lewis in *The Nutty Professor.*" Lewis also directly addressed his Jewishness in a made-for-TV version of *The Jazz Singer* (1961) and in a never-released film, *The Day the Clown Cried*, which he starred in and directed about a clown who entertains children on their way to the gas chambers.

In short, almost all of the comedians entertained both the Jewish and non-Jewish worlds even as they internalized their exclusion and accepted it. That is, until Lenny Bruce.

A tough outsider who not only mixed with strippers, junkies, and hepcats (in the minds of traditionalists, the dreaded goyim), Bruce also functioned as a social critic while openly referring to his Jewishness. Yiddish phrases and jokes and kamikaze-style humor that actually risked using the Holocaust as material were all hallmarks of Bruce's act—indeed, they were the components that often got the biggest laughs in his day, just as they continued to do decades later when Bruce was embraced by the emerging punks.

From the confrontational Bruce, there's a clear line to the social-critiquing Bob Dylan, the social-mocking Tuli Kupferberg, and the social underbelly–exposing Lou Reed. Dylan, who praised Bruce in song ("he was the brother that you never had . . ."), is the consummate outsider with a moral conscience, a "voice of a generation" who defended blacks ("The Lonesome Death of Hattie Carol"), immigrants ("I Pity the Poor Immigrant"), convicts ("Hurricane"), and even Israel ("The Neighborhood Bully"), all while preaching like an Old Testament prophet warning the people of destruction both actual ("A Hard Rain's Gonna Fall") and moral ("Frankie Lee and Judas Priest"). It's not too hard to imagine Dylan onstage reading court transcripts, as Lenny Bruce did near the end of his career, nor too difficult to envision Fugs cofounder and self-proclaimed "old time Jewish anarchist" Tuli (short for the Hebrew "Naphtali") Kupferberg being banned for gleefully shouting out Bruce's infamously dirty words. In fact, it's pretty easy to see early Fugs contemporary Lou Reed backing up Tuli on guitar while occasionally taking the mike to shout about being a white boy waiting uptown for his connection (a black man who provides both figurative and literal spiritual uplift) or his anger at the hypocrisy of onetime presidential candidate Jesse Jackson, who referred to New York City as "Hymietown."

These precursors helped create not just the setting, but also the musical and lyrical template for what was soon to become punk rock. They range from Jonathan Richman, a Boston acolyte of Reed's Velvet Underground who imparted his cool nerd, outsider sensibility to New York via the Modern Lovers, to Eric Bloom (singer), Sandy Pearlman (manager/lyricist), and Richard Meltzer (lyricist) of the Blue Öyster Cult, all of whom incorporated Nazi imagery, stripped-down power chords, and comedic purpose into their music, fueling an ironic strain of "light metal" that bore deep resemblances to punk.* Pearlman and Meltzer later played an integral role in creating New York punk by defining and championing it as critics, as did numerous other Jewish music writers, such as Lenny Kaye, Lisa Robinson, Jon Landau, and Billy Altman.

Punk architect Tommy Erdelyi pays tribute to these bands and others: "The Blue Öyster Cult was like an intellectual's version of a heavy metal band and they inspired me in many ways—just as did Leslie West of Mountain. When I was growing up in Forest Hills, West was still playing with the Vagrants, perhaps the first real band to emerge in the New York scene. I mean, there were the Rascals from Long Island, but the Vagrants were more like the real thing—a garage band with a monstrous sound. And they looked like us, like kids in my mostly Jewish neighborhood. They made me think putting together a band might be possible."

Others echo these sentiments and more. Here's Richard "Handsome Dick Manitoba" Blum on the creation of the Dictators' comic persona: "I'm a Jew. I grew up around lots of Italians and Jews in the Bronx and I understood the way we were an oppressed people who had to fight back to survive and how we often did that with comedy. The Dictators were funny—as were all of the early punk bands to varying degrees. You wouldn't be wrong to say that I was doing stand up onstage between songs—that's why we left the spoken word bits between tracks on the first album, the ones where I'm talking about making it big and retiring to Florida. I mean, just look at our name for Christ's sake! The Dictators! Get it?"

The Patti Smith Group's musical mastermind Lenny Kaye, originally a rock critic best known for compiling *Nuggets*, a collection of 1960s garage tunes that later influenced many of the punk bands, says: "Jews have always been a writerly race . . . what is the Bible but an explication of art's implications . . . and what are biblical scholars but critics of the Bible? I like to see

---

*A separate book could be written about the large number of Jewish performers in heavy metal, among them: Geddy Lee of Rush, who earned his stage name through his heavily accented Jewish grandmother's inability to pronounce "Gary"; Leslie West (Leslie Weinstein) of Mountain, best known for "Mississippi Queen"; Scott Ian (Scott Ian Rosenfeld) of Anthrax; and Gene Simmons (Chaim Witz) and Paul Stanley (Stanley Harvey Eisen) of KISS. In Twisted Sister alone, there's Jay Jay French (John Segal), who supposedly played in a pre-KISS band called Rainbow with Simmons and Stanley; Mark "the Animal" Mendoza, who helped transform Twisted Sister from a glam band in the mode of the New York Dolls to a metal one after coming over from the all-Jewish Dictators; and Dee Snider, who, though not Jewish, does have a paternal Jewish grandfather.

myself as part of that tradition . . . I like to think of myself as a scholar of the Talmud of rock 'n' roll."

Ultimately, the Jewish aspect of New York culture influenced to varying degrees even a non-Jewish band such as the Dead Boys—just as the non-Jewish aspect of the city's culture affected many of the largely Jewish bands. The Dictators (five-sixths Jewish), the Ramones (at least half-Jewish), and numerous other bands built on a tradition of cultural "collaboration" that stretched back at least as far as Irving Berlin's wedding of Jewish folk music (or klezmer) to American jazz (one of his early hits was "Yiddle on Your Fiddle Play Some Ragtime," 1909). The "immigrant" Dead Boys from Cleveland, an industrial city with a large German/Slavic population, arrived in New York looking and sounding like a heavy metal band. They quickly transformed themselves into crazed, sick, comically demented pranksters who liked to dress in Nazi regalia and, offstage, sleep almost exclusively with Jewish girls, often atop a Nazi flag while wearing a swastika. Lead guitarist Cheetah Chrome's half-Jewish former girlfriend Gyda Gash has the word "stigmata" tattooed on one arm and a Jewish star on the other. She comments, "What do you expect from a self-loathing half-Jew?"

There's no denying that, on some level, the "self-loathing" Gash half-jokingly describes deeply informed New York punk. The emergence of Israel as a national power* and an awareness of the Holocaust were of supreme importance to it. As audience members, performers, and behind-the-scenes players have revealed in interviews, these realities created a split Jewish consciousness that felt pride in the newfound power of Israel even as it experienced shame—and anger—at a history of victimization in Europe.

This transformation of Jewish consciousness couldn't help but have an effect on punk, as the New York audience that first accepted the music was either Jewish or, at the very least, schooled in Jewishness. So were the music's critics (Meltzer et al.), producers (child of Holocaust survivors Genya Ravan, etc.), deejays (Alan Freed created the term "rock 'n' roll"), managers (Iggy Pop and MC5 discoverer Danny Fields), executives (Sire Records president Seymour Stein) club owners (CBGB's founder Hilly Kristal), publicists (Orthodox Jew Ida Langsam, who before handling the Ramones, created the

---

*Following its victories in the Six-Day War of 1967 and the Yom Kippur War of 1974. It's also important to note that while the first victory established a new image of Jews as tough fighters, the second led to the unheard-of association of Jews with occupation and dominance.

punning *Apple Juice* newsletter as president of the Beatles New York Fan Club), roadies (Ramones "tour director" Monte Melnick), groupies (Nancy Spungen), "translators" (Sex Pistols "creator" Malcolm McLaren), and many, many others.

They all welcomed this new music and lifestyle that were both outside the mainstream, yet as close-knit (especially in the East Village) as a shtetl. It was a celebration of the degenerate (as Hitler termed Jewish art), the sick (as critics described Lenny Bruce), and the alienated (as Jewish writer Franz Kafka called himself), not to mention the socially outrageous (think the Marx Brothers with ripped T-shirts) and comic ("If it wasn't funny, it wasn't punk," says Snooky Bellomo).

Only in New York, that city where, as Lenny Bruce said, "It doesn't matter if you're Catholic . . . you're Jewish," could a "popular" art form like punk have found a birthplace. There, on that island of immigrants, where Jews formed such a sizable portion of the population, they could take their Jewishness and all its intellectual, nonviolent, comic-driven aspects for granted. Joey Ramone, a figure straight out of Kafka's *The Metamorphosis*, Richard Hell, a Jewish mother's worst nightmare, and Lenny Kaye, a kind of post-1960s Jewish mystic, rose up, ready to take over the world. They didn't, of course—at least not in their time. But for a few years, at least, they reigned as gods on that island where they had been born, raised, and nurtured, that city that had formed them, Hymietown.

Lenny Bruce's daughter, Kitty, who in the late 1970s performed at CBGB with her band, The Great Must Ache (The Great Mistake), comments, "My father was a very spiritual man, highly spiritual. Religious? No. But part of his Jewishness was he grew up in Long Island, he lived in Brooklyn—and he did comparisons between Miracle Whip being goyish and mustard being Jewish. So it's a way of life. . . . And punk? I think [my father] would have found it *very* interesting. It's a subculture that became a culture. It *also* became a way of life."

In other words, it didn't matter if it was known as punk. If it had those components of New York culture that Lenny Bruce epitomized, it was Jewish.

2

THE PUNK ZEYNE

Lou Reed: The Godfather of (Jewish) Punk

I wanna be a Panther / have a girlfriend named Samantha / keep a stable of foxy whores / and fuck up the Jews.

> —Lou Reed, "I Wanna Be Black"
> (*Street Hassle*, 1978)

Nico was fond of asking "Are there any Jewwwwwwwwwwwwws in the audience?"

> —Richard Witt, *Nico: The Life and Lies of an Icon*

Friday afternoon, just before Passover 2004, a phone rings in Michael Dorf's Tribeca condo. The former impresario of the Knitting Factory, for many years the leading venue for avant-garde music in the city, Dorf rolls his eyes as he pads along his throw rugs, wondering what this next call can be about. Tomorrow he will be hosting the Downtown Seder, a gathering of artists, writers, musicians, and other hip Jews coming together to celebrate the holiday, and he's nervous and frazzled and tired of calls.

"Michael, can you get me seats for the Seder? Laurie's relatives are in town. We need four spots."

It takes a second for Dorf to place that most distinctive of voices.

"Lou?"

"Yeah. You wanted me at this Seder, right? I'll need some seats."

Two months ago, Dorf tried to get Reed to take part, never to hear back from him. Now it's hours away from the event, and Dorf is exhausted. But this is Lou Reed, cofounder of the ultimate New York band, the songwriter who made the record players of America's youth safe for masochists, drug addicts, leather fetishists, and street punks.

"Of course you can come, no problem."

A half-hour later, Reed calls back.

"Michael," Reed says. "Mich-a-el. We need to bring our dog."

"You're kidding, right?"

"No. But it's a small dog."

"Well, I don't know."

Reed hangs up.

Twenty minutes later an e-mail arrives.

"So, just to let you know, our dog is really small. Really small, and it's a Jewish dog. So come on, let the dog come to the Seder."

Dorf spends the remainder of the day convincing the museum where the event is taking place to allow a dog on its premises. Then he gives Reed an assignment of sorts for the Seder, "four other questions" to complement the traditional four asked by the youngest member in attendance. These questions will be from Reed's latest album, a reinterpretation of Edgar Allen Poe's "The Raven."

When the *alter kocker* (old shit) indie rocker asks to take part, you grab him while you can. The *zeyde* (grandfather) of punk doesn't usually play the prodigal son. In fact, he rarely even refers to his Jewishness. If you can get him by mixing the Raven and the Jewish god, then that's what you better do, putz.

*   *   *

When Lou Reed was first making himself into the Godfather of Punk, he seemed to be doing everything he could to distance himself from his Jewishness. He had conked his "Jewfro" in the manner of black performers like Little Richard and James Brown who were trying to look whiter, and had written songs whose sadomasochism was the antithesis of socially responsible secular Jewish American morality. He'd also entered the world of Andy

Warhol's Factory—as blue-blood, Gentile, and moneyed as the social register or the DAR—there all but adopting Warhol as a father while falling "head over heels" in love, as John Cale puts it, with the German-born ice princess Nico, whose brother was a member of the Hitler Youth during World War II, and who eventually drove Reed to what appears to have been a suicide attempt when she told him, in front of The Velvet Underground, "I can not make love to Jews anymore."

Reed was not exactly the nice Jewish boy in those days. Or he didn't seem to be on the surface. And yet, in looking back at the years leading up to that pivotal event and then further ahead at much of what came after it, one can see that essentially Reed was always as Jewish as they come. As Jewish as that punk patron saint Lenny Bruce, to whom the teenage Reed had turned as a role model.

*   *   *

Born in Brooklyn in 1942 to George Sidney Reed (an accountant) and Toby Futterman Reed (a former beauty queen), Lewis Allen Reed was in many ways the All-American-Jewish-Kid. Growing up in Freeport, Long Island, where his parents felt they could find those all-important essentials to a brighter future—respectability and class—Reed, like so many others of his generation, found instead suburban alienation and resentment.

Less than a year after the Reeds moved to Freeport, the then twelve-year-old Lou embraced, to his parents' regret, the world of rock 'n' roll—or its initial manifestation, rhythm and blues. Reed's biographer Victor Bockris, in his book *Transformer*, describes the family as increasingly troubled by Reed's interest in the music, worrying that it would derail him from his, or rather *their*, plan that he become a doctor or, like his father, an accountant. Keeping a wary eye on their son's increasing moodiness, they hoped for the best, even as they indulged his more outlandish desires, such as his demand that he be given an electric guitar and, a couple of years later, a motorcycle.

In "Standing on Ceremony," a song Reed claims to have written for his mother, he answers his parents' fears with his own attack: "Remember your manners, will you please take your hat off, your mother is dying, listen to her cough. We were always standing on ceremony, we were always standing on ceremony" (*Growing Up in Public*, 1980). This sterile world of manners and propriety rankled Reed, as it did many of his generation. The so-called generation gap—all the wider for Jewish Baby Boomers—largely resulted from the disjunct these kids felt between their comfortable circumstances and those of their forebears. Like Reed, the grandson of Russian Jews fleeing anti-Semitism, the Jewish Baby Boomers knew that their grandparents and, to a lesser extent, their parents had known hard times. They knew that the lives they'd fled had contained ghettos, pogroms, and even death camps. Yet, at the same time, they knew that those lives had contained a multitude of positive experiences that were forever lost to their American descendants. As even Stalin had observed, albeit disparagingly, Jewish "cosmopolitans" had helped make European cities vibrant centers of cultural excitement.

Growing up in the suburbs, divorced from his past (his father had changed the family name from Rabinowitz when Lou was one year old), aware on some level that kids just like himself were being rounded up and gassed in Europe, Reed would have had plenty to feel angry, or at least nervous, about. Prominent anti-Semites only a few years earlier, such as radio preacher Father Coughlin and auto magnate Henry Ford, had reflected a general distaste for Jews among the American populace. As Bockris notes, even in childhood Reed exhibited that heebie-jeebies–like condition known as *shpilkes*. "The small, thin child with kinky black hair" perhaps suffered from the overprotective "Jewish mother syndrome" (according to a family friend), or perhaps was hurt by his father's "sarcastic Jewish sense of humor,"* which Reed clearly displayed on his album-as-stand-up-routine, *Take No Prisoners: Live*. Perhaps he was a taboo-breaking bisexual (though evidence suggests he may have been feigning effeminacy to torment his parents). Or, most damning of all, perhaps he was a victim of what Albert Goldman, in his biography of Lenny Bruce (*Ladies and Gentlemen, Lenny Bruce!!*) called "Jewish love": "Jewish love is love, all right, but it's mingled with such a big slug of pity, cut with so much condescension, embittered with so much tacit disapproval, disapprobation, even disgust, that when you are the object of this love, you might as well be an object of hate. Jewish love made Kafka feel like a cockroach."

---

*Lawrence Epstein says in his study of Jewish humor, *The Haunted Smile* (Public Affairs, 2001), "As the children of immigrants, [Jews] were neither insiders, privy to power or easy passage through American life, nor outsiders, living in a foreign country dreaming of America as the Golden Land. This precarious identity provided a particular perspective, a skepticism about life in general, a distrust of institutions, and a palpable anxiety that sometimes found its way into humor."

Whatever the case, one thing's for sure. When Reed began riding around his neighborhood on a motorcycle, a guitar strapped across his back, a sneer on his face in imitation of Lenny Bruce and Marlon Brando, his parents, who'd heard more than enough from their son about his intention to become a musician, reacted, determined to put him "right." They weren't about to see him turn into some sort of beatnik fag folksinger. They were going to nip this thing in the bud even if it meant subjecting their teenage son to procedures worthy of that Eastern European crypto-Jew, Dr. Frankenstein. They allowed doctors to administer electroshock treatments nearly twenty-five times during the summer between Reed's junior and senior years. They let those medical men play with his brain in an attempt to save the respectability of his soul.

*　　*　　*

Reed refers to the shock treatments as one of the pivotal events of his life. He says that on the one hand, they taught him the power of electricity and so of electric music, and that on the other, they wiped out much of his memory and left him despairing of ever becoming a writer. *Village Voice* freelancer Jim (Antonicello) Marshall, who was friendly with Reed's guitarist, Robert Quine, says the doctors at the clinic "would show him pictures of naked men, and if he got a hard-on he would get zapped with this electric pulse." Marshall goes on to say that Reed's mother was "an ex-beauty queen . . . and really uptight," while Bockris adds that Reed never forgave her or his father for their "treachery" in allowing the treatments. Reed refers to this directly in his song "Kill Your Sons" (*Sally Can't Dance*, 1974):

> *All your two-bit psychiatrists*
> *are giving you electroshock. . . .*
> *Don't you know they're gonna kill your sons. . . .*

As Bockris observes, Reed felt that if his parents really loved him, they would never have permitted the treatments.

Of course, the treatments backfired. Within months Reed was a student at Syracuse University, where he set about breaking with his past. And yet, being on some level a nice Jewish boy, he couldn't quite leave his old life behind. Instead, he danced back and forth between his old world and his new one. He chose to major in English rather than something more sensible that would lead to a professional career, but he did *go* to college. He refused to join a frat—much less a *Jewish* frat—but he did *allow* himself to be adopted as mascot by the "more socially progressive" Sigma Alpha Mu house, offering himself up to the nice Jewish "Sammies" as a vicarious, wild-eyed extension of their inner bad boys. Bockris notes that Jewish fraternities were not only "more socially progressive" during that time, but also that they "would provide some of the most receptive of Lou Reed's audiences throughout his career."

Perhaps most telling, though Reed skipped classes and played in black bars with his band LA and the Eldorados (for Lewis, his first name, and Allen, the first name of his childhood friend, Allen Hyman), he chose as his roommate the very Jewish New Yorker Lincoln Swados, and as his girlfriend the equally Jewish midwesterner Shelly Albin. As Bockris says, Lincoln came from one of those "classic New York Jewish intellectual families" that displayed all the interest in culture and thought Reed's parents had sacrificed in their effort to be socially acceptable. Shelly, on the other hand, though a wild child herself, was the daughter of parents much like Reed's own. When Lou finally brought her home for a weekend, an event he'd put off for months, his parents saw her as a perfect match for their son. Shelly understood that Lou had conflicted feelings toward his parents. He wanted to please them and prove that he was worthy of their respect, but he resented them, presumably for the electroshock and for their refusal to recognize his musical talent. She could also see that their efforts at welcoming her into the family were doomed because Lou was determined to upset them, no matter what. "He was just impossible," says Shelly. "I'd never seen so much anger in my life and it scared me." By the time she and Lou had returned to the Reed family for a second visit more than two years later, Lou had gotten his "revenge," as she puts it. Shelly now had dyed hair and dressed like "Miss Trash," Lou's new pet name for her. As Shelly says, Reed's parents "saw this nice, wholesome girl turned into trash and they said, 'Oh my God, Lou has done it again. He has ruined somebody, he has won.'"

In terms of his musical career, Lou's English teacher at Syracuse, Delmore Schwartz, influenced him as much or more than his roommate or girlfriend. Lou described Schwartz as "the wandering Jew," Bloom to his Dedalus (the lead characters in James Joyce's modernist classic *Ulysses*). A tragic figure in Jewish-American literary history, Schwartz is today probably best known through Saul Bellow's thinly veiled portrait of him in the novel *Humboldt's*

Gift. Bellow, himself Jewish-American, tells the story of a gifted youth who is accepted as a literary star in the 1930s despite the fact he's Jewish. Acclaimed for his poetry and stories, Humboldt becomes increasingly distrustful of his own talent. While others, both Jewish and not, follow in his literary footsteps, Humboldt the man begins to see anti-Semitism everywhere. Bellow shows that Humboldt's madness grows in part from his perception that the Nazis, anti-Semitic FBI men, and Holocaust victims he imagines on his doorstep do, in fact, populate 1950s New York, though they may not really threaten him.

Schwartz began his career like Humboldt, acclaimed for his poetry and short stories, then quickly saw his talent plummet. He, too, reacted by descending into bitterness, paranoia, and madness. Unlike Humboldt, however, Schwartz had been troubled even at the beginning of his career. In one of his earliest and best short stories, "In Dreams Begin Responsibilities," a narrator dreams that he goes to a movie theater and begins to watch a picture, slowly realizing that it tells the story of his parents' meeting and courtship. The movie quickly becomes a nightmare of the horrors that await his parents, including their psychic confusion as Jewish immigrants and his own birth and troubled life. In a story composed soon after as a sort of companion piece, "America! America!," Schwartz returns more explicitly to the troubled bond between Jews of his generation and their parents. "[He] was exhausted by his mother's story. He was sick of the mood in which he had listened, the irony and contempt which had taken hold of each new event. He had listened from such a distance that what he saw was an outline, a caricature, and an abstraction . . . but there existed also an unbreakable unity. As the air was full of radio's unseen voices, so the life he breathed in was full of these lives and the age in which they had acted and suffered." (*In Dreams Begin Responsibilities and Other Stories*).

When Schwartz met Reed, he was only six years away from his death in a Bowery flophouse (located, ironically enough, not far from what would later become CBGB). He shared Reed's dark oedipal vision, saw his talent, and encouraged him to write subversively. Reed has repeatedly discussed his close "friendship" with "Delmore," referring to their times together at the local tavern as important meetings of two deeply intellectual minds. He paid tribute to his former teacher at least twice during his career, first dedicating a song, "European Son," to him on The Velvet Underground's debut album, and then offering him a eulogy of sorts on his 1982 "comeback" disc, *The*

Blue Mask. These songs and others reveal Reed's ongoing preoccupation with his background as a Jew and as a New Yorker. Not long after he left college, he returned to the city his parents had fled.

*   *   *

By the end of his time at Syracuse, Reed had distanced himself from both Swados, who helped by suffering a nervous breakdown, and Shelly, who began dating someone else due to Reed's repeated sexual betrayals. Though he may have loved them—especially Shelly, who Bockris claims was "the love of his life"—Reed knew that if he was going to become the rebel artist he imagined, the combination "White Negro"/Dedalus/Delmore Schwartz, he would have to strike out on his own, going to the city where his grandparents had begun their lives in the Golden Land nearly a century before.

Like countless Jewish kids before him, Reed sought a job in songwriting, seeing there a path into music that was at once respectable (his parents could see him bringing home a paycheck) and reasonable (Jews could exist behind the scenes even if they couldn't get onstage). Carole King, Neil Diamond, and Joey Levine (composer of Joey Ramone's favorite bubblegum hit "Yummy, Yummy") ended up at the Brill Building—the former clothing warehouse at 1619 Broadway that held more than 150 pop music publishing companies at the time—but Reed went across town to the less prestigious Pickwick Records. Brill Building writers attempted to create new hits that would climb the charts, while Pickwick writers were directed to craft songs in the style of whatever was a hit at the moment. The job forced Reed to write songs in styles from garage to bubblegum to his beloved doo-wop. Thus, he began his career learning good old-fashioned Jewish song craft. In trying to churn out a garage-style tune with an animal name, imitating hits like "Do The Monkey" and "Do The Bird," Reed composed a song that would change the course of his life. "(Do) The Ostrich" was no great work of art, but when a television show asked if the band could appear to perform it, Pickwick put Reed to work creating such a band, then later sent "The Primitives" on tour. More than happy to move to the other side of the curtain, Reed recruited a group of talented studio musicians, among them his future collaborator and The Velvet Underground's cofounder, John Cale.

A Tanglewood-trained classical musician from Wales who was all but starving while playing avant-garde music in the lofts of the East Village, Cale proved a surprisingly compatible foil for Reed, and vice versa. Reed wanted to stretch the boundaries of rock so that it became art, and Cale wanted to stretch the art of the avant-garde so that it embraced rock's primitive and savage beat. The Velvet Underground in effect became the first art-rock band. It absorbed the lessons of innovative classical composers such as John Cage and La Monte Young (especially the latter's use of extended drones) as well as the similarly bold concepts of Jewish composers like George Gershwin, Leonard Bernstein, and Aaron Copland (Cale's teacher at Tanglewood), who had brought popular forms of American music to their classical work. Reed and Cale's Jewish contemporary, Philip Glass, was just beginning to do the same.

The first incarnation of The Velvet Underground—at this point still known as the Warlocks—included a bassist Reed knew and occasionally played with in college, a fellow Long Island native, Sterling Morrison. A student at City College during the early months of the band, Morrison later earned a doctorate in English and become a professor at the University of Texas, joining English major Reed and master of music Cale to create what has since become known as "the most highly scholarshipped band in history." Completing the intellectual tradition of this early lineup was a post-beatnik character named Angus MacLise, who undertook a kind of personal world music study of drums while sharing an East Village apartment with Ira Cohen. Ira, a hippie poet later famous for his photographs for record covers such as Spirits' *Twelve Dreams of Dr. Sardonicus*, had deep Jewish roots in New York. His cousin, Mayor Ed Koch, ran the city from 1977 to 1989.

MacLise was a true bohemian. He added a trancelike loop to the music, only to drop out of the band when he learned they were being paid for their first gig. In his place, Reed and company recruited Maureen "Moe" Tucker, a primitive in terms of musical education who nonetheless brought a strong, equally trancelike beat to the proceedings.

For all its intellectual credentials and melding of high and low art—a tradition particularly embodied by Jews in America—The Velvet Underground was equally important for introducing a new aesthetic of menace. Early rockers such as Gene Vincent, Jerry Lee Lewis, and even Elvis Presley had traded in the fear of sexualized juvenile delinquents bursting with potential violence. The Velvet Underground took this a number of steps further, creating a sense of menace that was as psychological as it was physical, threatening in part for the intelligence that showed behind it. The Velvet Underground was honing an image of cool, ironic disdain and a love for art that transcended warm and fuzzy emotion. It was the epitome of the unsentimental, and Reed, the band's lyricist and visual leader, embodied it best. How much was due to his childhood in the Jewish suburb of Freeport and how much he picked up from college nights reading the work of Sade and Céline is anyone's guess, but one thing's for sure—it was far from disconnected to his earlier behavior as a college student and teen. And it made him a figure of excitement and intrigue for the cold, calculating thrill-seekers at Andy Warhol's Factory.

Reed met the Factory crowd in 1965 when they saw the band perform at the Café Bizarre. Warhol in particular loved Reed's black-leather look, while his followers embraced the music. It was loud, hypnotic, yet driving enough to dance to, a mixture of primal beats, electric viola loops, and simple drum patterns that drew the listener up into a wall of sound-surrounding lyrics as self-consciously evil—and at times comic—as anything by Delmore Schwartz or Jean Genet. Warhol encouraged the band to play at the Factory, and before long was telling them that he would like to manage them and take them on his traveling multimedia show, The Exploding Plastic Inevitable. This was among the coolest names in the city, and the band could not afford to turn Warhol down.

Cale joined the show for pragmatic reasons. He found Warhol's Factory scene "petty" and "catty." Reed, however, was clearly drawn to the cutting and largely camp atmosphere that blossomed there. For one thing, he was the center of attention. As early rock talent scout Danny Fields says, "He was so beautiful, everyone wanted to sleep with Lou." And for another, he was again finding his literary—or at least "artistic"—ambitions being supported by a respected "father" figure. Warhol, though only fourteen years older, was an established name in the art world and more than happy to flatter Reed's ego.

Still, despite his growing power and importance at the Factory, Reed seemed at times quite lost there. Those around him began to notice that he got rattled and nervous for no apparent reason, as if he didn't know how to handle himself. Perhaps that's why he began to gravitate toward a figure that seemed completely out of character for him, the Teutonic goddess known as Nico.

Though many biographies and memoirs of the VU stress that Reed hated Nico for usurping him as lead singer of the band (then-manager Warhol had insisted on the change), their relationship was far more complicated, being predicated on love as much as hate. Sometimes it seems as if the Nico-Reed relationship has been intentionally expunged from the record, as if those involved in it were blind to what was happening, or had decided in retrospect not to see. Yet, Reed not only took up with Nico despite his anger toward her for joining the band, he also "fell madly in love with the tall European with long flaxen hair," as Bockris puts it. In fact, according to Reed's childhood friend, the Jewish Richard Mishkin (another member of the almost totally Jewish LA and the Eldorados), Reed told him that "Nico's the kind of person that you meet and you're not quite the same afterwards. She has an amazing mind." Before long Reed was staying at Nico's apartment, composing songs for her. One of these, "Femme Fatale" (1967), is among his most revealing. If Nico was his "Femme Fatale" who "built [him] up just to put [him] down," why was he attracted to her? Again, Reed's friend Richard Mishkin seems to hold the key. According to Mishkin, Reed loved the fact that Nico was big. The Velvet Underground's biographer Joe Harvard elaborates: "People who've only seen her picture don't realize what a large woman Nico actually was. She was huge, almost manly, and imposing with her icy stare and manner. Reed clearly was drawn to her, as if she were a towering presence that he needed to overwhelm. Considering the fact that he was a little Jew from New York [Reed is five foot eight] and she was a big woman from Germany with—at least in her family—a Nazi past, one can make assumptions. I don't need to spell it out."

If Harvard's assumptions seem to be off the mark, consider how the relationship between Reed and Nico ended. Continually threatened by the possibility that Nico would steal the spotlight, Reed abused her in public, even if he did continue to see her in private. For the most part, Nico seemed willing to take this. As she recalled later, what she most loved about Reed was that, at heart, he was "very soft and lovely. Not aggressive at all. You could just cuddle him . . . he was rather cute . . . and he said funny things." In other words, he was a nice Jewish boy. Then one day, after one of Lou's more strategically placed barbs, Nico fired back. Waiting until the other band members and an assortment of Factory regulars were present, she proclaimed in a strong, calm, clearly audible voice, "I cannot make love to Jews anymore." Whether Nico's comment was anti-Semitic (and it appears that it wasn't) is not the issue. What really matters is how Reed reacted. As Cale says, "It took a lot to calm Lou down after that. I think he went to a doctor at noon and got a full bottle of Placidyl, a full bottle of codeine and by nine o'clock that night was completely paralytic. He couldn't move. Everybody saw that and somebody took it upon themselves to relieve him of the bottles, but it was only for his own good" (*What's Welsh for Zen: The Autobiography of John Cale*).

Reed broke off from Nico and—aside from joining her and Cale onstage in Paris in 1972 and allowing her to stay with him briefly in New York in 1974—barely spoke to her again, even in later years when she was hooked on heroin, broke, and desperate for the songs he could have written. Cale, who did write and produce songs for Nico until her premature death caused by falling from a bicycle, says, "Right through the seventies I hoped Lou would write her another song . . . but he never did." Still, Cale understood how deep Lou's hurt went. "Andy and Nico liked each other's company. There was something complicit in the way they both handled Lou, for instance. Lou was straight-up Jewish New York, while Nico and Andy were kind of European . . . Lou was dazzled by Andy and Nico. They caught him time and again. She would say things so he couldn't answer back. Lou's affair with Nico lasted through January and halfway through February. By then she was finished with him. Nico just swatted him like a fly."

Was it his Long Island Jewishness and the self-doubt that it instilled in Reed that left him so vulnerable to Nico's attack? Was it in fact what drew him to the Factory in the first place, that atmosphere not exactly pro-Jewish even if it wasn't anti-Semitic? Most of the members of the Factory were wealthy WASPs with blue-blood pedigrees that Warhol, a working-class Catholic outsider of a different sort, seemed to crave. As Nat Finkelstein, a Jewish photographer and regular at the Factory during its heyday remembers, "Andy didn't talk to me much or seem very impressed by my presence, but then one day he asked me if I wanted to go to lunch with him uptown where he had to meet some women who were interested in buying his paintings. As it turned out these women were nice Jewish ladies of the Upper West Side variety, and Andy did everything he could to flatter them while having me sit next to him. After the women had left and we were sitting there in silence, I asked him outright if he had asked me along because he wanted to impress those women by having a 'friend' who was obviously Jewish. 'Oh, yes,' he said. 'You don't like Jews very much, do you, Andy,' I replied. 'Oh, no,' he laughed. But he wasn't really joking, he meant it."

Warhol was notoriously cryptic during his life, and rarely answered questions directly. His actions speak louder than his words. The Factory was a very un-Jewish place, considering it was originally located in the Lower East Side of New York. Though a number of Factory regulars were Jewish, such as Nat Finkelstein, Danny Fields, and writer Lynne Tillman, they were rarely more than bit players (Tillman, in fact, was only in the Factory because she was dating Cale). When Warhol did allow Jews to figure prominently in the Factory's affairs, they were either established celebrities like Bob Dylan (whom the Factory regulars mocked mercilessly behind his back) or pathetic types who functioned as "entertainment," like bipolar "superstar" Andrea "Warhola Whips" Feldman, famous for stripping on command at Max's Kansas City (and later leaping to her death from her Fifth Avenue apartment). Once Warhol became successful, he moved the Factory uptown, where he could escape from these crazies and take up with more pedigreed sorts like debutante/celebrity Cornelia Guest.

* * *

Nico or no Nico, Reed completed the first album with the band and was ready to do all he could to promote it. Though Warhol had nominally produced *The Velvet Underground and Nico*, many say he merely sat in the studio and nodded his head at what the band was doing. He gave his imprimatur by providing artwork for the cover—the famous banana that peeled to reveal pink—but the album tanked, the result of bad luck (Factory regular Eric Emerson sued to either be compensated or have his picture removed from the back cover), lackluster management (as Warhol by this point was becoming more interested in film), and audience resistance.

In fact, the album was about as different from "California Dreamin'," then sweeping the nation as the theme song of the Summer of Love, as any record could get. Where in Frisco, youths were wearing flowers in their hair and looking like Jesus, in New York—especially the New York of The Velvet Underground—they were discussing Sade and acting like true European sons, as Reed wrote in a song of the same name dedicated, not coincidentally, to Delmore Schwartz. A combination of romantic and sinister, *The Velvet Underground and Nico* was an aural and psychological assault that didn't go down well outside of New York. In the city itself, the message was loud and clear. Here was a band that meant business. A band that kicked ass and was cool.

It was Lenny Bruce all over again, the leather-jacket, snarling, sarcastic Jewish thing given a rock context. Like Bruce, Reed could be as funny as he was dark. In a later song, "The Gift" (*White Light/White Heat*, 1967), which Reed adapted from a short story he wrote at Syracuse, a college student mails himself to his girlfriend during summer break, only to have his head split when she attempts to open the carton with a sheet-metal cutter. Reed could also make Lenny Bruce–style commentary. His story-songs about New York characters such as the "white boy" waiting uptown for his drug connection ("I'm Waiting for the Man") presage a career-long interest in the people and places of the city. A reviewer for America's largest Yiddish daily, *The Forward (Forverts)*, Elizabeth Gold, ("How the Godfather of Punk and the Epitome of Cool Twists Stereotypes Around," April 21, 2000), compared his ability to explore the little people on the outskirts of society to Grace Paley's (an early feminist writer whose work was largely informed by her Jewishness). Capping off the album with one of the most beautiful ballads ever committed to vinyl ("I'll Be Your Mirror"), Reed seemed to bring to rock the sophisticated song craft and lyrics made famous by Jews on Broadway and Tin Pan Alley for decades. At the same time, he also tapped into his generation's latent preoccupation with the Holocaust in songs such as "Heroin" ("all the dead bodies piled up in mounds") and "The Black Angel's Death Song" ("sacrificial remains make it hard to forget / where you come from").

The Velvet Underground's second album, 1967's *White Light/White Heat*, took a sharp turn in a more avant-garde direction. Now free of Nico, and containing only one ballad, it favored manic, driving guitar work ("I Heard Her Call My Name," "White Light/White Heat") over story-songs, and was capped by a nearly twenty-minute, largely instrumental finale that exceeds most anything in the psychedelic canon for force, energy, and inventiveness, the wonderful "Sister Ray." Indeed, it is on this record—and with this song in particular—that the VU achieved their definitive avant-garde statement, its mix of rock, trance, risqué lyrics, and crystal-meth-driven guitar pushing pop into extremes never before achieved. It was an extreme that Reed refused to extend.

The critics hated it, and the public rejected it more thoroughly than the first album. Reed was in this for the long haul, as a business. Even more important, he was a rocker, a man of the people. He wasn't composing for an elite audience—he wanted to reach the very outcasts that he wrote about in the songs, the *kleine menschele*, as Jewish critic Irving Howe referred to them—*the little man*—beloved by Yiddish writers and Jewish socialists decades before Reed penned his best works. Despite his earlier allegiance with the cool, detached, and ironic, after *White Light/White Heat* it appeared that Reed wanted to reach hearts as much as minds, to move his public in an almost religious way. As Factory member Ronnie Cutrone put it, "Lou didn't want to be arty anymore. He wanted to be pure rock 'n' roll. You know, enough was enough" (*Please Kill Me*).

And so, as if born again, Reed fired Cale and toned back the avant-garde, naming the next VU album simply *The Velvet Underground* (1969), as if the band had been reborn as well. The insinuation was that the VU had been Reed's band from the beginning, long before it had acquired a chanteuse as lead singer, an anti-artist as producer, and an avant-garde classicist as co-composer. Reed's band, the *real* Velvet Underground, played in a lo-fi, casual style that was not only borderline acoustic in tone, but straight-up religious in content. What do we make of lyrics like "I saw my head laughing, rolling on the ground / . . . I'm set free to find a new illusion" ("I'm Set Free"), "Jesus, help me find my proper place" ("Jesus"), "it's truly . . . a sin" ("Pale Blue Eyes"), "the difference between wrong and right" ("That's the Story of My Life"), and "Wine in the morning, and some breakfast at night, well, I'm beginning to see the light" ("Beginning to See the Light").

We can't read these songs in the spirit of Bob Dylan's born-again albums. An ironic, undercutting humor pulls the rug out from under the sentiments they seem to profess. What sort of religion would demand wine in the morning and breakfast at night? That sounds like the church—or shul—of rock 'n' roll. So does a religion or "illusion" that sets you free to envision your all-too-happy disconnected head rolling like a bowling ball on the ground.

No, irony is the point. It must have grown out of Reed's place—or rather, nonplace—at the Factory. Nico proclaimed she could no longer sleep with Jews, and then Reed cut her out of his life. Warhol bristled when Reed questioned his handling of the group's finances, freezing out the suburban Jewish son of a businessman long before Reed announced his counter-rejection. Reed must have been stung by the insinuation that he only cared about money. If not laced with anti-Jewish feeling, certainly it echoed such feelings strongly enough to set off alarm bells in Reed's mind. Is this why Reed seemed to grapple with issues of a religious—and clearly non-Jewish—nature on his new album? Is this why the jokes lie embedded subtly in the songs, like time bombs waiting to go off amidst the gentle arrangements? The most affecting song on the album, the painfully sincere ballad to a lost loved one, lingers on that ultimate sign of goyish beauty, second only to blonde hair, "Pale Blue Eyes." "I thought of you as my mountaintop, I thought of you as my peak / I thought of you as everything / I had, but couldn't keep, I had, but couldn't keep." The regret, love, and self-loathing (or is that bitterness?) in this song is as deeply embedded here as in Philip Roth's 1968 novel, *Portnoy's Complaint*. Reed is expressing longing, but he also is expressing dissatisfaction with himself. He can't keep the figure with the pale blue eyes, the artist, the chanteuse, the flaxen-haired god or goddess that walks upon the surface of the earth on blue-blood feet. Before the song is over, he repeats his desire stated in the earlier ballad "I'll Be Your Mirror" to be the reflection of his lover ("If I could make the world as pure and strange as what I see / I'd put you in the mirror / I put in front of me"), yet the "if" in the clause makes it clear that he's no longer able to do this. No, now his lover has informed him—or accused him of not realizing—that "money is like us in time / It lies, but can't stand up." With shades of Warhol's rejection lingering between these lines, we learn that the singer does still "have" his lover at times, but only in secret, in "sin," away from her (his?) marriage. This exiled figure who is spoken to in monetary terms is allowed just so far into his former lover's life. He lingers on the periphery, in the realm of sin, but never again can he step into the mirror.

This eponymous third album by Reed's VU was a melancholy, bittersweet tour of spirituality gone bad. The next, *Loaded* (as in loaded with drugs or hits), was more upbeat and tuneful. *Loaded* (1970) returned Reed not only to the people (like Jack, a banker, and Jane, a clerk, both of whom save their money), but to *his* people, perhaps not the Jews as a whole, but the songwriters of the Brill Building tradition. In "Rock & Roll" Reed says, "One fine morning, she puts on a New York station . . . / She started dancing to that fine, fine music / You know her life was saved by rock 'n' roll." Yes, New York rock 'n' roll, the kind of rock 'n' roll Reed himself loved as a teenager when Brill Building, doo-wop-flavored hits were all you heard on the radio—all that you needed to hear.

On this album, Reed explores in depth the songwriting technique that would serve him so well in the years to come. He experimented with the singer-as-narrator conceit in "I'm Waiting for the Man" ("Hey white boy"), in "Sister Ray" ("like Sister Ray says"), and in "Candy Says" ("Candy says, 'I've come to hate my body'"). In "Sweet Jane" ("You can hear Jack say . . ."), "New Age" ("'Can I have your autograph?' he said to the fat blonde actress"), and "Head Held High" ("They said the answer was to become a dancer"), he takes it to new levels, presaging a whole series of songs to come in later albums. We see it in *Berlin* ("They're taking her children away / because they say she was not a good mother") and *Transformer* ("and the colored girls say"; "She said, 'Hey babe, take a walk on the wild side'") and *Coney Island Baby* ("I said, if I ever see Sharon again") and *Street Hassle* ("And there's nothing left to say / but oh, how I miss you baby").

The technique reaches its zenith in the album-as-novel that deals with Reed's most cherished subject, the city of his birth, *New York*. Here, all the little people get to speak, from the ghetto Romeo and Juliet to the queens in the Halloween Parade to the angry Lou himself, fed up with Nazi fugitives like Kurt Waldheim and anti-Semitic candidates like Jessie Jackson and even more deeply anti-Semitic political figures like the Pope. It's not exactly punk in volume, but it's still punk in DIY populist spirit. Reed gives dignity to all of his characters, who are just trying to get by, *doing it for themselves*.

But *Loaded* was a third failure with the public. Reed, the refugee from suburbia who fled to New York, found himself exiled once again. Or he felt that he was exiled, which amounts to the same thing. It's deeply Jewish, the feeling that one's skin is turned inside out so that emotions bleed at every pinprick, die at every insult. It's born as much from centuries of oppression by the church in Europe as from self-seclusion in the shtetl of the soul. But it's there, ready to swallow you up—just as it swallowed Reed soon after the public refused to clasp his album *Loaded* to its heart.

No, after *Loaded* Reed seemed a beaten man, briefly limping along with the band as he gradually turned it over to his new guitarist Doug Yule, then, after a show at Max's Kansas City, heading back to his parents' home in Long Island, where he either suffered a nervous breakdown, began working for his dad's accounting business, or both. One of his central conflicts during this period was his fear of becoming too strange, too odd, too much the rock 'n' roller who would never understand the simple pride and joy of working in the nine-to-five world like his father. Back on Long Island, he wrote a piece about Brian Epstein in which he describes both the life-and-death importance of music and the madness of the rock 'n' roll lifestyle. When he eventually returned to the city and to music to undertake a solo career, he did so with a new appreciation of his father. As if claiming it as his own, he began to refer to his Jewishness indirectly, and on occasion directly, as when he sang about his "friend and teacher . . . Delmore . . . the wandering Jew" on 1982's *The Blue Mask*, "Harry's Circumcision—Reverie Gone Astray" on 1992's *Magic and Loss* and "that New York Jewish elixir the egg cream" (as Robert Christgau calls it) on 1996's *Set the Twilight Reeling*.

Yet it wasn't till 2004, when Reed asked those "four other questions" at that gathering of rockers, klezmer musicians, poets, and other hip members of the New York Jewish scene known as the Downtown Seder that he really seemed to come home. For it was there, with his dog, partner, and a hundred fellow Jews looking on, that he combined Edgar Allen Poe with Jewishness, sounding as pissed off and bored as he had decades before, talking about servants named Severin and shiny boots of leather. Sounding, in other words, like Louis Rabinowitz, the spiritual son of Lenny Alfred Schneider Bruce.

3
A NICE JEWISH BOY

*Danny Fields Begets the Shaman, the Misfit,
and the Punk*

Detroit is the most *goyishe* hub of civilization . . . that's why I loved
it so much. [The MC5] were tall and big and butch, not like New
York Jews . . . They were macho men. They sort of marched, you
know? And they were literally the sons of automobile workers who
came from the Appalachians . . . I just thought the virility of it
was something—I mean, virility is not, shall we say, a characteristic
of the Jewish community . . . In Jewish [culture] the women are
the most important thing. . . . [these guys] were *echt* [authentic]
Americans.

—Danny Fields, 2003

Virile? You don't have to breed that out of New York Jews? I mean,
The Catcher in the Rye? My God!

—Danny Fields, 2003

Like Woody Allen's character "Zelig," a certain face pops up repeatedly
in the pictorial annals of punk. There he is between Lou Reed and Andy
Warhol on the back of that Jew-centric Reed bio, *Transformer*. And there he
is again with Joey "Hyman" Ramone, who later name-checked him in song
("Danny Says," *End of the Century*, 1980). Look, there he is once more with
Iggy Stooge before Stooge became Iggy Pop, and there he is again with Fred
"Sonic" Smith when Smith was still a guitarist with the MC5 and not yet Mr.

Patti Smith. Christ, you can even see him with a young Jonathan Richman years before he introduced "Jojo" to his future Modern Lovers, just as you can see him again with a young Edie Sedgwick who lived with him when she moved to New York. He's everywhere, the man of the moment, the man at the center, the great and powerful Oz. Or as Legs McNeil, who supposedly named the movement that he helped create, said in the dedication for *Please Kill Me: The Uncensored Oral History of Punk*: "To Danny Fields, forever the coolest guy in the room."

Yes, Danny Fields was forever the coolest guy in the room. An offstage master who discovered, supported, and promoted key talent, he was also forever at heart a nice Jewish boy who embodied punk's simultaneous reaction against yet embrace of New York Jewishness. If we go back to 1951, we can see the ten-year-old Fields in his parents' house in Richmond Hill, Queens, pressing his chubby face against the window as his neighbors pass on their way to work. It's an odd sight, considering how we know he will end up, and a sad sight, too. For like those neighbors—Irish-, German-, and Italian-American bar owners and laborers, for the most part—we can hear the Bach B Minor Mass and the Beethoven quartets issuing from behind Danny in that house, the house of his father, the neighborhood MD, second only to the local priest in status. And though we wave, we can see that he barely waves back. He's far away, in his own world, to which we have no access.

His classmates at Edgar Dubbs Shimer Junior High feel the same. They see Danny in line at lunch and wandering down the halls between classes, but they rarely interact with him. In fact, they barely notice he's there until he's skipped two grades and gone off at age eleven to become the youngest student ever to enter John Adams High School's sophomore class.

It's all in keeping with the plan as Dr. Fienberg (Danny changed his name after college) and the neighbors see it, young Danny preparing himself for a respectable career in the tradition of his father and his people. And yet, below the surface, tensions are simmering. Other kids ignore him as they stand beside Danny waiting for the bus, the Jewish kids especially.

"They were just so shrimpy and pathetic," says the now sixty-four-year-old Fields, sitting in his eighth-floor apartment overlooking the Hudson River and the now-vanished Twin Towers. "I'm reading *Catcher in the Rye*. I'm going out with girls who live on Central Park West and Park Avenue. I mean, I'm wearing Brooks Brothers clothes and I am out of Richmond Hill at every opportunity."

Heading off to parties in Brooklyn or dates in Manhattan, Fields became ever more enmeshed in the world of New York's elite. "Those were my kind of people. You know, they went to the Hamptons in the summer, and they were cool. And then they all went to Harvard and Cornell and Radcliffe and all of that, and I just felt more at home there."

Indeed, by fifteen, graduated and with an acceptance to the University of Pennsylvania, Fields was ready to make his break from Richmond Hill complete. "When my girlfriend gave me Bach's Mass for my birthday, I played it day and night. My father was berserk. 'He has become a Christian, he has become a goy. What is this *goyishe* music?' 'Dad, it's a mass, which is Catholic, but he was Lutheran. It's just music.' 'I was alienated from him, as much as I was from outer-borough values and Jewishness. I despised everything that I came from and had to get away."

At Penn, Fields made friends with "the wealthiest, coolest, and brightest kids" in his class, before long frequenting their summer homes in Switzerland and their winter homes in Italy, all the while planning his next step. He always found a few "weird Jewish people, like Billy Meyers, one of the richest Jews in Providence," and those were his friends. "You know, crazy, crazy Jews," Fields says. "And I saw Jewish society in Providence because of my roommate Billy . . . [His] mother was like really pretty with blonde hair, and [his] father was distinguished with gray locks. They didn't look like Jews . . . I mean, coming from New York Jewdom, there's nothing in the world like it. My aunt Jane ran a candy store, counting pennies every night . . . that's why I was so eager to go to Harvard Law School."

Fifth in his class at Penn, Fields had no trouble getting into Harvard Law and enrolled there immediately after graduating from college in 1959. Of course, he had absolutely no interest in becoming a lawyer or even in attending classes. He just wanted to be in Harvard's rarefied environment, most particularly the social scene surrounding it in Cambridge.

"Oh God, those people at Harvard were pathetic," Fields says. "They studied when they were on the toilet, asking questions back and forth while they took a crap. I spent all of my time on the other side of Cambridge, drinking and fucking and shoplifting. It was everything I'd ever dreamed Harvard could be."

Not surprisingly, within months Fields decided to drop out, even though he was passing most of his classes. His parents were devastated, but Fields was happy with his situation, staying on in Cambridge for another year or so to drink, fuck, and shoplift, all while heading down to Greenwich Village on a regular basis.

When his parents finally decided that he had to do *something*, Danny enrolled in NYU, ostensibly to pursue a master's degree in literature, but really so that he could become more involved in the extracurricular activities available in Greenwich Village. Here, he finally made his way into the social circles he'd always longed for, becoming first a member of the "gay elite," centered around the San Remo bar, then through the writers and playwrights he met there, part of Andy Warhol's art studio cum private club, the Factory.

"I wasn't really anything more than a B-list player there, but I made lots of friends and introduced the Warhol crowd to the Harvard crowd," Fields says. "Edie [Sedgwick] came down from Cambridge and moved into my loft."

While Fields might not have minded being a bit player, when he dropped out of NYU and moved on to work, first at *Liquor Store Magazine* ("very glamorous") and then the fledgling rock monthly *Datebook* ("who's your favorite Beatle?"), his status at the Factory quickly changed. "Suddenly, I was in the media and could write about them," Fields says. "There was always room in a limousine for me now and an invitation to the best parties. They liked getting their press, I'll say that."

While Fields had no background in journalism, he threw himself into making *Datebook* an exciting publication. He printed articles about The Velvet Underground and gleaned the foreign press for news outside the United States. And yet, being a member of the Factory, he perhaps made *Datebook* a bit too exciting. At least for the Beatles.

"In the second issue of *Datebook* that I worked on, I found the publisher had bought the American rights to two interviews, one with Paul and one with John. They had long since been published in the UK, and were barely commented on. But I found two quotes in the interviews that I thought deserved more attention, so I moved them onto the front cover. One was Paul declaring 'It's a lousy country where anyone black is a dirty nigger,' and the other was John Lennon predicting, 'I don't know—which will go first, rock and roll or Christianity.' *That* quote was part of a longer John statement, printed in the actual entire interview, and it was a zinger: 'We're more popular than Jesus now.'"

The "Jesus" issue, *Datebook* September 1966, went on sale in July of that year, and came to the attention of a deejay in Alabama, who pretended to go berserk at this impiety. He encouraged kids who owned Beatles records to burn them on Main Street, and soon the Bible Belt was alight with Beatles Bonfires. "Goebbels would have been proud of the vigor of the offended 'Christians'," says Fields.

This chaos was happening as the Beatles were beginning their stadium tour of the United States. At their concert in Memphis, instead of the boys humbly paying homage to the music created there a decade earlier, the Beatles were forced to confront the KKK, who filled the parking lot of the stadium with one of "those hate rallies that they do so well," Fields says. "There were death-threats, and during a soundcheck, the noise of a falling garbage pail in the distant stands had Ringo jumping under his drum set, thinking it was a rifle shot."

You could almost say that the Beatles' decision at tour's end to stop performing live, and John Lennon's murder fourteen years later, both stemmed in part from the *Datebook* incident. Lennon's assassin, Mark David Chapman, was a disturbed product of the fundamentalist Christian prayer groups then spreading like sleeper-cells throughout the South. In *Mark David Chapman: The Man Who Killed John Lennon*, Fred McGunagle writes, "Two events influenced the born-again Mark. When John Lennon was quoted as saying, 'We're more popular than Jesus Christ now,' he turned violently against his one-time hero . . . Also, his friend Michael McFarland recommended a book to him." That book ended up being the one Chapman sat down to reread immediately after shooting Lennon: *The Catcher in the Rye*. Blamed for everything from the rise of juvenile delinquency in the 1950s to the spread of freaky "alternative lifestyles" in the 1960s, *The Catcher in the Rye* was written by a half-Jewish New Yorker who on some level had chosen to run from his Jewishness. Jerome David Salinger placed not only Holden, but later Holden spin-offs like Seymour, Franny, and Miriam, right in the midst of liberal Upper West Side Jewishness, yet barely—and in the case of Holden, never—indicated whether they might be of the tribe (their names aside). As New York Jewish intellectual Maxwell Geismar famously observed, "The locale of the New York sections [in *The Catcher in the Rye*] is obviously that of a comfortable middle-class urban Jewish society where, however, all the leading figures have become beautifully Anglicized. Holden and Phoebe Caulfield: what perfect American social register names which are presented to us in both a social and a psychological void!"

Or as Paul McCartney later said to Fields upon learning of his role in the Jesus article's release, "So *you* were the one." Yes, this gay Jewish outsider from Richmond Hill in Queens, this grad-school dropout and Warhol acolyte who fled from his background almost like Holden Caulfield, was indeed the "punk" who helped put an end to live performance by the Beatles.

Not that being fired bothered Fields. As he says, he was an avowed Rolling Stones fan, and he'd recently been offered a much more exciting job elsewhere. "Elektra hired me to create a publicity department, but that didn't mean I couldn't also recommend new bands that I thought might be worth signing. The company had just hit big with the Doors' 'Light My Fire,' and they wanted to expand into the rock gold mine in a big way. Of course, most of the execs were straighter guys and Elektra had previously been a folkie label (As I had been a Folkie in college!), so they didn't know what would work. That's why later people like me became known as the record companies' 'house freaks.' "

In those rapidly changing times in the late 1960s when "identity politics" first reared its head and anti-war protesters like Abbie Hoffman, Jerry Rubin, and Paul Krassner (all Jews) pushed increasingly for cultural revolution, it isn't too surprising to hear that executives in suits were adding corporate-sponsored "freaks" to their staffs."I don't know if my Jewishness had anything to do with it," says Fields. "After all, most of the executives in the companies I worked for were Jewish. Entertainment in America has been highly populated by Jews almost from its inception. Still, I will admit that I might have had different likes than someone from the South or the Midwest. I don't know. As a gay, Jewish, Bach-loving intellectual in a Chopin-based family, I've always been an outsider many times over. I guess it isn't too much to say that in traditional American terms I'm not just an outsider, I'm an alternative being."

As if to illustrate this, Fields immediately began championing some of the darkest and most threatening bands on the scene: the Doors, followed by the MC5, followed by the Stooges, and Nico. All of these musicians would one day be seen as pivotal links leading to punk—and all were reviled by certain executives at Elektra (although never by the company's founder, Jac Holzman, himself the son of a New York Jewish doctor) who kept them on at Field's insistence that they would one day turn a profit.*

"Did I really think they would?" says Fields. "Aside from the Doors, not at all. But I liked what they were doing. I liked it extremely. It was wild and threatening and entertaining. It was great theater. And *so* American."

---

*Actually, the Doors were already doing so, though many Elektra executives were growing weary of their—or rather, Jim Morrison's—controversial antics.

Fields points first to the volatile, unpredictable nature of Jim Morrison's performances with the Doors, saying that they were the most central feature of the band's appeal. "There was this sense that anything could happen at any moment," he says. "You never knew what to expect."

But it was really with Detroit bands like the MC5 and the Stooges that Fields discovered a truly revolutionary music—a music that he believes he understood in large part because of his odd perspective as a New York Jew.

"Detroit is the most *goyishe* hub of civilization . . . that's why I loved it so much," Fields says. "[The guys there] were tall and big and butch, not like New York Jews . . . They were *macho* men. They sort of marched, you know? And they were literally the sons of automobile workers who came from the Appalachians . . . I just thought the virility of it was something—I mean, virility is not, shall we say, a characteristic of the Jewish community . . . In Jewish [culture] the women are the most important thing . . . [these guys] were *echt* Americans."

These "*echt*" Americans were alien to Woody Allenesque New Yorkers like Fields, but they were far less so to the country as a whole. If the fans were not ready to embrace them at that point, it was perhaps because the MC5 and the Stooges were still too clear a reflection of their inner lives. As Neil Gabler theorizes in his critically acclaimed study of Jewish Hollywood in film's Golden Age, *An Empire of their Own*, it's as if the American dream began as a projection of what these immigrant Jewish producers thought America was . . . or should be. When the audiences, seeing these images, adopted them as their own, it became difficult to tell which came first—the chicken (Jew) or the egg (dream).

America perhaps wasn't ready to see its white, angry, class-divided, *echt* self just yet. But considering the limited success of these scary Detroit bands (as opposed to their safer cousins, Bob Seger and Grand Funk Railroad), and the fact that their audiences continued to grow in the coming years, it seems the country was at least *open* to it.

Fields had set in motion a new movement in rock that seemed to take off from where Lou Reed's VU stopped, and that brought an infusion of America's street-vibe into the artistic, Jewish milieu of New York. In his embrace of the *echt* American vibe he helped create a template for the punk bands to come, whether they were the Iggy-inspired Jewish duo that made up the pre-punk band Suicide, the Jewish-infused garage rock–loving half-Jewish duo of Lenny Kaye and Patti Smith, or that ultimate punk band, the first and in many eyes the greatest, the largely Jewish "bruddahs" from Forest Hills who Danny signed and managed directly, the Ramones.

Fields first encountered the Ramones not long after he returned to New York from Detroit. It was a kind of limbo time for him, between his period managing the Stooges and the MC5—who'd been cut loose from Elektra along with him for "making trouble" (using the word "motherfucker" in an open letter against their record company, for instance)—and his return to New York, where he found a number of things had changed in the interim. While he was away, Max's Kansas City had gone from the center of the scene to a fading memory. It even opened an upstairs venue for live disco, a sign of the apocalypse to many. The Mercer Arts Center and its main house act, the New York Dolls, were literally falling apart (the first when the roof collapsed, the second as a result of drugs). Glam rock seemed to be falling by the way-side, whatever scene there had been rapidly changing as clubs opened and failed, leaving almost no room for live bands and upcoming performances.

Around that time, a little club in the Bowery began booking local bands few had heard of before, including one that Fields, now working at the *Soho Weekly News*, and fellow rock writer Lisa Robinson were repeatedly approached to review. They tossed a coin to see who would go, and Robinson won. She came back raving to Fields about its wondrous power. The Ramones, as they were called, were going to be huge, Robinson said. The next night Fields went to check them out himself.

*   *   *

When Fields entered CBGB, the force of the Ramones hit him like a revelation. It was like he was back in that "*goyishe* hub of civilization," Detroit, that place where his "short, funny, little Jewish" self had been adopted by the "*echt* Americans." Yet this time, the band he was watching was playing in that once most Jewish section of that most Jewish of cities. And it was featuring at least one Jew on vocals and perhaps another in the background, though at the time Fields wasn't sure.*

---

*Though Fields later became manager of the Ramones, he didn't know definitely that Tommy was Jewish until told during interviews for this book—a testament to the degree to which Tommy kept this fact veiled due to his childhood experiences with anti-Semitism.

"When the Ramones appeared on the stage, they were like something I'd unconsciously been waiting for," Fields says. "They were perfect. I didn't want to change anything about them. They were like the MC5 and the Stooges except that they were funny and ironic. And, like Jews, they were steeped in the showbiz tradition."

These Jewish American traits were especially noticeable against the backdrop of the former Yiddish theater district where CBGB was located. They were revealed in the Ramones' funny, biting lyrics, in their matching costumes, and in their over-the-top performances.

"You want to compare the Ramones to vaudeville?" Fields asks. "I guess you could do that."

For all their inherent Jewishness, the Ramones weren't completely separated from their *echt* American forefathers in Detroit. Like the MC5 and the Stooges, the Ramones ran on anger as much as on music. Like those ever-so-macho, uncompromising rebels, they thrived on being seen as hard, right down to their permanent scowls and matching leather jackets. They dressed like a street gang, a Puerto Rican one perhaps, as their name suggested. When they mentioned storm troopers in their songs, they made it clear they were angry, dark, and pissed off.

And yet, there was irony about everything. That name, for instance, so much like a street gang's, was actually taken from Paul McCartney's Beatlemania-era pseudonym, Paul Ramon. And then too, there was the look of the band, a kind of leather-jacketed conformity that seemed not only to speak of street gangs, but of early 1960s girl groups, too. Girl groups? What could be less macho than that? Well, perhaps song titles like "I Wanna Be Your Boyfriend" or the appearance of the lead singer, a tall, gawky, painfully thin mantis-like figure who hunched over the microphone as if without it he might collapse.

"They were like a funhouse mirror of a group," says Fields. "That was part of their appeal."

The Ramones enhanced the macho, big-guy theatrics of the Detroit boys into a concept that a nice Jewish boy like Fields could embrace all the more. They altered the whole idea of machismo, turning it into comedy, or at least irony, creating distance so that the viewer could project himself onto the performers, just as gay, New York Jewish outsider Danny Fields had projected himself onto the *echt* Americans in the swastika-sporting band playing behind Iggy Osterberg Pop. It was much the same irony adopted by other CBGB's bands of the time, such as the Dictators, with their Henny Youngmanesque one-liners, and Richard Hell–era Television, with its comic lyrics like "love comes in spurts." It was New York irony. For New York punks.

*　*　*

Before long Fields was managing the Ramones and trying to sell them to America, believing that this time he had gotten it right. He invited his friend Linda Stein, by then married to Sire cofounder Seymour Stein, to come see the band. When she paved the way for the company to sign them, he invited her to become comanager. Together, the two were able to get relatively low budget Sire to support their efforts. Seymour Stein gave them the funds to go to England, where the Ramones played a historic show at The Roundhouse that influenced almost every major U.K. punk act to follow, including the Sex Pistols and the Clash. When the group returned to the states only to find that they were still nobodies, Fields continued to do what he could. He attempted to interest journalists he'd become friendly with during his years as an editor, and he committed the band to a punishing tour schedule that took them on a blitz across America, one that he believed would ultimately spread the word.

"It was more than I had ever been able to do for the bands in Detroit, because now I was the manager and I had a real commitment from the record company," Fields says. "You know that song 'Danny says we gotta go / gotta go to Idaho'? That was a fiction, we never went to Idaho, but we went just about everywhere else. We couldn't get on the radio, so we needed to take the music to the audience."

The Ramones caught on to a certain degree and garnered a cult following almost from the start, but Fields quickly realized something wasn't right. When they played their first major gig outside of New York, opening for Johnny Winter in Westbury, Connecticut, the audience booed them so consistently they had to cut their set short. Fields realized that they were hated by Johnny Winter's audience, a crowd with old fashioned blues-y taste who were impressed by fast guitar fingering. "They just went over the heads of this dorky audience," he says. The same thing was repeated around the country.

As Linda Stein explains it, they were too much for folks outside of New York. "Being from New York and being Jewish is related, and they were definitely from New York," Stein says. "I can see now that it was the same for me. It's as if I'm an alcoholic and I can finally admit the truth: 'I'm a New

Yorker, I'm a punk." Stein rises to her feet, puts her fists in the air, and shouts jokingly, "And I'm a Jeeewww!"

New York Punk Jews or not, Fields did what he could. He continued the band's punishing schedule, encouraged radio stations to play the Ramones, and attempted to find other venues for the group. But as U.K. punk, with its attendant violence and anger, was spotlighted in the media, American audiences came to fear any band with the punk moniker, even those homegrown ones who'd originally created the genre. At the same time Fields saw Sire was not doing enough to promote the band on the radio. For the Ramones' second album, *Leave Home* (1977), Sire produced thousands of little baseball bats, a sly reference to the baseball bats clutched like arrows by the band's logo, a bald eagle. Of course, these baseball bats also referred to a song from the first album, the Joey-penned revenge fantasy "Beat on the Brat," in which the once-tortured misfit sang about pounding Babe Ruth–style on his former enemies. As Fields predicted, these gimmicks didn't work in getting air play; just as the logo itself seemed to cause problems. The bald eagle concept created by Ramones friend and lighting director Arturo Vega called to mind less the presidential seal than the fascist symbols of Nazi Germany, not too surprising considering that one of Vega's most frequent and provocative subjects was swastikas, presented in a variety of black light–bright pastels.

All of these high-concept, self-consciously designed motifs were either lost on the audience or, more likely, troubling to it in ways that weren't clear. As Fields says, "The Ramones were threatening or at least looked threatening, even if they were just babies at heart. Aside from Johnny, they couldn't hurt a flea—not even Dee Dee due to his paranoia. But they looked scary. They looked like something out of the SS. They didn't look cuddly or cute or hippie. They were too much for the rest of the country. The Americans just didn't get it—even if in every city they played there were always a few kids who loved them, kids who quickly went off and started their own bands."

Aside from these few followers, the Ramones just couldn't get a break. Fields couldn't figure out why at the time. The Ramones fired him, and he became separated from the scene. He couldn't figure it out even as he returned to journalism, editing *Country Rhythms* and then *Rock Video*, all while writing columns for the *Soho Weekly News* and *Hits*. Fields tried to break back into the business over the years. He tried to make something of the music he loved, doing everything from becoming a publicity agent and VIP host for the Ritz, to ghostwriting Warhol superstar and "Jean Genie" inspiration

Cyrinda Foxe's autobiography *Dream On*, to heading a rock 'n' roll bus tour in which he described scenes of interest while screaming through a megaphone ("horrible," he says, summing up this experience in one word). He never could figure out the problem, though, even as he entered his sixties.

Today, he thinks he's got it.

"I understand the Ramones much better now, because I realize they and I made the same journey," he says, gazing out the window. "To cross that river is much easier than to cross *that* river," he adds, pointing first to the Hudson, separating New York from the mainland, then to the East River, separating Manhattan from the boroughs of Brooklyn and Queens. "If you come across the Hudson River from Potato Salad, Idaho, you're a little infusion of America, and we can handle that. But if you come across the East River from Brooklyn or Queens, like I did and the Ramones did, you're bridge and tunnel. That transition isn't easy. Barbara Streisand and Woody Allen and thousands of others have done it, but there's a stigma and it's not easy to shake. The Ramones were the ultimate outsiders. They were too much for America and they were almost too much for New York. They were just too outside."

Now, of course, Ramones songs are used on commercials, and those who worked with them and other bands Fields helped discover are millionaires.

"But where am I?" he asks. "I'm not even making a living, and that's kind of scary when you're nearing seventy. So I was twenty-five years ahead of the curve. Wow! Great! Where does that leave me today? Those in bands ended up making it big. I'm writing my memoirs."

For all of his connections to Warhol and the Factory and the gay elite and the wealthiest Jewish families in the country, Fields is still an outsider—an outcast—a misfit, even in his adopted city. He's still the kid from Richmond Hill who was expected to do great things even as he was expected to keep a distance. He's still the kid peering from the window of his parents' house, though now it's not into the great beyond as classical music plays, but at the Hudson River, all the views easier to take in due to the absence of the Twin Towers.

Fields concludes, "Music? I don't have time for that. All that Christina Aguia-whore and metal and rap. I refuse to listen to it."

So instead he surrounds himself with silence. A monumental silence that swells like an anti-soundtrack as he gazes out the window, especially as his eyes light upon the bridge connecting Queens to Manhattan—the same bridge that he crossed long ago in search of a new life.

4
SUICIDE IS PAINFUL

Martin Rev and Alan Vega Bring the
Jewish Streets Indoors

In a way we were more of a CBGB's band than Max's. But the people that ran Max's made it more of an Italian, Jewish, Las Vegas
underground kind of thing, it was more like where we grew up, it
was a New York thing.

—Martin Rev, 2004

They used to say that "Frankie Teardrop" is the song that Lou Reed
wished he had done.

—Alan Vega, 2004

In that pre-punk venue Max's Kansas City, the same bar where The Velvet Underground once held court and Warhol socialites and freaks mingled
in the back, a new, even more abrasive avant-garde band is at work. This
band, a kind of *White Light/White Heat*–era VU in a post-apocalyptic mood,
is doing more than just playing for the audience. They're confronting it, abusing it, tearing down the fourth wall between it and the stage. With their sec-
ond-hand farsifa organ and crazy singer who bats the mike against his head
until it bleeds, they are performance art as much as they are performers, a
combination of Danny Fields's *echt* American, Iggy Pop, and Jewish New
York's Lenny-Bruce-on-speed, Lou Reed.

"We weren't theatrical, we were theater," says the once-bloody singer, Alan
Vega, sitting in his Brooklyn apartment today. "And we weren't entertainers, we

were artists confronting the audience. People came in wanting to escape the streets, and we threw the streets back in their faces."

Far out there on the rock horizons, where even the pre-punks hated them—and the punks when they returned to become part of that scene—this duo, Suicide, was so New York it was almost too much for even New Yorkers. They were smartass and more. Alan Vega blocked the exits when viewers attempted to leave the room after he and Martin Rev took the stage. Rev created a repetitive droning sound akin to that once churned out by the VU's John Cale on either keyboards or viola. The trancelike loops built a mounting tension as the singer screamed and shouted and abused the audience verbally while swinging a gang member's chain, a switchblade, or another knife. Blood regularly flowed at the shows, always that of the singer, Alan Vega. He was the center of the maelstrom that was brought from the streets into the theater where others watched. He was the ultimate sign of horror in New York and in the post-Holocaust world it reflected. He seemed to want to illustrate suicide for the audience. And he and his partner committed commercial suicide on the stage. They were who they were, who they couldn't avoid being.

For all their honesty, however, there was one aspect of their act that was never addressed, either onstage or off, not even decades later when they approved their first official biography *No Exit*, which appeared in 2004. Despite speaking honestly and openly about their lives on the streets, their working-class roots, their difficulties with girls, audiences, and club managers, they never once mentioned a pivotal aspect of their backgrounds. They were both Jewish, deeply so. Vega (Alan Bermowitz) grew up in a semi-Orthodox home, and Rev (Martin Reverby) later became involved in an orthodox branch of Judaism far removed from his secular, socialist upbringing.

They were both Jewish, yet it took numerous interviews to establish this fact. After initially denying his Jewishness, Vega eventually admitted that he is East European Jewish on both sides of his family. He continues to say that there is some Spanish heritage in his background, but won't be any more specific. Rev, who is also Jewish according to Vega, refused to take part in these interviews, saying he prefers to leave such questions unanswered. In the past, however, he has allowed, just as Vega did in our interviews, that since all humanity began in Africa, ultimately he is black or African on some level, and by extension, from near the Middle East.

* * *

Why this vagueness? To hear Vega tell it, he and Rev hate the hostility created by organized religion, the way it divides one group from another so that "us versus them" eventually leads to war, misery, and death. They don't want to be identified in any way, but rather to be free to define themselves, to create a new synthesis. They want to enjoy the ultimate opportunity of freedom, the ability to make—or remake—one's self. Like Richard Meyers Hell, who claimed his punk anthem "Blank Generation" was not a paean to nihilism but an inducement to the audience to fill in that blank as it wished, like all of those punk and pre-punk rockers who changed their names, whether they were Joey Hyman Ramone, Dick Richard Blum Manitoba, or Bob Robert Zimmerman Dylan, Alan Bermowitz Vega and Martin Reverby Rev were determined to escape the confines of constructed categories of ethnicity.

For all their elusiveness, however, both seem more than ready to be confused for black. And in that they're very much part of a Jewish tradition, one that ties them in with Lenny Bruce, Leiber and Stoller, the Brill Building, and countless others and makes them in some sense pre-punk. As Leiber, who, with Stoller, wrote more of Elvis's hits than did black writers, said in describing his ethnicity to a reporter, "I felt black. I *was*, as far as I was concerned."

Was it a desire to be seen as anything but Jewish, or an all-too-Jewish desire to identify with the group at the lowest end of the totem pole in America, a minority that had been as oppressed and maligned for centuries as Jews had been for a millennium in Europe?

Alan Vega, warming up to his pride in being Jewish once he admits it, says, "Jews were the ones who became so much a part of the civil rights movement. Two Jewish kids died with one black kid in Mississippi while fighting for voters' rights. The NAACP and many other black organizations of the period would never have begun without Jewish participation and money. That's what makes me so crazy when I hear kids today listening to Farrakhan and bad-mouthing Jews. It just tears my heart up."

In fact, Vega says, he thinks it is this sympathy and understanding that is in part the reason so many of his Jewish friends have married black women—among them his Suicide partner Martin Rev.

Or as Lenny Bruce put it, "My conversation, spoken and written, is usually flavored with the jargon of the hipster. . . . Negroes are all Jews."

*   *   *

Of course, back in the day none of this was apparent to Rev, Vega, or Suicide. When they first met and came together to form a band, it was in part through coincidence, and in part as the result of a simpatico understanding based on mutual backgrounds and experiences.

This isn't to imply that Rev and Vega were identical, for they were anything but. They were more like opposite ends of the same spectrum, two reactions to a classic Jewish New York experience that played an integral part in making them so perfect as a duo.

Vega grew up in Bensonhurst, the son of a working-class diamond setter. Rev's father, also working-class, was a socialist-leaning leftist and union organizer. Vega's parents continued, in modified form, the strict Orthodox behaviors of his grandparents. Rev's parents were secular in orientation, believing that the future lay in class struggle of the masses and political action.

They shared the experience of New York as a melting pot, where cultures were thrown together whether they chose to be or not. As Vega says, "It was still a ghetto mentality. You were supposed to stay with your own, and they were supposed to stay with theirs. My neighborhood was mostly Jewish and Italian with a little Polish. I liked the Italian kids because they were tougher, and I hung out with them a lot, though I wasn't supposed to. But I did notice that their parents didn't expect them to go to college or become professionals, whereas God forbid if I brought home a grade that wasn't decent. I was supposed to do better than my parents. I was supposed to become a professional that didn't have to work with his hands."

In the Bronx, Rev experienced much the same, according to Vega, though his exposure to other cultures didn't seem so divided in his mind. Vega says that Rev fell in love with the sounds of rock 'n' roll as a kid and that he began to pursue music almost immediately, eventually seeking out lessons from local jazz artists and taking up piano as early as his tenth year.

By the time he and Vega were on the verge of meeting, they embraced two competing aspects of New York musical culture. Rev, by this point leader of an avant-garde jazz band, Reverend B, was as in love with the free jazz explorations of Albert Ayler, John Coltrane, and Cecil Taylor, as Lenny Bruce had been with their bebop precursors. Vega, meanwhile, was a visual artist and sculptor who had come to the electronic sound through his love of doo-wop and the musical/performance style of Iggy Pop. He says it was doo-wop, the music of the streets, that introduced him to sound in the first place and a 1969 Iggy concert in Queens that forever changed his direction from visual art to music.

What he doesn't say, however, is that doo-wop was also the cherished music of Lou Reed before him, and countless New York punks after him, especially Jewish punks like Joey Ramone, Tommy Ramone, and Chris Stein. This doo-wop, bred of the streets and the confluence of Jewish, Italian, and black cultures in the city that it represented, was as pivotal to punk as it was to the Brill Building era. It intermingled with Vega's artistic sensibilities and Rev's avant-garde jazz tastes and helped form the sound of Suicide.

*   *   *

When Rev and Vega met in the summer of 1969, both were starving so that they could focus their energies on their art. To get by, Vega was working as a glorified janitor for the Project of Living Artists, a state-funded center for sculptors and painters that also served as his studio and residence. Rev was leading Reverend B and getting involved with his future wife, Mary (now Mari), a member of New York's groundbreaking Living Theater, which, like Vega's later approach to rock 'n' roll, erased the boundary between audience and performer in an effort to do away with the so-called fourth wall. (Mari was, in fact, the only black member of the Living Theater, "an enormous accomplishment at that time," according to Vega. "It was hard enough just being a woman and getting involved in a cultural landmark like that, but to be a woman and black just shows the extent of her talent and commitment." Interestingly, like her husband Rev, the theater's cofounder and director, Julien Beck, was a Jew from a progressive background whose productions regularly reflected his anarchist politics. Rev says that this, and Mari's early training with Jewish classical composers, may have played a part in her later conversion to Judiasm.)

One day, as Vega was taking a break from his sculpture, which by that point was being exhibited in respected galleries, such as OK Harris, he began playing around with some of the tape loops and recorded sounds with which he'd been experimenting, making a kind of futuristic noise that caught the ear of Rev, who was in the building visiting another artist. Without saying anything, Rev sat down across from Vega and began tapping along percussively on the top of a paint can. When an hour had passed and neither of the men had spoken, Vega turned to Rev and smiled.

After Rev appeared at the Project of Living Artists with his band Reverend B, amazing Vega with his combination of electric keyboards and brass instruments, the two, along with Mari, began working together, creating an unusual melding of free jazz, Velvet rock, Iggy pop, and primal shrieking. It was a blend of high and low culture, such as the two had experienced in their upbringings in their multicultural neighborhoods. It was a marriage of the exalted and the degraded, which had preoccupied Jewish musicians in New York from George Gershwin to Leonard Bernstein to Steve Reich. It was the street meeting the stage, and it was unique. As Rev and Vega prepared to take it into the clubs and concert halls around the city, they had no idea how disturbing its audience would find it.

* * *

Their first show was a 1972 performance at the Project of Living Artists, with guitarist Paul Liebgott. The angry audience threw chairs at them. A second show later that year at the Cafe Au Go Go, where Jimi Hendrix had appeared before being discovered by Chas Chandler, didn't go much better. This time, Suicide, now down to its essential form of Rev and Vega, began in fine form, only to have the electric plug pulled by the manager less than three minutes into its first song. At a third show at Ugano's in Greenwich Village, which had previously hosted such fringe notables as Iggy Pop and Captain Beefheart, the band played an entire gig, but afterward one of the club's owners told Vega and Rev, "Listen, I cannot have you guys here, you cannot play here, it is like having ninety-nine Iggies . . . people were scared."

Of course, when the club owner relented and allowed the duo back for a second night, the club was packed. Though the reaction was again not entirely receptive—Vega remembers things being thrown at the two onstage—Suicide did finish its second show, its art of confrontation clearly having power to intrigue if not seduce.

* * *

Suicide was all about confrontation—confronting the audience, confronting the horror of the streets, confronting reality, confronting themselves. The name derived from an issue of the comic book *Ghotstrider* titled "Satan Suicide," and it reflected Vega's and Rev's belief that the world around them was bent on self-destruction. The country was in Vietnam, the counterculture was in decline, and far too many of the people they knew were abusing heroin, which had begun to flood the city just a year before. Vega was then still going by the name Alan Suicide (he'd already ditched his initial stage name, Nasty Cut, as Rev had dispensed with Marty Maniac). And he was wearing a leather jacket with "Suicide" written on the back, which caused people to shout derogatory things after him on the street. Rev, meanwhile, was beginning to dress in a manner that recalled his youth in 1950s New York, when gangs were immensely popular and the leather-jacketed thug image was de rigueur. As Rev explains, "Growing up . . . it was really part of my culture, but by the time Alan and I got together I was beyond all that. But with Suicide coming together, being more intensely focused on rock 'n' roll, it brought that back to me as a kind of inspiration. It was kind of like starting from scratch again."

The duo brought this confrontational street culture, this punk look, into the behavior of the band onstage. If the audience threw chairs, Vega answered with insults, or calls to resistance, or reminders about homelessness and other ills of the street. As the band became regulars at the Mercer Arts Center, along with the New York Dolls and the Modern Lovers, Vega pushed this confrontation to the limits. At this daytime theater turned nighttime rock club, bands played in rooms named for great dramatists. While the dress-and-lipstick-wearing Dolls, a band that figured as the missing link between glam and punk, performed to packed audiences happy to dance in the Oscar Wilde room, and the Modern Lovers played a discordant yet danceable rock beat across the hall, Suicide worked its dark magic in the tiny and appropriately named Blue Room. Rev's tense farsifa and Vega's almost Yoko Onoesque vocalizations set most of those in attendance heading for the door. When Vega jumped from the stage to stop them, it wasn't just the fact that he was breaking down the invisible fourth wall separating the audience from the performer that made them apprehensive. And it wasn't even the wild look in his eye or his stream of consciousness lyricizing. It was the fact that he was brandishing a chain like a gang member, and displaying a switchblade in his pocket, though he never hurt anyone but himself.

The Mercer Arts Center collapsed one day, falling down into a heap of rubble, and CBGB was born as a result. But the audiences who came to CBGB to see Suicide even before Television or the Ramones had played there hated them even more than the Max's and Mercer Arts Center crowds. At the height of punk, when Suicide toured with the Clash as its opening act in 1978, Vega was not only in danger of hurting himself, but of being hurt even worse by the increasingly violent and anti-Semitic audience. "One night a bunch of fucking Nazi guys came to the show," says Vega. "I was in the dressing room and in walked all these Nazi motherfuckers with their swastikas and everything. I think they wanted to kill me. After the show everybody came backstage and they chased them out. It was a really weird sight, man, it was like being transported to Berlin circa 1936 with some brownshirts. History was flashing right in front of my eyes."

Vega was bloodied by some thuggish audience member nearly every night during that tour, even having his nose broken on one occasion, but he did not abandon his confrontational stance. He took to wearing an unusual costume, a vintage field marshal's uniform with a black armband, in protest of his treatment by the fascistic National Front and its sympathizers. It was history flashing before the *audience's* eyes this time. Vega, the confrontational Jewish kid from Brooklyn who'd had family perish in the Holocaust, marched across stage with that black ribbon, his arm appearing on occasion to rise in a mocking Nazi salute. Suicide began to call its show "a punk mass." Vega says, "It began as a poetry thing, and six years later it was a movement."

*   *   *

Like those later punk bands, the Patti Smith Group, the Voidoids, and even the Ramones, Suicide infused avant-garde art with a force that could reach a mass audience. In this, Suicide was continuing the tradition of Lou Reed's Velvet Underground as much as it was anticipating bands to come. It was doing so not just in its sound but in its stories, its lyrical emphasis on the street, making those who lived on it inescapable to the audience.

"Alan would write in character," says Martin Rev, discussing the origin of the tracks on Suicide's eponymous debut from 1977. "Songs like 'Johnny,' 'Frankie Teardrop,' and 'Cheree' were about street people." Or as Vega puts it, "They used to say that 'Frankie Teardrop' is the song that Lou Reed wished he had done."

No wonder Rev was wooed by bands as varied as Blondie and the Voidoids, not to mention Malcolm McLaren, who saw him as a great partner for Debbie Harry. No wonder Suicide was managed by Marty Thau, most recently of the New York Dolls, signed by Richard Gottehrer, formerly of the

Brill Building, and produced by Gottehrer with Craig Leon, at that point also a producer of the Ramones. And no wonder Suicide's songs were commissioned by German rebel director Rainer Werner Fassbinder, and its sound influenced by German bands like Kraftwerk and the Silver Apples.

As Thurston Moore says, "all the artists in New York owned [Suicide's first] record," among them Joey Ramone, doo-wop revivalist Willy DeVille, and New York Dolls frontman David Johansen. "Their first album really captured the underbelly of the city," says journalist and musician Kris Needs, while *Wire* magazine reviewer Steve Barker adds that Rev's solo work had his now "recognizable trademark twin influences of a doo-wop cadence swathed in the frumble, hiss and buzz of the city."

This urban melodism and discordance, this street beat epitomized by earlier Jewish writers such as Lou Reed and Jerry Leiber, and later Jewish writers such as Joey Ramone and Jonathan Richman, was inseparable from the city, especially the Jewish part of the city. It grew up somewhere between the street-corner doo-wop group and the street-corner gang fight—and later moved somewhere between the Brill Building and the Lower East Side shooting galleries. Eventually it created both the punk rock attitude and the punk rock conscience, those twin desires for confrontation and romance, angry rebellion and love for love's sake.

It also seemed to weigh heavily on Suicide. When Rev went on to embrace an intensely religious branch of Orthodox Judaism, in effect putting the band on hold for much of the 1980s, Vega, who continued to tour and record as a solo artist, slipped further from his own religious upbringing, yet never, despite repeated temptations, officially changed his name.

"I almost did a number of times, but something always held me back, this desire to honor my parents," he says. "I guess it's the whole Jewish thing. As much as I hate group identification and consider myself a new American individual, I still find myself rooting for the Jew when he does something good. Like Sandy Koufax not playing on Yom Kippur or Einstein winning the war against Hitler after he'd been forced to flee Germany or even Israel beating the Arabs in the Yom Kippur War. In fact, I almost signed up to go fight in that war. It was just so unfair, that sneak attack, the Arab nations threatening to 'push the Jews into the sea.'"

This Jewish New York link even leads Vega to believe that Suicide's work influenced Lou Reed. When the Godfather of Punk followed his 1974 attempt at a commercial breakthrough, *Sally Can't Dance*, with the double album of feedback and electrical blips he's alternatively described as his masterpiece and his practical joke on his record company, 1975's *Metal Machine Music*, Vega thought the similarities to Suicide were discernible. Both Reed's album and Suicide's were major influences on late 1970s industrial bands such as Throbbing Gristle and Cabaret Voltaire. And as Vega points out, Reed was very aware of Suicide in the early 1970s, even soliciting Vega's opinion on producers for one of his solo albums. It's certainly possible that Reed absorbed Suicide's lessons. And it would be all the more fitting if he did so. If Vega and Rev were continuing any sort of tradition, it was the musical and lyrical tradition of Reed's VU. Both bands wed avant-garde noise to confrontational story-songs of little people, street people surrounded by the harsh sounds of the city. And both bands were commercially unsuccessful in their time, only to be acknowledged eventually as pivotal innovators (it was the 1990s before Suicide's influence on everything from industrial music to synth pop was widely appreciated). How fitting it would be for the spiritual father to honor the spiritual son by being influenced by him in return.

Then again, it isn't as if Reed had only *one* spiritual son. The Punk Rock *Zeyde* also deeply influenced at least one other Jewish kid of the younger generation, a Jewish kid who started in the same place as Vega, yet ended up somewhere else entirely.

5

I'M STRAIGHT!

Jonathan Richman: Cool Nerd

My parents would sing little melodies to me once in a while when I was two or three years old, and the kind of melodies that my mother liked and her sense of wit and funny rhymes have found their way into the music I make.

—Jonathan Richman, 1993

Well the old world may be dead / Our parents can't understand / But I still have parents / And I still love the old world.

—"The Old World" by the Modern Lovers

They were wild like the USA / A mystery band in a New York way / Rock and roll, but not like the rest / . . . Biker boys meet the college kind.

—Jonathan Richman, "Velvet
Underground" (*I, Jonathan*, 1992)

It's the Summer of Love and Jonathan Richman's in a bad mood. Sitting in Harvard Square, a guitar in his lap, he sees nothing but tie-dye, long hair, and beads. Worse, the kids who wear these costumes have a look in their eyes that says they're not all there. Bloodshot, glazed, with huge pupils that look like eclipses, they stare off into space as if what was before them didn't count. And that makes Jonathan want to turn away.

He can't stand this absence, this willful removal, this desire to take one-self away from awareness and so from feeling and appreciation of the outside world. He can't stand the way they all smile the same at one another, as if they were so in love with everyone, they loved no one, the men especially, their smiles so transparently fake. Jonathan can tell with just one glance that these long-haired, buckskinned guys are not all they pretend to be—filled with love and the desire to spread that love through song. As they walk down the street with their acoustic or electric guitars in hand, Jonathan wants to go up to them and stare into their eyes. He wants to make them see who's the good guy here. He wants to make them see who's the chump.

He gets up from where he's watching the performers in front of the T station and heads over to the large grassy common across from Harvard. He's going to give his own performance. He's going to show them what music is really all about.

* * *

Is it any surprise that this performance does not go down quite as Jonathan expects that day? Does it amaze anyone that the hippies and acid-happy college kids are not interested in hearing his songs about mental hospitals and lost love and respecting your parents? Jonathan sports a close-cropped haircut that wouldn't look out of place on a doctor or accountant. And he wears a white button-down shirt and a pair of nicely ironed pants. A very present-able young man. Except for the goofy expression on his face. The half-smile, half-leer that makes him look a bit mad. Or like a misfit. A dork at the very least. What was it that he thought he would accomplish with that look? And why did he imagine the hippies and freaks would respond to it?

* * *

For Jonathan, dressing like the straightest of nice boys was a way of rebelling against rebellion. It was a way of honoring the Old World even as he lived in, and loved, the new one. Danny Fields and especially Lou Reed, Jonathan's idol, rebelled against their middle-class backgrounds by cultivating their punk look and image. Jonathan's rebellion was a bit more complicated.

Though he was born and raised in Boston, Richman was a New Yorker at heart. He moved there before he started his band so that he could be closer to Lou Reed and the atmosphere he craved. His band, the Modern Lovers, was best known and most influential in New York. It modeled itself on those quintessential New Yorkers, The Velvet Underground, even as Richman modeled himself on Reed. The New York band the Talking Heads achieved their distinctive sound and image through the Modern Lovers' keyboardist Jerry Harrison, and thus indirectly through Richman, the Boston native turned New Yorker.

Not that New York—at least, Reed's New York—was *that* far from Richman's Boston. Born in 1951 in Natick, a north Boston suburb at least as Jewish as Reed's Freeport, Long Island, Richman, like Reed, was raised in a largely secular fashion.* Most Jewish kids in both neighborhoods were bred to believe that professions of the safest and most conventional sort were the best bet, and the vast majority of their parents did everything they could to send them to schools where they could achieve upward mobility. As in Freeport, Natick residents tended to be liberal politically. A large segment of the population voted Democratic and unequivocally supported the State of Israel.

However, the differences between Richman and Reed's backgrounds are at least as essential as the similarities. While synagogue attendance in Richman's neighborhood was generally as low as in Freeport, Richman's parents went to shul every Friday night on *Shabbes* and, according to Richman's next-door neighbor, high school friend, and Modern Lovers cofounder John Felice, often took Jonathan with them. Perhaps more important, Richman's family was less affluent than Reed's. They had enough to support Jonathan and his older brother, yet they never achieved the levels of social or economic success that Reed's parents were so proud of. Saul Richman did not own a business or have a profession, but worked as someone else's employee. He was a salesman, just like Willy Loman, that quintessential, broken-down Jewish American in *Death of a Salesman*.

Richman is notoriously guarded about his past and personal life. He got up and walked away when I met him backstage and told him I'd like to profile him in this book, but he does repeat in interviews that it was while rid-

---

*Then, as now, most Jews remain largely secular. While recent surveys indicate that 79 percent of Americans believe in God, 10 percent of Roman Catholics, 21 percent of Protestants, and 52 percent of Jews do *not*. As Sigmund Freud said, "I am resigned to the fact that I am a God-forsaken nonbelieving Jew."

ing around with his father on business that he came up with his most famous song, "Roadrunner," a vision of the not-so-open road, cluttered with neon signs of businesses like the Stop & Shop grocery franchise. The anarchist Sex Pistols later covered it, perhaps not realizing that it has its origins in the life of a salesman.

Clearly, his father's influence bore directly on the young Jonathan, even if he had to reconfigure it to make it palatable in later life. "Roadrunner" is not just about riding the commercial strip of suburban sprawl America. It celebrates the transformative powers of the imagination, as the neon signs and grocery stores become visions of beauty in Richman's mind through an effort of aesthetic will. One can almost hear Richman saying beneath the lyrics, *Hey, my old man wasn't so bad, even if he did have to make a living as a hat-in-hand salesman.* Nevertheless, the divide between Richman and his family is wide, perhaps unbridgeable. Richman has commented throughout his career about how much he respects and appreciates his parents' support, but one notices that he never says "love." Felice says, "I had dinner with Jonathan and his parents a few times, and they [his parents] barely talked or showed any emotion. Jonathan is a colorful character, he loves life. They didn't even seem like they were from the same family."

Or as Biff, Willy Loman's alienated son, says to his brother Happy, explaining why he wants to flee home, "We don't belong in this nuthouse . . . We should be mixing cement on some open plain, or—or carpenters. A carpenter is allowed to whistle!"

*　*　*

And so the appeal of Lou Reed, Lewis Rabinowitz, Lou of the Jewfro and the nervous, *shpilkes*-ridden eyes, Lewis Allen steeped in a certain kind of Jewishness from which he rebelled in classically Jewish ways—a Jewishness that led him to be angry, mocking, and tough. Through The Velvet Underground in general, and Reed in particular, Jonathan Richman found the surrogate father he needed, one with whom he could share his admiration, if not love, by proxy.

Every time the VU visited Boston, Jonathan was there, hanging around backstage after the shows and hoping with all his might to meet his idols. Month after month he did this while in high school, and month after month the band noticed his awkward figure, the short-haired, dorky-looking Richman, an even stranger sight in the late 1960s than they were in their black leather. The Velvet Underground looked too angry and serious to be hippies, but they did at least look (accurately) as if they dabbled in drugs. Richman, however, had a truly unique look that seemed to advertise that he was deeply, proudly, straight.

"Jonathan was an odd kid," says Boston rock historian Joe Harvard, the author most recently of a book-length study of the VU's first album. "From what I've heard, he was completely alienated and alone, so much so that his parents wondered what might happen to him. Yet, unlike Lou Reed, they didn't give him electro-shock. They were just happy that he wasn't into drugs. You don't know how odd that was for a kid in those days."

Especially a Jewish kid. It is well documented that children of Jonathan's generation and background were more likely to be part of the social upheavals and rebellions that were sweeping the nation at that time than their WASP counterparts. The vast majority of those leading the student protest movement were Jewish, among them Abbie Hoffman, Jerry Rubin, and Allen Ginsberg. In fact, as Reed's biographer, Victor Bockris, points out, Lou was adopted as a mascot by the Jewish fraternity at Syracuse University (even though he wanted nothing to do with it), because "the fraternity environment still dominated the American campus . . . and there was . . . a vital cultural split between the Jewish and the non-Jewish fraternities. The Jewish fraternities were for the most part hipper, more receptive to the new culture, and more open to alternative ways of living" (*Transformer*).

Richman was a throwback, a Jewish kid straight out of an earlier generation, the kind of kid who epitomized "the nice Jewish boy." As was evident even then in the songs he was writing, Richman loved the Old World as much as he did the modern one. Like Ray Davies in England, he wanted to preserve the figurative village green, even if in Jonathan's case the green would have looked more like a simple split-level in Natick with a traveling salesman's car in the driveway.

From "Modern World" to "Dignified and Old" to "I'm Straight," we can hear Jonathan pining after a time when a girl "put down [her] cigarette [joint?]" so that she could be in love under "suburban rain," with a kid like him who wouldn't have to be "ashamed" for wanting to be "dignified and old," and "straight, not like hippie Johnny." A time and place where values were upheld and kids like him would be rewarded for working and studying hard, not to mention pleasing their parents. A time when it was better to be a scholar—or even a traveling salesman supporting his family—than a rebel dreamer chucking it all to go it alone.

* * *

Straight. Unlike The Velvet Underground that he so loved. Straight, but with the passionate longing that the hypnotic drumming of that band aroused. Straight, but "colorful," as John Felice put it. "A character," as Joe Harvard called him. A "poet," as fellow Modern Lover Ernie Brooks says.

Straight, but tortured, like the definitely un-straight Lou Reed. His surrogate father, his opposite, yet his reflection.

* * *

Though eventually Richman became disenchanted with the violent, even sadistic aspect of Reed's persona and work, in the beginning he seemed to tolerate it, to say the least. Finally able to meet his idols during their Boston visits, Richman always brought his poems and song lyrics with him, forcing them upon Reed, the VU member he most admired. Early Richman compositions such as "Hospital" and "She Cracked" are as disturbing as anything Reed ever put to paper. Though the first is couched in a maudlin tone that makes it partially ironic and the latter delivered in the style of a rave-up, both deal with the twin subjects of loneliness and madness, portraying the true lover as forced into antisocial withdrawal, if not breakdown. The kind of subjects Reed touched on later, though seemed to shy away from in the beginning.

Where Reed mythologized both sadomasochism ("Venus in Furs") and decadence ("European Son," "Sister Ray,") Richman went straight for the jugular, looking at the little lives of suburban girls and boys who were sent to mental hospitals and lonely rooms far out of sight. At the same time, he praised simple romantic love, acknowledging its healing power in "Hospital" and its possibility in "Someone I Care About." Reed did the same in many of his own compositions. Romantic love has perhaps never been better expressed in rock music than in Reed's "I'll Be Your Mirror" and in his dewy-eyed paeans to the "old world" such as "Sweet Jane" ("and those ladies, they rolled their eyes . . .") and "New Age" ("and when you kissed Robert Mitchum / gee, but I thought you'd never catch him").

* * *

Children of a history of oppression and exile, children as well of a new world where Hollywood romance and the Bill of Rights made everything possible, both Reed and Richman were as split in regard to their faith in romantic love as they were in their faith in human beings in general. This became all the clearer to Richman when he made his break from the old world complete, leaving Boston as soon as he'd graduated from high school (as his parents had begged him to do) and heading down to New York.

In the city, Richman attempted to further insinuate himself into the life of The Velvet Underground and their circle. Becoming first a messenger and then a "rack-puller" in the garment district, he eventually was able to secure a job as a busboy at that most famed of pre-CBGB hangouts, Max's Kansas City, the restaurant/bar that served as a kind of club for the Warhol set.

Opened in December 1965 by Mickey Ruskin, an impresario of the night who'd been running beatnik bars in the Village since the late 1950s, Max's was where the downtown elite met to greet, eat, and be indiscreet. Though bands like The Velvet Underground played up front and heroin (and later cocaine) was snorted in the private party rooms in back, at least part of the reason for going to Max's was to see who you could see and impress. On any given night a visitor could be treated to the sight of Warhol superstar Warhola Whips—the genuinely deranged Andrea Feldman—jumping up on her table to disrobe and dance while artist Larry Rivers and writer Terry Southern discussed the probability of her madness (she in fact leapt to her death from her fifteenth-floor apartment window in 1972) and Warhol himself coolly snapped pics. It was the sort of place that clueless Hollywood movies of the period portrayed as "wacky" and "wild," when in fact it was everything from exhilaratingly exciting to terrifying.

Richman saw it all, reveling in and expressing deep dissatisfaction with his experiences. Felice, who had stayed behind in Boston to finish high school (he was five years younger than Richman), remembers receiving as many as three letters a week from his friend. Richman was thrilled to meet Warhol and to be accepted later as an occasional visitor to the Factory, yet he was disturbed by how the famous artist distanced himself from people and kept them at bay, as if their feelings were his to elicit for the sake of observation.

Even worse, Richman told Felice, was the way his idol Lou Reed seemed to be doing the same, keeping himself apart not only from Richman, who considered Reed his mentor and substitute father, but from the rest of the band and the other Warhol associates, as if he were too good for them.

Richman had no idea that Reed was going through a crisis of his own, battling for control of his band with the guitarist he'd recruited after firing cofounder John Cale, and realizing he was losing not only that battle, but the one to keep himself together, his identity suddenly in peril.

"Reed seemed adrift as The Velvet Underground fell apart," says Bockris. "Before long he was heading back to Long Island to hide with his parents. It turned out that he was working for his father."

The article Reed wrote during this period on the meaning of rock 'n' roll is intensely telling. Repeatedly he praises the power of the music, only to undercut it, saying that it's "not fit for an adult to spend his time involved with it" and that it is more fitting for someone of his age to be working at a real job—"that's the real challenge," Reed says, sounding like an echo of his parents.

While Richman might not have seen this article, he did see Reed's retreat, and it didn't help to bring him out of his own inclination to withdraw. For weeks on end, Felice received letters from Jonathan concerning his alienation in the city, the loneliness he felt in his rented room. "I went to see him one weekend around then and he was surrounded by pizza boxes and dirty clothes and didn't look so great," Felice says.

Less than a month later, Richman decided to pack it in, heeding his parents' requests that he return to Boston. But only after he first went to Europe. And then Israel.

* * *

If there's a smoking gun in Richman's life, a before-and-after moment, a cathartic experience that resulted in revelation, it is this trip to Israel. Richman documented much of it for himself as well as for Felice, and it is clear that something very special occurred there.

"Jonathan was sending me these letters full of drawings of ancient ruins and sites, trying to describe the desert to me and how beautiful it was," says Felice. "I mean, man, the guy said he was having visions. Spiritual visions. It blew my mind."

Felice and others downplay the significance of Judaism in these visions, pointing out that Richman, like many at that time, adhered to numerous

Eastern philosophies. And yet, the connection seems obvious. Why did Richman go to Israel in the first place? Felice says that it was just part of his European tour, but as anyone knows who has attempted such a journey, Europe is not exactly a stopping point on the way to Israel. Felice says Jonathan had a cousin in Israel whom he was going to visit, though he acknowledges that Jonathan never mentioned the cousin after arriving in the country, and in fact repeatedly complained about his loneliness there. Even if he went to Israel primarily because his parents were willing to fund the trip, the Jewish homeland would have had associations for him beyond his interest in Eastern and other forms of religious thought. The clearest evidence for this is his description of his visions and his explanation of their message.

"When he was out in the desert and seeing these beautiful sights, Jonathan said the main thing he regretted was that he didn't have anyone to share them with," Felice says. "In fact, he said that he had decided he had to change that. He had to start a band. He wanted people around him."

Felice pauses and then repeats what he just said to stress its importance.

"He said that he wanted to start a band. I had been encouraging him to do just that for years already. Every day I would bug him. 'Let's start a band, let's start a band, come on, we should start a band.' But it wasn't until he went out in the fucking desert and felt alone that he changed his mind. All of sudden he wants to do it. 'Let's start a band,' he says. And as soon as he got back, we did it."

*   *   *

Is it too far a stretch to say that Jonathan's visions in the desert—as beautiful as they might have been—primarily reflected his own loneliness? His revelation was not that he had to pursue music or that he had to write songs or that he had to sing them. He'd already been doing that as a solo performer for years. Rather, he realized that he had to create a group, a community, a place where he would feel at home. And he realized it in the one place where, as conventional Jewish wisdom has it, all alienated Jews will feel accepted, where the wandering people of the diaspora will feel at peace, where even a Jewish nerd can get laid: Israel.

Jonathan may not have understood the depths of his alienation until he visited the Jewish homeland and found he felt out of place even there, suffering all the more greatly when he realized that he had no connection to "the land of his fathers." His anguish forced him to act. Rather than continue to be an outsider in Israel, as he had been in New York and in his largely Jewish neighborhood growing up, he decided to create his own thoroughly modern world of love. He had to fit into that world, for he was its creator. There he would lead like a god—he would be the ultimate Modern Lover.

*   *   *

Back in Boston, Richman and Felice began putting their band together. Among their initial recruits were David Robinson, a drummer Jonathan met while posting an ad for a drummer, and Rolfe Anderson, an acquaintance of Robinson's who played bass. While they practiced, Richman continued performing in Harvard Square, much as he had as a teenager before moving to New York. There he met Danny Fields, who introduced him to Harvard students Jerry Harrison and Ernie Brooks. Initially, Harrison was more interested in casting Jonathan in a film he was making for his student thesis than he was in playing music. "It was a documentary about three outcasts: a woman who lived on the streets and thought everyone was out to get her; a man who collected newspapers and didn't know how to relate to others; and Jonathan, this weird kid who seemed to make his own reality and to be quite happy doing so. Jonathan was the one happy person."

But before long, Harrison and Brooks found themselves intrigued by "the weird kid in the white leather jacket," and they joined Richman in his band. When Felice decided to leave and Anderson was dismissed, the classic lineup of the Modern Lovers was complete.

Like The Velvet Underground, the original Modern Lovers was an intellectual's dream band. Made up of two Harvard graduates, a high school student, and a Jewish kid who preferred clear thinking and dark subjects to good vibrations and California sun, it produced songs with sophisticated lyrics and strangely moving music that was garage rock in style, yet complicated.

The lyrics—written entirely by Richman—portrayed girls suffering mental breakdowns and cars driving down the neon-lit highways of suburbia at the start. As new songs appeared, their topics broadened to take in unpleasant characters such as hypocritical hippies ("Old World") and macho assholes ("Pablo Picasso"). The new Jonathan Richman was doing more than just chronicling breakdown and withdrawal. He was actually speaking back, answering those who had made him suffer as a teenager. (Some claim that

Richman failed to meet girls in high school not because he was shy, but because he was obnoxious, leading one to wonder if perhaps the blame in these songs is more inner-directed.) In "Pablo Picasso," for instance, Richman denounces the "schmuck" and "bell bottom bummer" who is "obnoxious" when trying to pick up girls, explaining to him that the girls can't resist Picasso because of his "stare," his gaze, his focus on them rather than himself. Picasso may appear to be passive, but he's really just making the women he sees the center of attention, staring at them in appreciation of their beauty and worth. By doing so, he doesn't only avoid getting called an asshole "like you," he avoids having that epithet hurled at him in the most cool—and tough—of places, that future center of punk: New York.

And yet, as the lyrics attacked the loud, obnoxious, and aggressive, the music did something quite different. With its mixture of VU-style repetition (just listen to the insistent sameness of the beat in "Roadrunner") and garage-style simple chord patterns, the Modern Lovers brought out the savage, primitive elements of the Velvet Underground's sound, while reducing its avant-garde weirdness. At the same time, it reintroduced the organ, the instrument Cale played to such terrific, and transporting, effect in the VU's avant-rock masterpiece "Sister Ray." Now the organ was less attuned to the avant stylings of downtown New York than it was to classic garage bands from the mid-1960s. As rock critic and Patti Smith Group guitarist Lenny Kaye would soon note in *Nuggets*, his collection of psychedelic garage tunes from this period, this organ sound was "rinky dinky" but created rock at its most "skeletal." Just listen to ? and the Mysterians' hit "96 Tears." Then turn to the Modern Lovers' "She Cracked" and you'll see the similarities. No? OK, turn "96 Tears" up to 78 rpm, then try again. There, that's the Modern Lovers' sound, a mix of menacing VU-styled aggression and hysteria-driven garage rock sped up to delirium proportions.

This sound and the lyrical style that later became so pivotal to punk grew from a split in Richman's consciousness. Like other punks to come, Richman seemed torn between a disdain for power and a desire to indulge in its pleasures. He also seemed tortured by the forces that had driven him to withdraw from the world, the same forces that historically had damaged Jews like him, making them retreat from a power they couldn't hope to fight.

This split became destructively apparent as the band progressed (or regressed?) in its career. Interest in the band had been all but immediate once the Modern Lovers began to play around Boston, and representatives from various labels courted them with record deals. But a great stasis seemed to set in on Richman's part as success approached, driving the band apart before its first record ever appeared. In fact, no formal album was ever recorded—what we know of the original Modern Lovers today is the result of a series of "informal" demo recordings.

The first of these took place in 1971, but resulted in only one usable song. In spring 1972 came the two sessions (one with John Cale, the other with Alan Mason) that formed the bulk of the album – including the classic "Roadrunner." Runaways Svengali Kim Fowley arranged a third session (but didn't produce it—Dinky Dawson did) in summer 1972, and Cale's second session and Fowley's own session were both summer 1973, but between those initial sessions with Cale and Mason and the subsequent ones nearly a year later, things had clearly changed. When the band attempted to re-record some of their earlier songs, Richman exhibited the same signs of disenchantment that they had begun to see from him in concert. His performances were lackluster and halfhearted, at times barely audible over the music. The new songs he brought were quieter and quirkier than those that had come before, and presaged the whimsical hymns to mosquitoes and abominable snowmen that would soon drive the band to distraction with their cutesiness. Even the presence of Cale didn't help. Richman repeatedly resisted the elder rocker's efforts to get him to pick up the tempo and the volume and get back to what he did best. In fact, Cale made things worse, for Richman was clearly rethinking his role as a rocker, beginning to tell others that he couldn't sing music that was so aggressive and violent—the same things he had actually been saying in his lyrics from the beginning.

In retrospect it appears that the breaking point had come in the fall of 1972 when Miss Christine—of the all-female Zappa creation the GTOs (Girls Together Outrageously)—overdosed in the house where the Modern Lovers were living while preparing for their next session. Richman was disgusted by the waste of her life. After retreating into passive resistance at the Cale sessions, he announced that he wouldn't play certain songs any longer, he wanted the volume turned down in the future, and he still wasn't sure which label he would sign with. Felice, who'd briefly returned to the fold, became so upset that he quit on the spot, leaving to form his own punk-era band, the Boston-based Real Kids. Harrison, Robinson, and Brooks tried to stick it out, but by 1974 the band was finished. Harrison went to teach at Harvard for a year, then joined the Talking Heads in 1976. Robinson soon did the same with the

Boston-based band the Cars, and Brooks played around in various local groups until Richman finally came around in the mid-1970s and formed a new incarnation of the Modern Lovers that became quite popular in Europe.

Of course, by then the Cale-produced album from 1972—demos and all—had been released to critical acclaim and joy among a select audience. Songs such as "Roadrunner" and "Pablo Picasso" became staples on the CBGB's jukebox, spinning away beside The Velvet Underground's "White Light/White Heat," the Patti Smith Group's "Gloria" and ? and the Mysterians' "96 Tears."

The songs the Modern Lovers created during this period are among the most exciting in rock, as important to the development of punk as anything by the Velvet Underground, the Stooges, the MC5, or the Doors. In fact, these songs—odes to suburban sprawl, attacks on macho assholes, paeans to girls suffering mental breakdowns—were a blueprint for punk. And, coming from the post-Israel, Natick-born Jonathan Richman, lyrically they form a template for the emotional concerns of the Jewish New York punk bands.

Denunciations of the macho, identifications with the mentally ill, and rejection of hippie anti-intellectualism were all integral to New York punk in ways that resonated with its Jewish milieu. The Ramones, for instance, weren't much different from Richman in their focus on the broken and wounded psyches of their era, or in combining traditional notions of love with thoroughly modern disappointment and angst. Just as Richman wanted a "girlfren," so the Ramones sang "I wanna be your boyfriend." And just as Richman eventually went on to insist his band was too loud and that he couldn't play music that would "hurt the ears of children," so Joey and Tommy Ramone, the band's two Jewish members, often softened their massive guitar attack with the soothing melodies of the most joyous and romantic Brill Building pop.

Jonathan's Jewishness cannot be separated from his music. First, as became apparent only in 1994, with the release of *Precise Modern Lovers Order*, during the glory days of the band, Richman sometimes introduced the song "Hospital" with the comment: "Someone once asked me recently if I understood the Jewish Princess concept and in evidence I told them how I wrote this song." And as Ernie Brooks told me, marveling at the fact himself, in the early years of the Modern Lovers, the band practiced and even demoed a song called "There Is No Such Place as Scarsdale or New Rochelle." Though since lost, Brooks says that this song—"a quite good one, actually"—was very interesting lyrically. "I can't remember the exact words now, but it had something to do with the commuter trains being like the trains going to the death camps during the Holocaust. As you know, Scarsdale and New Rochelle are clearly identified as Jewish suburbs. Jonathan knew that, too."

Yes, all those New York Jews in the suburbs north of New York City got the Jonathan Richman treatment. The kid from the Jewish suburb north of Boston saw the darkness of the rails running past their homes—even if the darkness was supposedly long past.

THE TEN NUGGETS

Lenny Kaye and the Compilation of the Ten Punk Commandments

In some ways, I like to think of myself as a scholar of the Talmud of rock 'n' roll; to untie those knotty questions, and those small arcana of B sides and discuss them with my fellow yeshiva rock students.

—Lenny Kaye, 2004

Jesus died for somebody's sins, but not mine.

—Patti Smith, 1974

Around the same time that Richman broke up the original Modern Lovers and set about making a softer, less aggressive music that wouldn't hurt the ears of children, another Jewish kid, much closer to New York, yet not quite there either, began creating something new and provocative and aggressive from his love of the old world.

This kid, at least as gawky as the early Richman, was Lenny Kaye, the compiler of the Ten Commandments of Punk, a rock critic later turned punk avatar. As the editorial mind behind the essential pre-punk collection *Nuggets* and the musical mind behind that early, all-but-punk band the Patti Smith Group, Kaye is the missing link between the word and the deed, the thought and the action, Jewish criticism and Jewish performance that brought Jews from behind the curtain and onto the stage.

Nothing seemed to indicate that Kaye would end up in this role. Though born in Washington Heights and raised in both Queens and Brooklyn (in the latter case, the predominantly Jewish Flatbush area), Kaye spent his pivotal teen years in "foreign" New Brunswick, New Jersey. "When I moved to New Jersey [at the age of thirteen], there were not that many Jews there. It was the first time I really felt like I was not part of a dominant ethnic group. Actually it spooked me a little bit, because I don't think I was even inside a church until I was thirteen or fourteen. I never saw it. It was a different world."

While doing his best to adjust to this new world, Kaye in essence remained apart. He revolved around his circle of outsiders—a quartet including an Italian, an Arab, a Jew, and himself—and he read science fiction and created sci-fi fanzines, even as he dreamed about making music.

Of course, music, at least rock music, was not the expected route for Jewish kids from Jersey via Queens and Brooklyn. "I probably was prepared for 'better'," says Kaye. "I didn't really find myself being specifically chosen for it . . . I didn't really feel like that was what I could be. I mean, obviously looking back, that's all I really wanted to be. But from my background, which is middle-class somewhat, to seek [it] out . . . I didn't see me doing that."

Instead, Kaye went to college, where he did the expected thing and concentrated on his studies, focusing on an understanding of European history and the changing distribution of capital. Even then he continued playing music on the side, indulging his dreams of rock stardom as just that, dreams. He was like dozens, hundreds, probably thousands of other kids who did the same—except for one thing. Kaye had an uncle in the music industry who wrote songs. When Kaye was a junior in college, his uncle gave him one of these, "Crazy Like a Fox," a folk rock protest piece that Kaye recorded with his uncle's assistance. It became a small hit, and suddenly Kaye was a star. Or at least kind of. Actually, a guy with a different name got the fame. Kaye was in the background. A no one. A secret.

When Lenny was one, his father changed the family name to Kaye from Kusikoff. Lenny's uncle and the music men behind him did it again. On the record, they gave Lenny Kaye the name Link Cromwell, a faux Brit Invasion rocker. As Kaye says, it was a classic example of Write Yiddish, Cast British.

"This was just at the beginning of the British Invasion," Kaye explains. "I guess they thought they'd sell more records with that name than my own."

Kaye wasn't too upset. He now had an image, something that could take him beyond the scrawny middle-class kid for whom music was not an option.

He could be a star. He could "put on the cape" of Link Cromwell, as he describes it. Like that crypto-Jew in hiding, Superman, he could become someone else.

In fact, when Kaye joined the popular Rutgers band the Zoo, performing at frat parties backed by the Zulu Girl dancers, he began wearing a cape of another sort, an animal skin thrown across his shoulder in the manner of an African native. He was a Wildman in the noble savage mode, no more Jewish than the fake Brit-rocker Link Cromwell. Or so he liked to think. In truth, one of his bandmates had gotten those costumes from his father, a furrier in the garment district. In other words, they'd obtained them in the classic Jewish manner—via a *gonnegtion in de bidness* who'd offered them wholesale.

* * *

As much as Kaye liked the idea of pursuing music as a career, it seemed to him that it just wasn't a possibility. He was a Jewish kid, expected to continue with his studies, and no one wanted to see him onstage. Maybe as Link Cromwell, but even that was a stretch. What could he do instead of performing? He wasn't sure, but he knew it was going to take place in the city. That's where things were happening—back in the East Village, back near Ratner's and the picklemen and the Fillmore East. He entered the NYU graduate program in history so he could go back to New York.

Kaye's plan had been simply to get to the city, but once he was there it became more than that. It was the fall after the Summer of Love, and change was in the air, revolutionary change that Kaye was as swept up by as anyone else. He'd already been an SDS (Students for a Democratic Society) member in college and marched against the Vietnam War. And though he was against the recent move to violence by the SDS splinter group, The Weathermen, he was definitely committed to the kind of revolution in consciousness that Yippies like Abbie Hoffman and Jerry Rubin were promising, where materialism would come second to self-expression and compassion, and art would supersede commerce—a revolution for a new generation. Like so many then, he felt rock was part of that.

"What really put it over the edge was when the whole garage rock thing started to permeate into the progressive rock, hippie thing, and all of a sudden music became in the forefront of cultural revolution," says Kaye. "At least from my perspective, music, and especially rock music, was driving the sense of possibility that the '60s represented, and I went for it hook, line, and sinker. I embraced the hippie philosophy and incorporated it into my life . . . You could believe that love could change the world, which seems incredibly naive now, but that's what being twenty years old was about and it kind of caught me at a good cusp."

Though he loved the music world and spent his spare time at concerts, Kaye didn't immediately try to join it. He was still one of the people of the book, not of the guitar and amp. So what did Kaye do? He wrote. Even in high school he had been interested in writing as much as in music. And not just science fiction writing or even songwriting in the manner of his uncle, but writing *about* music. In other words, rock criticism.

"One of the things I really enjoyed about finding *Crawdaddy* as a kid fascinated with music, and especially rock 'n' roll, was the fact that here were writers attempting to speak about the music with the same intensity as the music itself offered. When you would read Sandy Pearlman and his history of Los Angeles, you would get into the psyche of the Doors and Love much more than reading a straight interview or a kind of concert review. Meltzer especially used the music as a jumping-off point to make his own music, quite a sense of poetry."

Like so many others, he took a hobby that had come to him naturally as a clever, word-oriented kid, and began, almost accidentally, to make it into a career.

"In college, I'd written a couple of things for the school newspaper, so when I went to graduate school at NYU (which was really just a way to move to the city), I continued to do the same . . . As a result, a girlfriend of mine referred me to a friend of hers in the industry who gave me my first job as a critic. It all just sort of happened."

Well, maybe not. As Kaye himself puts it, "Jews have always been a writerly race . . . what is the Bible but an explication of art's implications . . . And what are biblical scholars but critics of the Bible. I like to see myself as part of that tradition . . . I like to think of myself as a scholar of the Talmud of rock 'n' roll."

Beginning as a freelancer, Kaye was soon—on Danny Fields's recommendation—writing a monthly column for *Cavalier* magazine. As a result, he was thrown in with the first generation of rock critics working at new music magazines such as *Crawdaddy* (Meltzer, Pearlman, Paul Williams) and *Creem* (Jon Landau, Ken Fowley, Lisa Robinson), and before long *Rolling Stone* (Greil Marcus, Nik Cohn) and *New York Rocker* (Andy Schwartz, Alan Betrock). As he says, these critics were a new breed, a group that "was trying to create writing as musical as the subject they wrote about." They were underpaid, driven, messianic to some extent, seeing in their new endeavor a continuation of the revolutionary social politics they had worked for in the 1960s.

And, oh yes, one other thing. All but Fowley were Jewish.

"I went to my first press party, and kind of got introduced to the world of rock writing. It was a very tight-knit group, Richard Meltzer and Sandy [Pearlman], Bobby Abrams, another Jew, and a bunch of other people, you know, who were kind of like on the press party circuit . . . So then I kind of got deeper into that, and was befriended by Lillian Roxon, who made quite a fuss over me, and Danny Goldberg and Ronnie Finkelstein. There's three Jews for you, three rock writers . . . the media has always been a nice home for the Jews."

Even Lester Bangs, the infamous punk critic and—with Joey Ramone's brother, Mickey—performer (their band, Birdland, recorded one album, which Mickey eventually released independently in 1998), owes an enormous debt to these pioneers. As former Sire general manager Howie Klein says, "I used to visit Meltzer's apartment in the Village, and he told me there is this crazy kid, he's actually a stalker from the Midwest somewhere, and he's writing me all of these fan letters, and he'd take them out and read them to me, and it was Lester Bangs, who no one had ever heard of at the time. And he was just completely absorbing Meltzer's writing style, which he was very successful at doing."

I won't go into the stories of these other critics—including pre-liberated writers such as the *Datebook*-era Danny Fields. Of Kaye's personal "big five"— Meltzer, Pearlman, Landau, Williams, and Richard Goldstein (who wrote mostly for the *Herald Tribune*)—the most important two, Meltzer and Pearlman, will be addressed in Chapter 8. For now, what's important is Lenny Kaye and his transformation from writer to performer. The story perfectly illustrates how all of these critics had a deep and abiding influence on the music that soon came to be known as punk. It reveals how they both directly and indirectly helped to create the genre, often as conceptualizers creating a theoretical basis for a new punk aesthetic, other times as songwriters yet another step removed from their typewriters and desks.

* * *

Working at *Cavalier*, Kaye championed a kind of basic rock 'n' roll that he remembered from his own youth, playing in the Zoo. It was primal, three-chord, stripped-down, honest music. It was what he felt was missing from rock, an opinion he shared with other critics at the time who were disgusted with the increasing pretentiousness and remove of their earlier idols and the reigning genres of AOR (Album-Oriented Rock) and progressive rock.

"It was in the wind," Kaye says. "These things were talked about. The idea of punk rock had been kind of mentioned, even though nobody really knew exactly what that might mean."

Yet, for all the credit he gives to others, it was Kaye who ended up bringing down the tablets inscribing the Ten Commandments of Punk. It was he who actually set in stone—or at least vinyl—the grooves that would remind the new rockers of their past and would inspire them to resurrect it. Within months came the first stirrings of what would eventually be called punk.

"In 1970 I got a call from Jac Holzman over at Elektra, who wanted to know if I wanted to work as a kind of a freelance scout for them, which I did," Kaye says. "Unfortunately, as with my predecessor Danny Fields, they never really liked any of the groups I brought them, still Jac did have an idea for this album called *Nuggets*,* which in his mind was an album that was made up of cuts from all those albums that only had one big song on them . . . He gave it to me, and over the course of a year, I kind of spun it into this appreciation of music that was simple and basic, but which carried a great deal of energy and excitement.

"I based it on kind of two things," says Kaye. "I always liked the Mr. Maestro oldies albums in the '60s, which kind of gathered songs from the '50s, and had motorcycle guys on the front cover, and like twelve great songs, like your top-40 albums. But also, I used to like Yazoo's blues records, you know, *Music of Georgia from 1927 to '32*, and the scholarly notes. So I always think of *Nuggets* as being a kind of combination of those two strains."

---

*Holzman actually had to convince Kaye to stay with the name *Nuggets* rather than his choice at the time, *Rockin' and Reelin' USA*. "And thank God he did," says Kaye. "*Nuggets* is such a great little mnemonic for it. It's just like a great one-word title. It really defines the era so well. And you know, it had that aspect of digging up things that perhaps had been buried by the sands of time."

In combining these two strains, Kaye was pursuing the semi-revolutionary agenda that had been pushing him since college. While championing the little guys of his own generation—what Irving Howe might have referred to as *dos kleyne menshele*—he was also offering them a better world where they could become liberated from their oppressive pasts and allowed to express themselves in the manner they felt was right. If he couldn't actually gain for them effective political change, at the very least he could give them a voice. His compilation of garage rock classics was more than just a gathering of like-minded sounds, but also of like-minded feelings and circumstances.

That's why the album was so filled with an almost cartoonish take on snotty rebellion, and why it favored psychedelic freak-outs of mind-bending intensity over surrealist trips into pastoral landscapes of kingdoms past. This album transformed teenage anger into an artistic expression of joy, desire, and hope. The bands on *Nuggets* weren't looking for great philosophical truths or entering an introspective place of withdrawal and doubt. Like Jonathan Richman, a lower-middle-class son of a salesman, they were simply trying to establish a place in the world, their songs shout-outs of pride that said *I'm here* as much as anything else.

As they did so, the *Nuggets* rockers were careful to avoid the grandiose gestures of seriousness that seemed the domain of "artier" rockers intent on proving their cultural credentials (think post–Syd Barrett Pink Floyd). These garage-styled freaks shared with their punk descendents a determination to avoid being pretentious or aloof. If, like the punks, they did occasionally pursue the grandiose, as in the "Journey to the Center of Your Mind," by Ted Nugent's first band, the Amboy Dukes, or "Psychotic Reaction" by the Dracula-caped Count Five, they did it mockingly, in a spirit of satire or farce. If the collection now seems relatively tame, it is a reminder of the state of music before punk broke.

In *Nuggets*, Kaye in effect created the Ten Punk Commandments, a template for the genre to which Jonathan Richman and Lou Reed—not to mention the other critics then propagating a vision of the future—could wholeheartedly subscribe. In no particular order, here they are:

 I. *Thou shalt return to basics.*
 II. *Thou shalt do so with ferocious energy.*
 III. *Thou shalt be young.*
 IV. *Thou shalt be sick.*

V. *Thou shalt be snotty.*

VI. *Thou shalt play hard and break all taboos.*

VII. *Thou shalt keep no other gods—especially fucking dinosaurs like Eric Clapton and so called "progressives" like Emerson, Lake & Palmer—before thee.*

VIII. *Thou shalt be revolutionary.*

IX. *Thou shalt be cartoonish.*

X. *Thou shalt remember thy rock past and keep it holy.*

For promoting these values, Kaye was championed by the almost exclusively Jewish rock critics listed above and hailed as a seer by a woman from working-class New Jersey who had plenty to rebel against and plenty to prove. Combining aspects of Keith Richards, Bob Dylan, and Janis Joplin, Patti Smith was what Kaye had been looking for.

*   *   *

Smith and Kaye met through the conduit of words. She read a piece of Kaye's about the evolution of doo-wop ("The Best of Acapella," now anthologized in *The Penguin Book of Rock and Roll Writing*, 1992) and sought him out at his new job at the Village Oldies record store. A freelance critic herself at the time, Smith was also a poet and a songwriter for the Blue Öyster Cult. At one point, the BOC had discussed using her as their lead singer, but most of the band were opposed to the idea of a "chick" singing lead and had nixed the idea before manager Sandy Pearlman and songwriter Richard Meltzer could get it launched. As a result, Smith was still looking to express that musical part of herself, to wed her words to rock and get them across to a vast audience. She was a woman in a man's world and, like Kaye, a Jerseyite in New York. She was trying to find a way to leap from the page to the stage. Once she met Kaye, things began to click.

No one is quite sure now how the friendship between Kaye and Smith developed into a partnership. As Smith began to branch out as a performer, appearing in a number of plays, including one she wrote with then-lover Sam Shepard, Kaye moved gradually from music criticism to music making, joining a band with fellow critic Bob Palmer. Soon Smith and Kaye found themselves inching closer to a professional relationship.

Initially, their collaboration was a bit diffuse. Smith read her poems and Kaye provided sonic assaults between them. Before long, Kaye played *while* Smith read, and then he played while she *sang*. Within a year of their first appearance at the East Village's Saint Mark's Church (February 10, 1971), the two decided to form a band in which Kaye, the musical ear behind *Nuggets* (which appeared in 1972), served primarily as arranger for Smith's poetry.

After a series of auditions they settled on three players: Richard Sohl, who'd already begun to sit in with them, piano; Jay Dee Daugherty, drums; and Ivan Kral, guitar and bass. They then commenced to put together some songs with Smith basically chanting her lyrics over riffs laid down by the other three, who, as often as not, followed Kaye's lead. In this way they came up with signature tunes like "Birdland" and "Land" that would later be included on their debut album. More important, they continued the path already begun by Smith and Kaye on their first single, "Piss Factory," Smith's diatribe against the limited choices she faced as a working-class teenager forced to labor on an assembly line despite her artistic inclinations.

This early collaboration seems to reflect an intersection between Smith's working-class anger and the generally leftist politics of Jewish immigrants to this country. Socialism influenced many who went on to create punk, among them Chris Stein, whose father wrote for leftist papers like *The Masses*; Richard Hell, whose Jewish father raised him as a "communist and atheist" in 1950s Kentucky; and Mark Suall (of the Revelons), whose father Irwin was a teenage member of the Young People's Socialist League and later, after becoming disillusioned with what he saw as anti-Semitism on the Left, director of fact-finding for the Anti-Defamation League. Kaye's own roots were in leftist politics, and later in life he supported all manner of liberal causes. As Kaye says of American Jews, "You're talking about an ethnic group that definitely leaned left. And despite the doctrinaire aspect of American communism and socialism and its fellow travelers, many of the moral points that were brought up about equality, and fairness and truth and justice for the workers, and bringing to scale some of the corporate excesses, are themes that the Jews have lived for centuries and centuries and centuries . . . as the seventies began, I began seeing just how deeply they had influenced who I was becoming, you know, in terms of what I would write about, in terms of the music I would be drawn to, and in terms of the music I would make. Especially when I began making music with such a heightened consciousness as Patti's."

Of course, for Smith and Kaye, as for almost all of the musicians in the early punk movement, politics with a capital *P* was in the background. Much more important was the politics of personal freedom, expressed in a variety of musical forms under the banner of a nameless ideology that we know as *punk.*

Bands as diverse as the Patti Smith Group, Television, and the Ramones were all opposed to the doctrinaire, overly formatted, elitist form of rock 'n' roll that had come to dominate the airwaves. They brought rock back to its original democratic impulse, one that allowed any kids with enough gumption and attitude to take the stage and make names for themselves. Indeed, they opened the doors even wider than they'd been in the original rock revolution, because now women, intellectuals, weaklings, and Jews were also accepted. (If punk hadn't also been rebelling against the choreographed rhythms of disco, it might have showed equal openness to black performers who—at least in NYC—were not intentionally excluded. In fact, Ivan Julian of Richard Hell's band, the Voidoids, which also included Jewish Robert Quine and Italian Marc Bell, who later became Marky Ramone, was an integral part of the scene.)

Punk celebrated the outsider and rebel, the individual who would, to paraphrase Dylan, live outside the law to be honest. It attracted the spiritual children of Verlaine and Rimbaud (Tom Verlaine, Richard Hell, Patti Smith) and populist groups like the Ramones (trash TV), the Dictators (cars and girls), and Blondie (comic books and the Brill Building). Smith and Kaye were all *but* punk—"Piss Factory" was an evolutionary link. As a result, their band was both of the scene and yet, not of it, a fact that became increasingly apparent on the first album.

*   *   *

Hooking up with the perfect punk producer, the post-VU mountain known as John Cale, Smith, Kaye, and company set about making their debut. Already Cale had produced debuts for both the Stooges and the Modern Lovers. As he entered the studio with the Patti Smith Group, he was just about to release his own intermittently melodic and caustic solo album, *Fear.* Though the stories surrounding the making of *Horses* (1975) have stressed the difficulties between Cale and the band, this first album is in many ways its best, even if the music isn't pure punk. Cale may have robbed the songs of the "live" feel the band was after, but he provided structure and power, making the group define its sound while adding his own production techniques to help bring out the instrumentation. The layers of noise on *Horses*, dissonant and melodic, simple and intricate, are beautiful. Cale may have seemed to fight with the musicians, but he got their best work out of them despite the accusations of Smith and, to a lesser extent, Kaye that he tampered with their sound.

Kaye was largely responsible for the touches that made that album a precursor to punk. While Smith's declaration that "Jesus died for somebody's sins, but not mine" didn't seem out of place in a punk context, nor her emphasis on violence in the story of male rape to which the eponymous horses refer, her literary seriousness did feel a bit off the mark, as did her shamanlike declamations and her overall attitude of superior poetic awareness.

In fact, without Kaye's Ten Punk Commandments, the Patti Smith Group might never have been considered a punk band at all. Cale expanded the group's sound and tried to rein in some of the longer songs, but it was Kaye who added a cover of the *Nuggets*-era classic "Gloria," by Van Morrison's early band Them, as well as punk references to garage rock chestnuts such as "Land of a Thousand Dances," which is musically quoted in "Land." Moreover, Kaye insisted on keeping the chord progressions simple, the beat insistent, and the overall sound redolent of classic rock in the style of the Doors, the Stones, and The Who.

One great quality shown by almost every band on *Nuggets*—a garish cartoonishness of sound and image—did not carry over to *Horses*. It is difficult to say who was responsible for that, but the omission did not hurt the album's sales. Kaye's references to old songs lighten the mood enough. In fact, if it weren't for "Gloria," "Kimberly," "Free Money" (which sounds like a *Killer*-era Alice Cooper outtake), and perhaps "Redondo Beach" (a bit of faux reggae), the album might have flopped.

"Gloria" was the song that captured the public imagination and most closely aligned Patti Smith with the nascent punk movement. Like the music Kaye compiled on *Nuggets*, it was straightforward garage rock powered by simple chords and beats. The song was also about sexual excitement. Smith describes seeing a girl on the street and putting a spell on her so that she walks up the stairs and into his (her?) room at midnight. It's like Roy Orbison's "Pretty Woman" transposed into a pulp novel—or like a bit of overheated comic raunch in the style of that middle-core (not too soft and not too hard) novel from which The Velvet Underground took its name. By having a woman sing the song, Smith and Kaye made "Gloria" into both a joke and a semi-pointed commentary on sexual politics, all the while playing with the taboo subject of lesbianism. In short, they kicked off their album in pure punk fashion, shouting out a bit of provocative, sexy, taboo-breaking, old-time rock 'n' roll amped up and twisted for a new generation.

*   *   *

Of course, part of what put the group over the top was the sight of Patti Smith out there in front of those male musicians, a woman in control who looked less sexual than powerful, a woman who was independent, almost manly. Actually, manly is the wrong word, for Smith looked androgynous. She was clearly a girl, but she also had boyishly thin features. She looked a bit like a cross between waifish poet Arthur Rimbaud and guttersnipe guitarist Keith Richards. And in that she had merely switched the tables on the rock dynamic. For in fact, both Rimbaud (a kind of pre-rock rock star) and Richards (an artful dodger all grown up) were male versions of androgyny themselves. They took the old look of macho, muscular power and subverted it with the menace of the hermaphrodite, creating a kind of ultra-sexuality.

Ultimately, Smith was all about sex, right down to her comment during an interview that she didn't mind the idea of teenage boys masturbating to her picture since she masturbated to her picture herself. She was not only a woman claiming (and proclaiming) her sexuality when she said that. She was a woman who sounded like a man lusting after a woman. She had both sides within her and so, presumably, was lust incarnate.

*   *   *

In the world of New York Jewish punk, Smith never would have been able to achieve this gender merger if Kaye hadn't become her partner. In America during the early 1970s, men were generally not interested in playing back-up to women, either literally, as in supporting them as musicians, or figuratively, as in providing them the spotlight. Yet Kaye, a long-haired Jewish kid in the whippet-thin, anti-muscular mode, was a mirror of sorts for Smith. He, too, bordered on the androgynous both physically and temperamentally. Disinclined to go onstage where he "didn't belong," he initially took what some might see as a passive role, standing in front of the stage rather than on it so as to write about rather than experience the performance. When he actually began playing music, he was uninterested in being the lead singer. He wanted to make his music in your head, not in your face. As loud and rocking as the Patti Smith Group may have been on occasion, in essence it was head music that took you on an internal journey rather than got you out of your seat to move about and dance. While the Dictators, the Ramones, Blondie, and Talking Heads were sure to get you dancing (or at least pogoing), the Patti Smith Group would more likely have you there glaring at the stage, clenching your jaw with the energy of the music, seeing the images go by in your head as Smith spoke about jugulars being cut, white opals staring out, Arabian seahorses lapping. This was a more internal, cerebral experience, one that the naturally internal sci-fi reading Kaye could get behind.

*   *   *

Kaye and Smith were indeed a merging of opposites, complements to one another, whose geniuses brought out something new and different in each. If Smith was able to express her less traditionally feminine characteristics with Kaye, then Kaye was able to do the same in reverse with Smith. If Kaye was able to raise his love of basic rock to the level of rough-hewn art, then Smith was able to do the same in reverse, wedding her love of words and imagery to three-chord rock. Perhaps most important, Kaye was able to pursue an area of rock not previously so open to Jews—or at least Jewishness—and Smith, a Jersey-bred Jehovah's Witness, was able to do the same. Each found in the other the perfect collaborative partner, a fellow traveler on a completely different road who somehow came to the same junction at the same instant.

Just as Gershwin, Berlin, and Jolson dipped into black culture to get in touch with their own sense of otherness, so Kaye and Smith dipped into each other's backgrounds. As Kaye says, explaining his almost mystical relationship to the music he's made with Smith over the course of their thirty-two-year-collaboration:

> Certainly when I started playing with Patti and we transformed her poem which starts "Jesus died for somebody's sins but not mine," I realized there was a lot of overt Christian imagery in her work. You can make more or less of it, depending on your outlook. But basically, I didn't feel like I was carrying a Jewish torch. I was carrying my own sense of outsiderness, of which

Jewish is a part, of which being a hippie is a part, of which being a kind of person who likes extreme music is a part.

I mean, with the Patti Smith Group the whole thing, really, was beyond definition. Patti didn't think of herself as a male or a female. To play with her, I couldn't think of myself as a male or a female. I couldn't think of even our music as rock 'n' roll.

We weren't punk rock—we *were* punk rock. We weren't progressive rock—we *were*. We had as much to do with the Grateful Dead as we did with John Coltrane. We loved the Shirelles. We loved all of those things, because we'd resist definition. . . .

I think with a group like ours, we've consciously tried to provide ways in which we could grow. I mean, a lot of the bands, especially if they define themselves too heavily, are done once they've made their statement. I like to think of us, and also, you know, my own art, and my own sense of growth and the many things that I've done over the years, as a way of escaping from my own sense of stereotype, of who I'm supposed to be.

I mean, in a way being Jewish creates certain expectations of what you *can* be. And I like to think that I've moved beyond all of that . . . that I've been able to become myself; that I haven't fallen into any rock 'n' roll clichés. And I think playing with Patti all these years has had a lot to do with that. And I like to think that maybe the same is true for her."

Smith once told Kaye that she had wanted to convert to Judaism as a child and had even gone so far as to try and find a rabbi. The blurring of boundaries between their worlds—whether they are based on gender, culture, religion, or ethnicity—shows an openness to newness and inclusiveness and self-definition that is part of the classic Jewish American dream. In America, you have a chance to become whoever you want to be. If Patti wants to become a Jew, that's fine, just as it is fine if Kaye wants to become a rocker. After all, what is a Jew or a rocker or a woman for that matter? What does the future hold in the punk capital of the East Village? What was the purpose of punk in the first place?

This is the ultimate question, especially for the Jewish outsiders who helped make up the new scene that coalesced around a little biker bar in the Bowery by the mysterious name of CBGB.

7

THE FIDDLER ON THE BOWERY

Hilly Kristal Sets Up a DIY CBGB OMFUG

The violin, of course, maybe because of the size, maybe because it's easy to transport, was always symbolic. I mean, somebody in almost every Jewish home played the violin. But don't forget, it's like why money was important to Jews in Europe. You can't own land, you've got to have something. And whatever you can carry around that's worth something when you go, if you're chased away, you've got to take it with you. You can't take your furniture. You can't take your house. You don't own the land; money. And the same is true with the violin. The violin is pretty small. You can't take a piano. You don't take a cello. But the violin is very small, it really is small. You put it in a box. And also, there is a lot of beauty. It's a very human-sounding instrument, so you can make the human sound with the violin.

—Hilly Kristal, 2005

It's a cold December night in New York in 1973. Up on Broadway, Zero Mostel—playing Tevye, the Old World Jewish dairy farmer plagued by anti-Semitism and pogroms—raises a glass of brandy to toast his daughter's engagement to a local butcher with a great deal of money. Meanwhile, downtown, in the area known as the Bowery, another muscular Jew with a past as a farmer raises his own glass to toast a bum on the sidewalk who's lifting a bottle to his trembling lips.

"Here's to you," says the man with the bottle.

"No, you," says the standing man, a flash of pained mischief crossing his face.

Who is this second onetime farmer? Like Danny Fields, he falls into a tradition of Jews working behind the scenes in the music business. And yet, whereas Fields was like countless producers and promoters before him, drawing upon his culturally inherited understanding of the middle ground between high and low culture to tap into the zeitgeist, this man is more concerned with the *Folk* (Yiddish for "the people") impulses of the common man and how to bring these out into the world. This man understands both high and low culture as well as Fields, but he leans toward the more personal music created by individuals rather than that created by artists. He believes, without ever saying so, that there is a place both for artists and for those who think differently about their role in performing music—those who think *Fuck art, let's dance.*

Hillel "Hilly" Kristal not only founded the club where art bands like Television and Patti Smith were outnumbered by entertainers like the Shirts and the Miamis by at least two to one, he promoted and in the end managed the Dead Boys, the ultimate expression of dancing for fun—even if said fun involved goose-stepping and *sieg heil* salutes.

Kristal's own tug between high and low culture gave him a deep understanding of the *echt* American vibe that Fields sought. His upbringing in the countryside made him a kind of Danny Fields in reverse. Kristal was a Jew who went to the city from the country, yet never lost his American-bred toughness.

Kristal's story begins decades before his birth, when his father and his mother's uncle immigrated separately to America from Russia in the early 1900s. Unlike Fields's ancestors, who came to America from Eastern Europe determined to pursue professions like medicine, Kristal's forebears, especially his uncle, were determined to claim the land rights that centuries of European oppression had denied them.

"My uncle, Benjamin Brown, started this cooperative farm around Hightstown, New Jersey, known as the Jersey Homestead," says Kristal. "It was a place to get Jewish people out from the city, Philadelphia, New York, the surrounding area, and bring them out to the country. Albert Einstein was one of its most visible advocates—I remember he once patted me on the head."

This back-to-the-earth movement for land-disenfranchised Jews had less to do with the socialist agrarian movements then sweeping the country than it did with a specifically Jewish land movement occurring at that time in the Middle East. Brown's Jersey Homestead shared a good deal with the original Zionist dream of Israel. Though some early Jewish immigrants to Palestine moved there for religious reasons, the vast majority were motivated by a romantic desire to become physically strong and spiritually connected to nature by developing the land.* While it was only a short step from this to nationalism—what is love of "motherland" but the ultimate expression of right of place?—initially the immigrants to Palestine were looking for something more along the lines of a Rousseauistic innocence. So were the farmers of the Jersey Homestead who followed Kristal's uncle's example. They wanted to get back to nature so as to be more natural. In a sense, they were proto-hippies, and like them, many later back-to-the-earth bearded sorts were also of Jewish descent.

As young Hillel—namesake of the talmudic scholar during King Herod's reign—came of age, his father's love of the land was not the only vision guiding him. As in some tragicomic version of *Green Acres*, Kristal saw that his mother had a quite different perspective on the Jersey Homestead. It separated her from the life of the mind and its creations, culture and art.

Kristal's mother had been something of a bohemian when she met his father in Greenwich Village. While the senior Kristal had been an insurance salesman who enjoyed playing chess in the park, she'd been a lover of the arts who loved the clubs where you could hear jazz and meet artists. Though she did in fact love the Jersey Homestead and the wonders of nature that it afforded, she never really felt at home there. Despite herself, she increasingly missed the excitement and stimulation of her earlier life. She deeply longed for the city, and so, Hilly began to realize, did he.

Like his mother, Hilly was a natural artist. He revealed talent as a musician almost from birth. Before he could speak, he was conducting along with

---

*Today, these farms continue to exist, though they are no longer exclusively Jewish. The Jersey Homestead, now known as the municipality of Roosevelt (after the New Deal president so instrumental to its survival), counted among its most visible advocates Albert Einstein. It was also home to numerous artists, including Ben Shahn, the famous Jewish liberal whom Woody Allen refers to in *Annie Hall* while reducing Allison Portchnik (Carol Kane) to "a cultural stereotype." (See chapter 12, "The Shiksa Goddess.")

Kristal's Zionist father was fully aware of this, having fought with the British in Palestine before America entered the First World War. He later helped raise funds for the new state after the Second World War.

Toscanini on the radio, and as soon as he entered school he began playing the violin.

"My mother was more supportive than my father," says Kristal. "My father was not that interested in music . . . I began to go once or twice a week to the Settlement School in Philadelphia, where I studied with Johann Grolle, hitching or taking the bus . . . but I had to do a lot of hard physical work on the farm, and it didn't mesh too much with being a violinist . . . Bad for the hands."

Sitting at his desk at the front of CBGB, the gray morning light filtering in, Kristal pauses and stares straight ahead, his brow furrowing as if in pain.

"You know, there were times when there was nobody on the farm but my father and me. We had to harvest the wheat ourselves . . . And it was all right, I liked it actually, but it was very difficult . . . I needed six hours a day to practice to really progress as an instrumentalist. It was very difficult."

Suddenly Kristal begins to tell a story about the first time he ran away from home, a story that seems to lighten his spirits in the way such an interlude would for an audience in a theater. All of sixteen, Kristal went to Montreal, then to Chicago and Arizona, spending six months traveling before returning to New Jersey. Along the way he took what odd jobs he could, attempting as much as possible to make a living through music. In Montreal he gave his first professional performance, though it wasn't as a violinist in the classical mode, but as a crooner of pop standards of the day. Singing at a wedding and a couple of other social functions, Kristal was less Toscanini than Frank Sinatra or Mel Tormé—the pop stars of his own generation.

"Oh, the girls liked the singers," he winks. "I had a lot of fun. There were many adventures in those days."

The adventure eventually took Kristal as far away as Mexico, but when his parents finally got wind of where he'd gone and begged him to come home, he did so, understanding that he was making a sacrifice that would affect his entire life.

"My sister had cerebral palsy and she had become sicker and my parents needed me to help," he says. "I loved her, we all did, and it was difficult. But I'm glad I did it. You have to do these sorts of things."

Nonetheless, Kristal attempted to keep up with his music, traveling back and forth to New York at least once a week, where he studied opera and took voice lessons, having decided there were too many obstacles to becoming a concert violinist. By the time he was twenty, he was ready to move to the city permanently, with the understanding that he would help out on the farm when needed. He was just out of his teens, but he was hardened from work and practice and delayed dreams. And he was ready to make, if not a name for himself, then most definitely a life. A life rich in excitement—heebie-jeebies—*shpilkes*.

*   *   *

The next few years of Kristal's life were a round of practice sessions, rehearsals, performances, and odd jobs to support them. For a time he was an usher in a movie house, which got him interested in the lounge singers who began performing in venues like the Paramount, the Capital, and the Roxy after the Second World War. He saw just about everyone, from Tony Bennett to Nat King Cole to the Velvet Fog to Lady Day. But he says, "standing in a uniform was not my style." So after that, for about a year, he got a day job working for music publisher Carl Fischer, then located mere blocks from what would later become CBGB. He was a "rack jobber"—someone who helped to fill the racks of department stores with sheet music—just like another saint of the church of CBGB, Seymour Stein, founder of the label that signed the Ramones, Talking Heads, and Blondie, among others.

After leaving Carl Fischer, Hilly worked "under a crane" at an Army base in Brooklyn, and soon after entered the Marine Corps. He stayed for a number of years, never seeing combat, but learning about radio and serving as a deejay for Marine-affiliated stations throughout the country. It was a wonderful time that added to his musical training—except for one thing. Kristal remembers a troubling incident involving the only other Jewish member of his platoon:

> On Parris Island, there was one chubby little man, Bill Boy. How he got in the Marine Corps, I don't know. He was a refugee from a concentration camp, a Nazi concentration camp. I know there was a little brutality then, to put it mildly . . . He used to boast that you could hit him in his stomach with all your might and he wouldn't blink. He learned to control his emotions in the concentration camp, showed no emotion. And I don't think they hit him with all their might. I don't know what they did. I never saw it, but I know they did hit him, they did, and he got transferred out.

After serving his time, Kristal returned to New York, where he did everything from drive a cab to work in restaurants like the Four Seasons to serve as a sales rep for a shipping room company that assigned him the territory below 14th Street.

"You had the Lower East Side, all the pickle barrels out in the street," says Kristal. "I mean, it was like you think of Manhattan in the good old days, but it was still there. It was still segmented in these little things. And I went from place to place, and I really learned a lot about just people and different things."

It was around this time that Kristal got the musical break that he'd been waiting for. While singing at a coffeehouse, he landed an audition for a show at Radio City Music Hall. With his bass baritone voice, he turned out to be the perfect person for the spot—especially considering the number he was to be singing: the Jewish prayer Kol Nidre.

For close to three years, Kristal sang with the chorus at Radio City Music Hall, fraternizing with the orchestra and the producers and especially the Rockettes. It was a fine time and he was making a living through singing, yet ultimately the entire chorus was let go, so he had to return to restaurant work, becoming head cashier at the Brasserie, which was directly across from his old job at New York's equally prestigious Four Seasons.

Kristal continued to get occasional gigs through his agent Irvin Arthur (whose secretary in those days was Joan Rivers), traveling as far as Texas for extended engagements as a soloist. He was clearly making headway, having attracted the notice of many agents and managers through his Radio City gig, but he was getting older and less enthusiastic about travel and seventy-hour workweeks. When Allen approached him with an offer that combined his music and business skills, he leaped at it, becoming manager of the famed Village Vanguard.

Every night beginning in 1959, Kristal worked with the biggest names in the business, among them Miles Davis, Charles Mingus, Thelonious Monk, and Lenny Bruce. And every night he experienced the life of the Village, taking deeply to its bohemian vibe—and even more to its music. He was living the life his mother had left behind, becoming part of the city's musical heart and then a prime mover in it.

When the bottom dropped out and he suddenly found himself unemployed again, Kristal wasn't upset.

"My father had always said that I was lucky to work the land, because it was in working the land that you learned how to be strong," Kristal says. "When my time at the Village Vanguard ended and I was looking for the next thing to do, I knew he was right and that I was lucky in a way."

He was tired of working for others, tired of trying to make it in a career that wouldn't have him, tired of running around from job to job. He would start his own club, something that only the toughest sorts in the city could undertake. He would support the music from the other side. And he would use the tough skin he'd developed to survive.

*   *   *

The club world was indeed tough, just as it was a melting pot. In an interview, *Tough Jews* author Rich Cohen explained how Jews and Italians grew together in the world of popular music, functioning at once as gangsters, club owners, and musicians. This dynamic—touched upon in *The Godfather II* (Havana casino impresario Hyman Roth, based on Meyer Lansky), *Goodfellas* (Las Vegas casino manager Sam "Ace" Goldstein, based on Franky "Lefty" Rosenthal), and *The Sopranos* (former rock promoter Herman "Hesh" Rabkin, based on Morris Levy)—formed much of the basis of musical entertainment in New York, not only in clubland, but later on in the streets and in the Brill Building, where doo-wop emerged as its ultimate artistic expression. Richard Meltzer once joked about doo-wop: "You know how you get the perfect group? You get a black guy to provide the rhythm, an Italian guy to sing the song, and a Jewish guy to write the words and arrange them."

The music of the streets before hip-hop, doo-wop was as democratic and DIY as you could get. Kids from all manner of neighborhoods, too poor to buy instruments, would get together on street corners to sing a cappella arrangements that drew on gospel, crooning, and Tin Pan Alley pop. They rarely crossed racial or cultural lines except in their music, where they created a vision of America in which kids from all backgrounds could employ and enjoy each others' musical styles. Think *West Side Story* minus the fancy dance numbers, or a movie like *The Wanderers,* where gangs of Italians, blacks, and Puerto Ricans are out to kill one another even as they sing songs almost identical in content.

Or one could look to jazz, where almost all the performers who weren't black were either Italian or Jewish, among them Stan Getz, Art Pepper, Eddie Lang, and Artie Shaw. As Lenny Bruce observed, "Every Jew or Italian wanted to be Benny Goodman or Gene Krupa" (*Ladies and Gentleman, Lenny Bruce!!*). Or as Sam Raphaelson, author of the play on which the film *The Jazz Singer* was based, put it: "I have used a Jewish youth as my protagonist because the Jews are determining the nature and scope of jazz more than any other race—more than the negroes from whom they have stolen jazz and given it a new color and meaning. Jazz is Irving Berlin, Al Jolson, George Gershwin, Sophie Tucker. These are Jews with their roots in the synagogue."

Raphaelson's contention that "negroes" disappeared from jazz makes sense only if one equates jazz with popular song—and even then it is arguable. But he understood the importance of Jews in American popular music, just as Lenny Bruce understood the combined influence of Jews and Italians in jazz. Likewise in punk, blacks have almost vanished while Jews and Italians predominate, drawing on their doo-wop origins as they trade each others' skins. The Dictators, five Jewish guys from Queens and the Bronx who, to varying degrees, tried to pass as Italian, and the Ramones, four kids from Jewish Forest Hills, who modeled themselves on an Italian or Puerto Rican street gang, drew on the street culture and sound of doo-wop to create a new New York–based cultural exchange. Numerous other punk-era groups did the same. It was all about synthesis, all about collaborations among people of different backgrounds, though in almost every case Jews were in some way involved.

Hilly Kristal was all about synthesis. At his new club—Hilly's on Ninth Street—he created an atmosphere where old-time nightclubbers of the Jewish-Italian Rat Pack era could meet and indulge in nostalgia for the bad old days of gangsterdom. On folk nights, Kristal catered to the regular *Folk* who were born and bred in a world much like his own, where Old World longing for a simpler life on the land combined with Old World notions of social progress and personal—if not economic—justice. An heir to both the artistic and the agrarian, the highbrow and the middlebrow, the Old World and the New, Hilly magnified the twin impulses at Hilly's on Ninth Street to see how they might translate to a new generation that had missed out on both.

*   *   *

In 1973, more than ten years after leaving the Village Vanguard and nearly a decade since the reign of the folkies and white Jewish blues artists like Mike Bloomfield, Al Kooper, and Barry Goldberg, Hilly set up a second club in the lower-rent East Village.

Still far from the hipster paradise it would become, the East Village—especially the Bowery area, where Kristal chose to open his club—had been growing steadily since Warhol had decamped in the late 1960s. It had seen initial settlers like Tuli Kupferberg of the Fugs, who, along with the rest of his beatnik friends in the band, performed radical political songs as informed by Yiddish melody as by Jewish humor. Lou Reed of The Velvet Underground had lived there; so had Abbie Hoffman, Paul Krassner, Jerry Rubin, and Larry "Ratso" Sloman of the Yippies, headquartered in the Second Avenue offices of the *East Village Other* newspaper. Allen Ginsberg and William Burroughs had reinhabited the no-man's-land of the formerly Jewish Lower East Side across Houston Street. At the same time, the first punk rockers-to-be were beginning to move in, among them Lenny Kaye, Patti Smith, Chris Stein, and Andy Shernoff. But none of them ever expected the area to become fashionable enough or wealthy enough to support a club—especially one that played the kind of music popular in the West Village, the country, bluegrass, and blues that had proliferated in the late 1960s and early '70s.

But Hilly believed it was possible. When he opened his country (C), bluegrass (BG), and blues (B) venue—CBGB—he included another series of letters in its name: OMFUG, for Other Music For Uplifting Gourmandizers. He wanted a club where customers could sample all manner of city music, so long as it was created by the folk—the regular people of the metropolis.

So when the Hell's Angels began to hang out at CBGB, Hilly let them stay and watch the rare harmonica or fiddle player who came in to perform before sinking his dimes in the jukebox and burying his mustache in a foamy pint of beer.

And when a couple of underfed kids with short haircuts and bad skin offered to play, he didn't turn them away with the demand that they be either C or BG or B musicians. He didn't even require that they audition. He simply said that it would be OK, with one all-important provision.

"You have to play your own music. You have to play original songs."

Your music. Original music. The music of the people. New music created by the folk.

He underplays this, and few if any have made note of it over the years, but herein is Hilly Kristal's most important and unique contribution to punk. Play your own music, he said. And so the pimply band, Television, did.

Within weeks, so did the Ramones, the Patti Smith Group, and Blondie.

None of these bands would have had a chance anywhere else. Their members could barely play their instruments. Kristal didn't even like their sound. But they were creating their own original music, and for Hilly Kristal, that was enough.

"I just felt that's what I would have liked done for me," Kristal says. "I don't know if I would have been a success, but I would have liked that . . . It's about being given a chance to express yourself and to be heard. That's basically it. It was just let them have their say. See what happens. And I encouraged the ones who really had the desire. I mean, a lot of people say, 'Why did you keep putting the Ramones on if they weren't so good at first?' They really had a desire to do it. They were compelling because it was a unit. I mean, they might have all been from Queens, but I don't know what brought them together. Somehow, they just wanted to do this, and they were just insistent. And that was a good enough reason for me, at least at first."

*   *   *

In setting the stage, literally, for punk to begin, Kristal cannot be credited enough. Yet in true DIY fashion, he's continued making CBGB a place where the urge toward individual expression and the desire to just do it come first. Rather than booking only headlining acts, Kristal continues to provide a venue for up-and-coming bands so they at least have a shot at reaching an audience. He's let such strange mixtures of high art and popular culture invade as No Wave artists Lydia Lunch, James Chance and the Contortions, and Glenn Branca (Static and Theoretical Girls), the last of whom appeared onstage with classical composer and Jewish product of the Lower East Side Philip Glass.

Even today, Kristal makes DIY the byword of his club. Next door to CBGB is the CBGB's Gallery, where paintings and photographs are displayed and sold, as solo musicians with acoustic guitars perform amid them in the traditional coffeehouse style. It's a return to his roots in Greenwich Village, where Kristal once traded his violin for a six-stringed guitar that he played at home between voice lessons. It's also the continuation of something he's never given up, an attachment to music whether it be classical, folk, or popular song. It's all music to him, music that can be enjoyed by any, even by the back-to-the-land farmers of his uncle's great agrarian dream.

In fact, Kristal resembles nothing so much as the Fiddler on the Roof that Zero Mostel portrayed uptown when CBGB first opened. Or maybe he is the Fiddler on the Bowery, scratching out a mournful tune even as he dances on the crumbling knife's edge of his old club. He's the Fiddler in the Capital of Punk who can flee with his instrument at any moment if things get any worse.

JUDIOS 'N' DECAF ITALIANS

Irony, Blasphemy, and Jewish Shtick

At CB's, basically my passion just became the Dictators. I went from being a New York Dolls fan to being a Dictators fan. I always looked for the kind of passionate intensity that those bands really provided. And whereas the Dolls were really flirting with this whole sort of effeminate affect, you know, the Dictators were really sort of super-macho guys, and the rock 'n' roll was killer, and that's what made it so great.

—Camilla Saly, 2003

I knocked 'em dead in Dallas, and I didn't pay my dues / Yeah, I knocked 'em dead in Dallas, they didn't know we were Jews . . .

—The Dictators, "The Next Big Thing"
(*The Dictators Go Girl Crazy*, 1974)

Where did punk begin? In the piss-hole of CBGB? In the cross-haired scars of Iggy Pop's chest? In the Sturm und Drang of The Velvet Underground or Jim Morrison's cry or Lenny Bruce's smirk? Most would pin the prize on the pinhead brow of the Ramones and the big-bang moment of their first aural assault on the stage of CBGB. Yet no event is without its precedent, and no precedent to the Ramones is clearer than the one established by an album that came out one year before that band's own debut, foreshadowing the first Ramones album right down to the selection of songs and comic content.

Who are these heroes of the underground, these pre-punk punkettes below the radar in the cut-out bins? A gang of tough guys from the Bronx, slaves of passion and anger who knocked down the walls between insider and outsider, members of a Jewish tradition expressed in Lenny Kaye and the Ten Punk Commandments, and epitomized in the Ramones. These happy-go-lucky yet angsty punks are even more Jewish than the Ramones. They are more Jewish than the management and creative team behind them, more even than the average New Yorker. They are the Dictators.

Yes, the Dictators, a band that included "Master Race Rock" as a song on its debut album and danced that Springtime-for-Hitler dance behind a strong man as comical as he was invincible: a Jewfroed wrestler/cook/roadie denizen of the yeshiva *bochur* school, a madman named Richard Blum—better known as Handsome Dick Manitoba.

✳ ✳ ✳

To look at Handsome Dick and his band in the early days, one would have thought not Jewish but Italian. Despite their names—bassist/lyricist Andy "Adny" Shernoff, rhythm guitarist Scott "Top Ten" Kempner, lead guitarist Ross "The Boss" Funicello, and drummer Stu "Boy" King—they were all 100 percent Jewish.* But most who saw them thought otherwise.

"I always thought they were Italian," says legendary rock chick (and girl-friend of Todd Rundgren, Steve Tyler, Elvis Costello, Stiv Bators, et al.) Bebe Buell.

"I thought they looked like a street gang," says Snooky Bellomo.

"Oh come on, Jewish? I don't believe it," says onetime CBGB's regular Susan Wegzyn.

Was this confusion intentional? No one will say. When I asked the band's founder and songwriter, Andy Shernoff, about this, he simply smiled. "We wanted to be tough," is all he would allow.

Wanting to look tough was what led them to form a band in the first place. It put them in leather jackets and made them tolerate Dick Manitoba, roadie, cook, and part-time wrestler, as their lead singer. They wanted to be seen as powerful, stylish, above intimidation. The Jewish half of the

---

*None of the drummers after Stu "Boy" King were Jewish—a kind of unintended homage to *Spinal Tap's* series of exploding percussionists.

Ramones and countless Jews across the country shared this desire. Especially in New York.

"Have you ever heard the term *Juido?*" asks the Dictators' most recent drummer, J. P. "Thunerbolt" Patterson (not Jewish). "I've heard Howard Stern use it. It refers to a Jew who wants to seem like an Italian, or *Guido.* I think that there's something to that in relation to the Dictators. Handsome Dick still talks the lingo of an Italian street kid even though he wears a Jewish star in the middle of his Yankees cap."

While Manitoba didn't wear the star of David in the middle of his cap in the beginning, he did advertise his Jewishness indirectly, in improvised bits between songs onstage, and his producers included many of these riffs on the band's debut disc, *The Dictators Go Girl Crazy* (1974). Here's Manitoba only a second or two after the record's scratchy start: "I don't have to do this, you know, I don't have to show up here; with my vast financial holdings I could be basking in the sun in Florida! This is just a hobby for me . . . a hobby!!!"

Then comes the song that inspired John Holmstrom and Legs McNeil to start *PUNK* magazine—"The Next Big Thing":

> *I used to shiver in the wings, but then I was young,*
> *I used to shiver in the wings, till I found my own tongue.*

> *I sock 'em everywhere that I sing,*
> *'cause you know baby,*
> *I'm the next big thing!*

> *I knocked 'em dead in Dallas, and I didn't pay my dues,*
> *Yeah, I knocked 'em dead in Dallas, they didn't know we were Jews.*

> *I sock 'em everywhere that I sing,*
> *'cause you know baby,*
> *I'm the next big thing!*

This mix of comic bluster and Jewish toughness is essential to the song's success. "The Next Big Thing" combines the sarcastic humor of the New York Jew and the macho bluster of the New York Italian. It is the hybrid offspring of the matriarchal, expressive, family-oriented but physically unimposing Jew

and the equally matriarchal, expressive, family-oriented but physically imposing Italian. Born of a desire to seem less vulnerable, more sexy—to be anything but an emaciated, sexless Holocaust victim—the song's tough humor
puts the spice in the schmaltz, the chocolate in the *mandelbrot*. It transforms
the Dictators from Decaf Italians to Espresso Jews ready for their close-ups.

*   *   *

"The Dictators are great because even though they *are* Jews, they're cool,"
said Miriam Linna, original drummer for the Cramps, in 1978. "They turn
every 'uncool' thing about them into an overwhelming asset and thus are true
Dictators."

Or as Camilla Saly, longtime fan of the band and eventually its press
secretary, puts it, "They were so irreverent, and so funny, and so willing to
poke fun at themselves. You know, they had songs like 'Master Race Rock'
and their whole thing about, 'We knocked them dead in Dallas, they didn't
know we were Jews' in 'The Next Big Thing.' They were constantly sort of
saying 'Here we are.' It was like that Rob Reiner movie, like Spinal Tap before
Spinal Tap, but with a Jewish kind of sense of humor . . . this kind of self-
effacing, very in your face kind of humor. And there is a relief, a certain
degree of relief that you feel from hearing stuff that's all around you anyway,
and to say, OK, here are all of these people pretending they're not Jewish, and
then here is a band going 'Ha, ha, I'm calling myself *this*, but I'm really *that*.'"

This Jewish sense of humor and the duplicitous face that it wears is as old
as the tales in the Bible, but its most direct link is to the Borscht Belt comics
who so appealed to an earlier generation of New Yorkers. In the 1950s and
'60s, weekend worriers like the Dictators' parents would head up to the hotels
of the Catskills to watch *tumlers* such as Jerry Lewis, Alan King, and Henny
Youngman perform a kind of shadow dance. In Grossinger's and the Aladdin
and the Pine, these comics both abused and amused themselves. They pulled
the rug out from under all in attendance, mocking their claims to respectability and class like a merciless peanut gallery of the subconscious, while at
the same time excusing them for everything—it was all just a joke.

So it was with the Dictators. For if this entirely Jewish band played up
its more ridiculous aspects—particularly through Handsome Dick Manitoba,
who, former associate Richard Meltzer says, executed "magical . . . moves" by
staggering "from stage left to stage right, and knock[ing] into the cymbals"—

then it also *mocked* its own self-effacement, both denying and embracing its Jewishness.

The Dictators exemplified a more extreme version of an older dynamic, in their case the outrageously comic and obnoxious Jew rather than the Patti Smith Group's refined and morally artistic one. They were the low culture of the streets put up against the high culture of the elites. And they got that way through a mixture of authentic experience and conscious molding undertaken by the very critics one might have expected to denounce them, Sandy Pearlman and Richard Meltzer.

❋   ❋   ❋

These critics, the same two who proved so inspirational to Lenny Kaye of the Patti Smith Group and to rock scribes in general, pretty much created the new genre of rock criticism—or, as it probably would have been called in the beginning, rock *writing*. Between 1967 and 1968, when revolution both political and musical was in the air, Jewish kids like Meltzer and Pearlman were suddenly at home in rock. They weren't strutting onstage like Mick Jagger or Rod Stewart, but they shaped performances through words, their cultural inheritance.

As Meltzer says, "When I was in high school—where essentially everybody was a Jew—I didn't know anybody in a band and I didn't know anybody who knew anybody in a band . . . By '67, I knew twenty, thirty, forty people in bands. I knew members of the Jefferson Airplane on a first-name basis. I got to know Jerry Garcia, blah, blah, blah."

And why was that? Because by then Meltzer had become a rock critic.

"I was writing for *Crawdaddy*, which predated *Rolling Stone* by about two years," Meltzer says. "Nobody got paid, so they couldn't very well tell you what to write . . . There were three or four people writing the stuff—me, Sandy Pearlman, Jon Landau, Paul Williams. Everybody picked his own little niche. I remember doing a piece at the time on *Between the Buttons* and 'Strawberry Fields'/'Penny Lane' that was twenty pages long, talking about just those two events. At the very least, it didn't feel anything like journalism. If anything, it was like ringside coverage of the sun coming up. It felt like being nurtured, like being constantly invigorated, like the maximum hand you could expect to be dealt by Life Itself. It was such an occasion. The human race, it seemed to me, thrived for a moment—for all those who were paying attention, at least. 'Psychedelic,' which was defined as mind-mani-festing . . . suddenly you had this manifestation of mind in a very conspicu-ous way."

In that psychedelic moment—that year when the Beatles died and were reborn as Sergeant Pepper, when the Stones disappeared to become Their Satanic Majesties, when Lennon was in granny glasses, Jim Morrison in leather pants, even Neil Diamond in a Nehru jacket—everything changed overnight. It was the year of "house freaks" like Danny Fields. The year Jonathan Richman withdrew further into himself so as to remain straight. The year Lou Reed freaked out in White Heat and White Light. The year there were suddenly all these magazines. And critics.

In this atmosphere, rock writers could make it new. They were found-ers, trailblazers, pioneers. And perhaps most important of all, they were co-conspirators.

"To be writing about this stuff just felt so normal," laughs Meltzer. "It was the easiest thing in the world to just think about it and let 'er fly. Jimi Hendrix and others *thanked* me for writing these things. Marty Balin of Jef-ferson Airplane. These people dealt with me as a co-conspirator. Imagine writing about rock 'n' roll! Wow, far out! For about ten minutes, writers *were* considered co-conspirators. By the eleventh minute, writers were just the serv-ice trade. 'What can you say about us?' It was over in a flash."

*   *   *

For those ten minutes, however, young men who'd grown up hunched over notebooks and curled around novels found themselves at the forefront of the action. As Lenny Kaye says, "When we'd walk into the Fillmore East, girls swooned; rock writers were like rock stars! . . . Who wouldn't be flattered by that?"

Most of these early rock writers, especially the really talented ones, came from Jewish backgrounds. Founding Fathers of rock criticism like Richard Meltzer, who published the first book on the subject, *The Aesthetics of Rock*, Sandy Pearlman, whose essays appeared in numerous collections, and Richard Goldstein, author of *Goldstein's Greatest Hits*, had a lot of company, especially in New York. Lisa Robinson, Danny Goldberg, Ronnie Finkelstein, and Danny Fields (yes, the same Danny Fields) were all instrumental in the scene. They may not have been thinking about it, but like Abbie Hoffman (*Steal This*

Book), Philip Roth (*Portnoy's Complaint*), Gloria Steinem (*Ms* magazine), and Kathy Acker (*Blood and Guts in High School*), their families were Jewish.

As Kaye says, "I think that Jewish people have always prized book learning and placed their learning in books. What's their holy book? It's kind of an explication of artistic experience. What are biblical scholars if not biblical critics interpreting and hopefully achieving the same sense of heightened sensibility that you would get from reading the Bible?"

So the People of the Book rewrote the Book of Love.

"One of the things I really enjoyed about finding *Crawdaddy* as a kid," Kaye says, "was the fact that here were writers attempting to speak about the music with the same intensity as the music itself. When you would read Sandy Pearlman and his history of Los Angeles, you would get into the psyche of the Doors and Love much more than reading a straight interview or a kind of concert review. Meltzer especially used the music as a jumping off point to make his own music, quite a sense of poetry. Nick Tosches is another one. People who were not necessarily musicians . . . were able to make their wordplay as musical as those they wrote about."

Adds Victor Bockris and Roberta Bayley in their biography of Patti Smith (herself a critic before becoming a performer), "They wrote about [rock] with an intensity that matched the Beats writing about sex, drugs, and Zen."

Even those early rock critics who weren't Jewish shared their tastes and some of their experiences. In addition to Italians like Nick Tosches, there were full-blown WASPs like Robert Christgau, who says of himself, "Well, I'm not Jewish, and I ended up not marrying a Jewish woman either. But my wife is the first woman I've ever been in love with who wasn't Jewish. And as a New Yorker, I identify very much with Jewish culture." Lester Bangs, like Patti Smith, was raised as a Jehovah's Witness, and like Patti was an outsider twice over—rock fan and religious freak. He may have been white, but as a lower-middle-class kid he wasn't right. Besides, he was a thinker and an intellectual. He was batting zero. No wonder that, like Meltzer—the person who most influenced him—he could flourish only in New York. And no wonder he became a rock writer and champion of punk. He had nothing else.

* * *

This psychedelic moment ended in a shakeout, of course. Some rock writers ended up as record company publicists or flacks. Others, like Greil Marcus, became professional authors, and still others made the leap from page to stage, like writer-turned-performer Lenny Kaye. Meltzer and Pearlman became *rock* writers, composing words for rockers to sing and audiences to hear.

They honed their craft with the early 1970s metal band, the Blue Öyster Cult, tapping what Pearlman called the "fascistic possibilities" of the rock concert for ironic purposes. The Blue Öyster Cult was a particularly Jewish take on Nazis, cabals, and conspiracy theories, delivered with a knowing, if perhaps not entirely humorous, wink. Here Pearlman in particular gave free rein to his preoccupations with twentieth-century madness, cloaking them in his lyrics with quasi-medieval references to astrologers, alchemists, and Freemasons that served as a kind of code to the initiated. Listeners who were familiar with the ravings of Aryan Brotherhood sorts picked up on the allusions to powerful elites who swore to nefarious "secret treaties" during the Second World War and before.

Secret Treaties (1974) was the title of BOC's third, and probably best, album. It refers to alleged agreements between German and American businessmen who wished to profit from the war at any moral cost. Hitler blamed similar elites for selling Germany down the river after the First World War. Pearlman's references to ZOG-like forces (ZOG stands for Zionist Occupation Government of America) are not hard to pick up once one begins paying attention. Both the German government and the Jewish Defense League (JDL) protested when *Secret Treaties* came out. They were frightened that the album could incite neo-Nazi apologists on both sides of the pond. While Pearlman probably didn't intend this—he probably merely meant to shock—there is no doubt that his preoccupations came naturally to a Jewish child of the post-Holocaust diaspora. Who better to see the devils in the architecture than the son of a people all but wiped out in his lifetime? Certainly not Allen Lanier, the "wannabe Nazi" child of southern aristocrats, as BOC biographer Martin Popoff refers to the group's keyboard player (*Blue Öyster Cult: Secrets Revealed!*). Certainly not the kids in the audience who thought the BOC were to be taken seriously. They weren't in on the joke. But Tomas Erdelyi smiled along with the reaper and dreamed about his own future band, the Ramones. He got it, and so did Pearlman, Meltzer, Andy Shernoff, and the Dictators' Richard Blum.

*　　*　　*

If we take out our old copy of *The Dictators Go Girl Crazy* and gaze at the cover, we see an early version of Handsome Dick frozen for the ages. Pumped up with muscles, wearing a wrestler's leotard, and stretching a manic angry-happy grin across his face, the thing that perhaps stands out most about him is the size of his enormous Jewfro. Dylan had already made the Jewfro cool; Dictators founder Andy Shernoff remembers it as a mid-1960s "black is beautiful" moment, but Handsome Dick's mop of hair is something else. Big, black, bushy, it looks like a clown wig on a macho wrestler. How tough is this guy?

The back cover mixes the message further. Here we have the other four original members of the Dictators, lounging in bedrooms papered with rock posters like the rooms of teenage girls. There's Top Ten (Scott Kempner), acting gonzo with his tongue out, and both Stu "Boy" King and Ross "The Boss" FUNichello (Ross Friedman, though dig that crazy Italian name), lying back like Hugh Hefner's man of sensuality; and then there's Adny (Andy) Shernoff, the Dictators founder, songwriter, and intellectual linchpin, looking, in his own modified Jewfro, almost as tough as Handsome Dick. All four have the same black-and-white poster of Handsome Dick displayed prominently on their walls, the one picturing Handsome Dick propping his elbow on his knee like a beefcake bodybuilder.

That back cover expresses the image the band was trying to project through its look and through its music as well. Song titles such as "Back to Africa," "Cars and Girls," and "Master Race Rock" speak to a comic-ironic take on American culture that is inherently Jewish. They also speak to darker, and equally Jewish, experiences: Nazis, racism, and anti-Semitism. Songwriters Sandy Pearlman and Richard Meltzer made their grand leap into uncharted territory with the Dictators. By combining their talents with Andy Shernoff's and using Handsome Dick Manitoba as their mouthpiece, they created the link between pre-punk and punk itself in the persona of the Jewish tough guy, the Italian-acting, Nazi-referencing wiseass and holy fool.

* * *

Born in the Bronx in 1952, Handsome Dick was raised in a largely Jewish neighborhood. Unlike the remaining Dictators, who (except for Queens native Shernoff) were raised in the borough's better sections, Dick's district belonged to an earlier generation. More like the tough streets of the Bowery Boys or the Dead End Kids than the small lawns and Sundays-at-the-deli of almost suburban Brooklyn/Queens, Handsome Dick's hood in the Bronx was more like that of Richard Meltzer's paternal grandfather, an immigrant Jew who traveled the country challenging all comers to wrestling matches.

Surrounded by yeshiva students and Italian hoods, Dick, like Meltzer's grandfather, had to learn how to fight, but *his* weapon was the street-smart attitude of the wiseass with the comic put-down.

Over in the part of Queens that would later give us the Ramones, Andy Shernoff was coming of age feeling that he, too, needed to learn how to be tough. He was mildly embarrassed about his origins, especially in relation to the Holocaust. "It made you feel kind of weak in a way, like how could your ancestors have allowed that to happen to them," he says. Surrounded by nice boys and girls who were planning to become doctors, lawyers, and housewives, Shernoff felt the lure of both the gang and rock cultures during his teens. "There was this energy in the air, with bands like The Who and the whole working-class thing," he says. Like Handsome Dick attempting to be tough in words whether or not he actually got into fights, Shernoff began playing around with writing rock songs like those of The Velvet Underground and the Stooges—songs that would make him feel badass even if they didn't force him to cause violence. Then, in 1967, when he was fifteen, Shernoff suddenly had an experience that made him proud to be Jewish. "That was the summer that Israel defeated a combined Arab army of six nations," he says. "They were 'going to push the Jews into the sea,' but the tiny Israeli Army not only beat them, it did so in less than a week. It made you feel tough to see that. It made you feel kind of proud."

Even then adopting the costume of leather jacket and half-scowl, Shernoff was well on his way to being a tough guy in the traditional mode. First, though, he had to pursue another avenue, one that lockstepped him into another tradition. He had to go to college. Like so many other Jewish kids who would later help to create punk rock, he had to pursue a degree—and hopefully a doctorate—before he could rock out. As he did so, he fell in step with a newer—and in some ways equally Jewish—tradition. He began to write about rock music even if he wasn't actually playing it.

At the State University of New York in New Paltz, not far from Woodstock, Shernoff walked the same road that older Jewish kids, such as Lenny Kaye and Richard Goldstein, had before him. He contributed record reviews to his school paper, and he started getting freelance assignments from *Creem* and *Oui*. He also began editing, printing, and distributing his own "magazine," a sheaf of mimeographed sheets stapled together using supplies stolen from his college. This collection of record reviews, comics, and jokes about fellow classmates, *Teenage Wasteland Gazette*, was not only the epitome of the

DIY spirit, it was one of the first zines. Perhaps even more important, it also served as a door to performance, for it was through the *Gazette* that Shernoff met Richard Meltzer, and through Meltzer, fellow rock journalist turned manager-producer Sandy Pearlman.

Actually, it was Shernoff's friend Scott Kempner who had first met Meltzer, going up to him at a Stooges' show in New York and boldly shaking hands at the bar. Aware of the connection, and now an official publisher via *Teenage Wasteland Gazette,* Shernoff invited Meltzer to give a lecture at New Paltz, an event that was cut short when the rock writer staggered offstage after only a few seconds to drunkenly puke behind the curtains. What followed was a bender of mythic proportions, the three Jewboys drinking and drugging their way through the remainder of the week and so creating the ultimate bond. As Meltzer recalls, "It was one of the best five-day parties I ever had."

Not long after that, Shernoff handed the editorial chores of *TWG* to Richard "Chinacat" Blum (effectively putting an end to it) and joined with Kempner and Ross to start the Fabulous Moolah (a step up from Shernoff's name for an earlier band, Grand Funk Salinsky). Contacting their new friend Meltzer, who, like the rest of the soon-to-be Dictators, also took a nickname, "Borneo Jimmy," Meltzer alerted his old BOC collaborator Sandy Pearlman to come check them out. After hearing some demos of the band, Pearlman expressed a bit of interest, but he didn't make anything official. So, to hone their chops, the Dictators began playing in any clubs that would have them. One of these was called the Coventry, a Queens lounge that was hosting performances by local glam band Sniper, whose drummer Joey Starship would later morph into Joey Ramone. The Coventry later showcased another Jewish-dominated punk-era band, KISS, whose Nazi-loving guitarist Ace Freehley sometimes jammed with Scott Kempner. For nearly a year the Dictators played there, and at other worse dives like the derelict bar Popeye's in Sheepshead Bay, Brooklyn. Then one night—not long after *TWG* cub reporter and editor Richard Blum had come onstage at Popeye's to give a manic reading of "Wild Thing"—the Dictators gears finally clicked. On May 3, 1974, with both Pearlman and his business partner Murray Krugman looking on, they played a party where they did something right—they invited Blum onstage for the entire performance. This kid with the giant Jewfro and muscles, who couldn't sing and couldn't dance, was knocking the crowd out—and that was because he was a riot. He was a travesty of a rock star, a joke and yet rock's essence. He was rebellious, tough, unselfconscious, and insane. He was a thug possessed of chutzpah, a Jew and a Nazi. He was *fachacht* in the head, and funny in a way that was almost frightening. Pearlman realized that he was the Dictators' secret weapon. He signed the band immediately, convinced they could be the next big thing.

* * *

While the core Dictators, Ross, Andy, and Scott, couldn't understand what Pearlman and Krugman saw in Handsome Dick, they agreed to their new management's stipulation that he become a permanent member. It was that or surrender more royalties. And yet, almost from the beginning their reservations seemed confirmed. It wasn't so much that Handsome Dick was untalented—it was more that Krugman and Pearlman in particular seemed determined to play up his more ridiculous aspects while also encouraging darker undercurrents in the band. Pearlman told Dick to exaggerate his onstage rants, and he advised the rest of the band to toughen up their sound. To Pearlman, Dick was the key player in the Dictators—but it wasn't only because he was funny, but because he showed strength. Power. An almost insane power, something that could overwhelm.

Richard "was a madman [then]" recalled *PUNK* magazine's John Holmstrom in an article published in 1977. "He ate twenty eggs a day. Restaurants couldn't fill his orders for lunch 'cause he ordered so much. He wore a giant Afro haircut and had a bad skin problem. He caused a lot of the trouble that got them thrown out of the press parties they'd connive their way into 'cause [he'd] eat so many 'ludes. He cooked for The Dictators and worked as a roadie—smashing equipment, totaling the rented equipment trucks, losing amplifiers and screwing up the sound."

Dick led the Dictators in being offensive to other bands in the glam scene. During shows at the Coventry, for instance, he was among the loudest of the Dictators to heckle the other groups, calling out that they were "fags, wimps, and homos." Indeed, it was just this sort of behavior at a Wayne County show at CBGB that later resulted in the Dictators being banned from Max's where Wayne's manager doubled as booking agent.

But Pearlman didn't mind. In fact, he loved it. The Dictators, especially Handsome Dick, were macho guys in unmacho times. They didn't buy into all that gender-bending bullshit. They were men's men, the antithesis of what was usually thought of as Jewish.

* * *

With Handsome Dick firmly in place, Pearlman kicked his contribution into high gear, quickly, almost unbelievably, getting the newly christened Dictators a contract with Epic, then one of the coolest major labels in the business. It wasn't just Pearlman and Meltzer's BOC connections that convinced Epic to sign the unknown band. "Glam," or as it was sometimes known in the United States, "glitter," was ascendant in New York at the time, and the half-glam, half-punk New York Dolls led the pack. Battling it out with the mostly British glam triumvirate of David Bowie, Sweet, and T. Rex (led by English Jew Marc "Bolan" Feld), the New York Dolls were punk before there was such a thing. Their costumes went beyond the tease and wink of gender-bending English glam to a mock-and-threat style that was quintessentially American and New York. They were fronted by David Johansen, a son of Czech immigrants, who was described by many, including himself, as "an honorary Jew," and supported by a rhythm section that was one-third Jewish (Ronald "Sylvain Sylvain" Mizrahi) and one-third Italian (the all-important tough-guy Lothario Johnny "Thunders" Genzale). The Dolls seemed to hint at a new direction for glam, one that was harder-edged, party-oriented, violence-prone and, perhaps above all, non-WASP.

The glam factor played into the Dictators' appeal for Epic. Their cheeky humor and leotard-clad frontman made them look to Epic like just another pack of gender-benders rather than tough-guy New Yorkers with a sarcastic edge. Of course, as it turned out, the similarities between the New York Dolls and the Dictators were all but nonexistent. Aside perhaps from the crypto-Italian connection to actual Italian Johnny Thunders, the Dictators were Juidos in the truest sense. And they weren't even very good looking.

They were pretty obviously Jewish, and so were their themes, the Dictators introducing topics that—as the Ramones found later—the average American simply couldn't abide. Songs like "Master Race Rock" and "Back to Africa" were funny in New York City, but beyond its environs they didn't play. Neither did Handsome Dick's Don-Rickles-on-speed shtick. Nonetheless, Pearlman insisted that Handsome Dick's harangues be part of the album, secretly recording them without telling the band. He couldn't see that the Dictators were too much for most Americans. Too comic. Or perhaps too tough. As Andy Shernoff says today, "In hindsight, I do think it was a mistake to make the humor as central in the marketing of the band, but at the time I was all for it."

* * *

In the end, Pearlman pushed his preoccupation with the darker aspects of Jewishness too far. If the Blue Öyster Cult had gotten away with its emphasis on Jewishness and nefariousness and Nazis, it was because that band had masked its obsessions. Even then, Pearlman had occasionally gotten carried away. He encouraged the BOC to perform his song "ME 262," about the first operational jet fighter, Hitler's Messerschmitt 262, while projecting images of wartime imagery during a concert in Berlin. The result was that the BOC were banned in Germany, a country that, ironically, has the strictest anti-Nazi policy in the world. The sleeve for the single "Hot Rails to Hell" depicted a German military figure, hinting that the rails were carrying victims to the death camps, and the band wore black armbands in one of its publicity shots. The BOC's own logo was red and black, the colors of the Nazi swastika, and the band alluded to the swastika in one of its songs. And of course there was the band's "mildly anti-Semitic" keyboard player Allen Lanier, as Meltzer refers to him today with mock understatement. Even that umlaut, the first in rock, begins to look more genuinely ominous than the fake Black Sabbath mood the BOC was supposed to project. Up until the Dictators, this had all been hidden in the spooky mysteries of the secret organizations and fraternal handshakes and evil cabals of Pearlman's obsessions with Masons, illuminati, and *cults*. Only the initiated could understand the Kabbalah-like code, as secret as alchemy or numerology.

The Dictators made these obsessions glaringly apparent. Their references to the master race, dictators, and Jews were right there for everyone to see. Andy Shernoff was the songwriter, so he created this material, but as producer and manager, Pearlman could have reined him in. He could have kept the Dictators masked as Italians. But he chose not to. As Richard Meltzer says, "If Pearlman could rule the world, he would like to be an Egyptian Pharaoh or something like that. He would like to have control of the godhead, and control of the coding, the hieroglyphics. He always was somebody who was fond of power, of the iconography of power, but his connection to things naturally was that he loved Rommel, that he fancied himself as a student of military history, and he was King Rommel and through Rommel, he got through a lot of the rest of it." BOC drummer Albert Bouchard adds, "Did Pearlman ever talk about his Jewishness? He seemed to conspicuously try to not talk about it. I don't want to say that he was an anti-Semitic Jew, but if there was ever such a thing, he was it."

*   *   *

And so what did the Dictators do? After their debut bombed and they were dismissed by Epic, they quickly set about redefining themselves. No longer would their act be so full of the shticky humor of Handsome Dick. And no longer would their songs be as offensive or troubling. No, now the music and the band would be simply tough.

As if bleeding themselves of both the positive and negative aspects of their Jewish preoccupations—the Jewish shtick and the Jewish horror—the Dictators went about making themselves tougher- and meaner-looking and harder than hard rock. They put out first *Manifest Destiny* (1977), then *Bloodbrothers** (1978), two albums containing *rawk* songs like "Steppin' Out," "Exposed," "Faster and Louder," and "Slow Death." They also let Handsome Dick gradually take over as lead singer, substituting his comic rants and drunken klutz antics with a guttural approach to singing and shouting at the audience. They didn't release another album of new material until Shernoff reconstituted the group as Manitoba's Wild Kingdom in the late 1980s (originally with "Fifth Ramone" Daniel "Rey" Rabinowitz on board) and "focused the image" of the band so that it returned to the black humor of the early days, yet also included the dark horror that had made that comedy so striking in the first place. "And You" sold more than any of the Dictators albums, received MTV airplay, and, when Ross the Boss joined, led to a Dictators reunion.

The fine line between humor and horror, catharsis and darkness, self-mockery and self-hatred can easily be crossed. The Dictators missed out on being the first real punk band because they failed to find the delicate balance between aggressive and ironic, violent and comic, threatening and camp that was so pivotal to that new genre. Yet they did pave the way for a band that nailed the balance perfectly, a band that was like a blood brother or a twin, right down to the Italian/Latin associations, neighborhood origins, and cover songs and styles on its first album. These wiseguys, these jokers in leather jackets, an equal collaboration of Jews and non-Jews, were, of course, the Ramones.

---

*Interestingly, the band by this point was associating itself with novelist Richard Price, perhaps best known for his first book, *The Wanderers* (1974), a tale of Bronx gangs in the early 1960s that features an Italian narrator clearly modeled on its Jewish author. Price's second novel, *Bloodbrothers* (1976), meanwhile, apparently inspired the Dictators' album of the same name.

9

A JEWISH AMERICAN BAND

The Hebraic Foundations of the Ramones

He loves John Ford movies, and the John Ford Irish myth of America. I think sometimes Johnny confused Americanism with Irishness, which doesn't make sense, especially historically, but to him it's one and the same. His vision of America was very John Wayne, John Ford.

> —Tommy Ramone speaking (in present
> tense) about his recently deceased former
> bandmate Johnny

When people talk about the Beatles, they often say that none of them alone could have created the group's magic without the others, that it was the combination, the interplay, the synergy that made them so special.

Ask the same people who was the leader of the Beatles, the one without whom the group could never have approached its heights, and they'll snap, "John Lennon. He was the heart and soul of the band. He was the one who created it."

Now ask fans of those latter-day Beatles from the seventies, the ones who started a revolution of their own, in fact created a whole new genre of music—the Ramones—the same question, and what will they say? "Umm, wasn't Joey the leader? Or Dee Dee? Were any of them?"

In short, they won't know. There's a good reason for this, one that speaks to the core meaning of the band and marks them as a Jewish American group whether anyone—including the band members themselves—is aware of it.

For the man who almost single-handedly created the Ramones was the most mysterious member of the group, the one whose past remained vague and uncertain, in large part because he never once brought it up. Who is this? Not Joey Ramone, though the man born Jeffry Hyman was in fact the figurative representative of the individual we're talking about. No, it's Tommy Erdelyi, born as Tamas in Hungary, best known to us today as Tommy Ramone.

Tommy-Tamas-Erdelyi-Ramone dreamed up the Ramones in the darkness of his childhood bedroom, then took it to a darkened studio in Manhattan, where he enlisted the talents of his "friends" from back in Queens to help realize it. As first manager Danny Fields says: "[Tommy] designed the band . . . It was Tommy that told us, you know the guitarist stands here, the lead singer never moves, there is no spotlight, all of that. Tommy was the architect." Or as Ramones tour manager Monte Melnick puts it, explaining why the other Ramones treated Tommy so badly: "They were jealous that he formed them. It was his concept . . . he brought them together." The band fulfilled a fantasy of his, provided a lifeline to surviving in an America where he often felt an immigrant. It was a way of getting rid of the violence and romantic longing in his head and a way of shedding the turmoil and angst that he'd acquired as a Jew living in exile.

Having fled anti-Semitism and persecution in Eastern Europe, Tommy knew that his Jewishness made him an outcast at least twice over. He apparently suspected that it did the same for his lead singer and, to an extent, his guitarist and bassist. All of them, Tommy, Joey, Johnny, and Dee Dee, emerged from that crucible of the Jewish American experience, that little-ghetto-within-the-larger-ghetto-of-New-York known as Forest Hills, Queens. All of them had come up from there and tried to insinuate themselves into Manhattan through the classic outsider's route of rock 'n' roll.

Ultimately, though, only Tommy understood the conflicts that had formed him and that kept him from announcing his pivotal role in the Ramones, much less proclaiming his Jewishness. Why else would he have been so calm the first time we met—answering my question as to why I'd never heard he was Jewish with unintentional punchline, "No one bothered to ask"—only to seem so nervous the second time we spoke, stopping suddenly to demand, "Are you trying to out Jews with this book?" Fear and its cousin, humor. That is the answer. Humor and fear, those twin poles of the Jewish American experience.

*   *   *

To really understand this fear we need to go back a bit. Most stories of the "bruddahs" focus on the classic American attributes of their childhoods—the concrete parks and playgrounds, the chain-link fences, the stoops—ignoring the plethora of Jewish delis, community centers, and synagogues in their beginnings. These were Jewish American childhoods that had their origins in Central and Eastern Europe.

A subway ride will prove it. Simply get on the F train from Houston Street in the Bowery (just gobbing distance from CBGB, in case you get lost), and ride it over bridge and through tunnel, as so many B&Ts do each day, until you get to the G train. Then take that to the 63rd Drive subway stop on Queens Boulevard in Forest Hills. There you'll find where the early B&T-like Ramones caught their own pre-Ramones trains into "the city," where the genesis of punk took place and its exodus to Manhattan soon followed.

Come on, come up from the underground and breathe the Jewish essence. It flows from the bagel and knish shops still dotting the area. It visually assaults you from the window of the nearby Forest Hills Jewish Center. With its Hebrew letters above the doorway and cheerful signs advertising Yiddish classes and Hadassah meetings inside, it looks just the way it did when the four Ramones used to pass by here as teenagers. In fact, it looks no different from how it did that day in 1965 when Johnny first met Joey's brother—and through him, Joey—at one of the Battles of the Bands that took place each weekend in the Center basement.

The Jewish presence continues as you move into the residential part of the neighborhood, historic sites popping up at regular intervals like tourist spots on a B'nai B'rith bus tour of Europe. First there's the synagogue where Joey Ramone (Jeffry Hyman) was bar-mitzvahed in 1964, followed soon after by the synagogue where his brother Mickey Leigh (Mitchell Hyman) went through the same ceremony of "becoming a man" three years later. Just beyond is the childhood home of Tommy Erdelyi, and near this the home of Ritchie Stern, an early Ramone who was let go before the band ever recorded because, as Tommy jokes, "he would have made us too Jewish." Surrounded by apartments adorned with mezuzahs on their doorposts—those talismans of Jewish fear in which the first two paragraphs of the Shema, Judaism's most holy prayer, are inserted to protect those inside—these homes speak of child-hoods embraced by Jewishness. It's a deep irony, considering that Tommy Erdelyi once felt alienated from this area because the "good Jewish girls" ignored guys like him, without money or prospects. Or as Joey's brother Mickey puts it before we head out from his house for our own tour of these spots, "My wife Arlene was a JAP [Jewish-American Princess] whether she likes to admit it or not. And she still is. She wants to me to get a job." "Stooooop," Arlene jokes from the kitchen, before switching tones entirely and whining, "And while you're out, be sure to pick up some nuts. I don't see why I have to do it. Why can't yooouuu?!"

Yes, these are historic sites, brick-and-mortar remnants of what was. And though they are interesting—just as are the nearby homes of Charlotte Lesher (Joey's mother), Ira Nagel (Joey's childhood friend), and Monte Melnick (the Ramones' tour director)*—they tell only half of the story. Perhaps not even that.

To get the full story, we need to go back still further, back to where it all began, into the past of that recent immigrant, the Ramones' key member and founder, Tommy Erdelyi.

*   *   *

"I was born in Budapest in January 1949, barely three years after the end of World War II," says Tommy, sitting in the living room of his low-lit Forest Hills condominium surrounded by hundreds of albums and dozens of Ramones session tapes. "My parents were professional photographers and they had liberal, artistic friends who protected them. But most of my family was murdered in the Holocaust. I am barely here."

---

*It's also interesting to note how many other key players in the Ramones story were Jewish and came from Jewish neighborhoods, among them Danny Fields (first manager; Redwood, Queens), Gary Kurfirst (second manager; Kew Gardens, Queens), Andy Shernoff (Dictators founder, guitarist on Ramones albums; Flagstone, Queens), George Seminara (Ramones video producer; Lower East Side, Manhattan); Daniel Rey (Daniel Rabinowitz, Shrapnel founder, guitarist/producer on both Ramones' albums and Joey's posthumous solo release *Don't Worry About Me*; Redbank, New Jersey), and Ida Langsam (Ramones' publicist, Orthodox Jew, and former editor of the Beatles' New York fan club newsletter, the punning *Apple Juice*; Washington Heights, Manhattan).

Tommy's final comment—that he is "barely here"—has a dark double meaning in light of the story to follow. For not only does Tommy believe that his parents should never have lived through the war considering the circumstances, he seems also to believe that he should never have been in Hungary in the first place, nor have ended up in America after that. He seems to believe, in fact, that he barely belongs *any* place.

"In Hungary it was sort of like a stigma to be Jewish," Tommy says. "There were very few Jews, and they knew you were Jewish because you were circumcised and nobody else was. You felt like there was something wrong with you. I mean, people made it known. It was a stigma that I felt."

In reaction to anti-Semitism, Tommy's father changed the family name from the Jewish-sounding Grunewald to the more Hungarian-sounding Erdelyi (both translate to "Greenwood"). It wasn't that he was ashamed of his Jewishness, Tommy says. He was just tired of constant discrimination. He thought that perhaps by reinventing himself, he would be able to free his family from that curse.

But with the Soviet invasion of 1956 and the increasingly repressive and anti-Semitic political climate that accompanied it, Tommy's father decided it was time to leave. Packing what belongings they could, the family escaped across the border to Austria, where they spent months going through the process of immigration before flying to America. It was an uncertain, frightening move filled with major cultural adjustments, not the least of them for Tommy himself. Yet, in many ways it was the youngest of the Erdelyis who was most excited. It had only been a few months since he'd discovered his first love—rock 'n' roll. Now he was going to the land that had created it, the land of Chuck Berry, Little Richard, and Elvis.

"I remember in Hungary I'd seen a film about the 'decadent West'," Tommy says. "They were telling us about this 'animalistic' music from America that was playing in the soundtrack, and as soon as I heard it, I loved it. It had this driving beat."

After living for a few months as refugees in New Jersey's Camp Kilmer army base, Tommy and his parents were finally able to settle into an apartment in the Bronx. Unsure where to put Tommy, the Erdelyis sent him to a local yeshiva, a major shift for a seven-year-old boy who had been raised in a completely secular—albeit *culturally* Jewish—home.

"It wasn't so bad," says Tommy. "But then, when my Orthodox relatives came to the United States from Israel, we moved with them from the Bronx to Brooklyn, and they insisted I be put into a hasidic yeshiva. That was another story altogether. That was too radical a change. To the kids there, I was like a goy."

Ostracized twice over for entirely opposite reasons, Tommy began to think of himself as a perpetual outsider. Still, he had his rock 'n' roll and his love of bands like the Comets and the Crickets. And he had his growing collection of instruments and the crystal radio that he'd built. He had his refuge and hobby—his music that he listened to and played. And then he discovered the Beatles, and his life changed forever.

"I knew what I wanted to do," Tommy says. I wanted to be in a band. I'd been in love with rock 'n' roll since I was six, but this was something really special."

Even as Tommy examined the faces of the Beatles, hoping that one of them might be Jewish ("you kind of thought maybe Ringo was, with that nose"), he continued practicing his guitar, gradually improving his skills. As if in league with his efforts, outside events began to turn in his favor. After "an endless year" at the Orthodox yeshiva, Tommy's parents told him they were moving again, and within months he was gone from Brooklyn and headed for Queens.

"I guess it must have been around this time that Tommy's family moved to Forest Hills," says childhood friend and Ramones tour director Monte Melnick. "I remember seeing him riding around the neighborhood on his bike and waving him down to talk to one day. We both liked science. And we didn't like contact sports. I tried to teach him golf and he tried to get me involved in music."

Though Monte would eventually get a record contract three years before the Ramones and put out two country rock albums with his band Thirty Days Out, at the time music was a low priority for him, so he and Tommy never got very far with their efforts. Instead, they discussed biology and chemistry and occasionally went out to shoot a few rounds, all the while hanging with their mutual friend, the son of the Indonesian ambassador to New York, one of the few kids in the area perhaps even more alienated than themselves.

Then, one day as the three were sitting together at the back of the lunchroom, a kid named Bob Rowland came over and said he wanted to introduce Tommy to someone. Tommy followed Rowland to a table not far away and saw a bunch of guys sitting around their beans and franks and milk cartons.

They all had that wary look that teenagers get when they're about to meet a stranger—yet there was one in the middle who seemed particularly distant.

"Here's the kid plays guitar," Rowland said.

"Oh really?" went the guy in the middle. Then, after asking Tommy if he'd like to jam that night, he returned to his beans and franks.

When Tommy arrived at Rowland's house later that evening, he didn't think much of the band that his new friend called the Tangerine Puppets. And yet, as he plugged in and began playing his guitar, his opinion of at least one of the members quickly changed.

"The sarcastic guy from lunch started jumping around and going kind of crazy," Tommy says. "He was charismatic and alive onstage. And I could see that we had immediate chemistry."

Indeed, the chemistry was so good that Tommy not only joined the band, he ended up becoming best friends with the "sarcastic guy," too. During the remainder of high school, the two were all but inseparable, Tommy serving as de facto leader of the Tangerine Puppets and the sarcastic guy as a kind of figurative avenger for Tommy. Like that invincible man of clay created by the sixteenth-century Prague rabbi, Judah Loew, the Sarcastic Guy, John Cummings (aka Johnny Ramone), became Tamas Erdelyi's personal golem.*

* * *

Like Tommy, John Cummings was an outsider's outsider. The son of a construction worker of Irish descent (what Danny Fields would have called one of those *echt* Americans), he was a member of the nation's majority culture and so should have felt at home most anywhere in the United States.

And yet, Johnny was in that part of America known as New York, that island just off the coast of the mainland that seems as if it could float back to Europe at any moment. Worse, he was in one of those sections of New York—like the Upper West Side in Manhattan and Flatbush Avenue in

---

* After Loew creates the golem to protect the Jewish community from annihilation, the monster turns on him and threatens to wreak havoc. Like Frankenstein's monster—born of the human desire for power—the golem constitutes a Faustian bargain that ultimately leads to self-destruction. (For further insight see the 1921 German expressionist film *Der Golem*, an award-winning retelling of this fable now complete with a new score by Jewish avant-garde punk Gary Lucas.)

Brooklyn—that seemed particularly alien to white Christian Americans (John's mother was of Lithuanian or Ukrainian descent and his father Irish Catholic). He was in Forest Hills—a largely middle-class, Jewish, shtetl-like place—where he was the anomaly, the outsider, the minority.

Where he was, in effect, Jewish.

"When I formed the Ramones I was sure to have Johnny, not just because he was my friend, but also because he added color," Tommy laughs. "Only in Forest Hills would a guy like Johnny have been considered exotic."

No wonder that Johnny—the Republican, Catholic, working-class kid with a disdain for intellectuals and weaklings—wanted to escape Forest Hills. And no wonder Tommy used him as a vehicle for doing so himself. It was as if Tommy had found a "shadow other" who, in his alienation, mirrored Tommy's own sense of displacement.

While being a misfit in a Jewish neighborhood might seem to identify Tommy as far from a typical Jew, the fact is that Jews are so expert at being outcasts that the truest products of the culture—the *echt* Jews as it were—often become alienated from their own people. Consider the old Jewish saying, "Two Jews, three opinions." Jews are so analytical and able to see so many sides, they often cannot identify with any. As no less a Jewish authority on alienation than Franz Kafka noted in his diaries (January 8, 1914): "What have I in common with Jews? I have hardly anything in common with myself and should stand very quietly in a corner, content that I can breathe."

With his long hair and gruff manner, Johnny seemed like an oddity in the rec-room jam sessions at Bob Rowland's house. But to a short, frizzy-haired guy like Tommy, he represented an alternative to traditional Jewishness—an alternative based on size and strength. Like those other Jews, Danny Fields, Robert Frank, and Bob Dylan, this Hungarian immigrant with the funny accent went in search of the "real" personification of America.

"Johnny was a big guy and tall and he was very different," Tommy says. "He looked rural and not very cityish. He always liked to arm wrestle me and play stickball. And I wasn't physical. It wasn't a very physical neighborhood. It wasn't the type of place where kids would have regular fistfights. Forest Hills was an intellectual place."

While Tommy stresses that he "did not want to be like John" and that he "did not like John's culture of sports and tough-guy bravado," he does admit that he found him "fascinating, charismatic, and exotic" and it seems that his new friend's anger was at the source.

"When the Tangerine Puppets played, John put on this great show," Tommy says. "He would wear his bass very high like a machine gun, sort of like Wilco Johnson [guitarist for Dr. Feelgood] later did, and he would move around, just go crazy on the stage . . . He was angry, a very angry guy. He was an angry person, and a lot of that violence came out in his music."

For this most internal and seemingly peaceful of Ramones, Johnny's explosions of anger were almost synonymous with his musical bombardments. Each provided Tommy with a much-needed emotional release.

As much as Tommy might have been impressed by Johnny's musical tastes and strength, however, it was Johnny's sense of humor that ultimately sealed the bond. Though Tommy has trouble remembering specific jokes today, he says that Johnny had a viciously surreal sense of humor, one—like the comedy of Lenny Bruce—that noted the darkness in the world, yet seemed to deflect it through cool strength. This sense of humor brought Tommy and his "shadow other" all the closer.

(Referring to a related, softer strain of Jewish-American humor prevalent during that period, Tommy says: "I started reading *MAD* magazine when I was either nine or ten, and it was a wonderful magazine, because it had so much intellectual humor in it for a young kid. You know, the farce and the—what do you call it—the satire. And yeah, it was a major influence on my sensibilities. . . . In fact, I have it on one of the shelves still. *The Brothers Mad* was one of the first paperbacks I bought, and that's all Harvey Kurtzman. And Kurtzman was all Yiddish stuff, you know, *meshuggener* and whatever, that whole sensibility. But *MAD* magazine was very influential on my sensibilities, my thinking, my sense of humor, probably my outlook on life. And then later on underground comics were, Robert Crumb and *Zap* comics and that stuff, which is really a continuation, in a way, of that, the hippified version of that.")

Ultimately it doesn't matter that Johnny never physically defended Tommy. For one gets the sense, in speaking to this seemingly mild-mannered Ramone, that he loved being friends with the most violent member of the band because it provided him with an outlet for his frustrations. A vicarious outlet, but one that maintained him nonetheless.

Like so many other Jews throughout the ages, both mythic and real—Rabbi Loew with his golem, Shuster and Siegel with their Superman, Brian Epstein with his leather-clad Beatles, Danny Fields with his MC5/Morrison/Stooges—Tommy got off on his association with this powerfully physical being, this powerfully American being who served as his unofficial avenger.

And so it should come as no surprise that when Tommy went to start his music career in Manhattan, working first as an engineer at the Record Plant, then later as a cofounder of Performance Studios rehearsal space (after the movie starring Mick Jagger), he called and called and then called Johnny again, telling him over and over that he should come to "the city" to start a band with him—that he, Tommy, would serve as the producer. He would help to create the sound, the look, the image. He would do it all—if only Johnny would come and join him.

* * *

When, nearly two years later, Johnny finally heeded Tommy's call, he didn't go alone. He brought with him another outsider from the old neighborhood that Tommy recognized as perfect—a kind of Jew-in-German's-clothing who underscored Tommy's own thrice-alienated consciousness and mirrored it back to him.

Raised in Berlin by an American soldier father and a blonde, blue-eyed German mother, Douglas Colvin (Dee Dee Ramone) was in some ways the ultimate expression of divided consciousness inherent in the band. Brought up amidst his parents' constant fighting—itself deeply driven by their cultural differences—Dee Dee came to see himself as the man without a country, an alienated soul who didn't know what to call home or how to form an identity. He was as divided inside as East and West Germany, as a Jew and a Nazi, as an outsider living in a land he could never really call his own. He both hated and loved everything that made up his self.

"Dee Dee was generally a paradox who would blow with the wind," Tommy says. "He would be left wing, right wing—he was very schizophrenic depending on what mood he was in. Ultimately, he was very childlike; his persona was that of a child."

While Tommy doesn't say so, it appears that Dee Dee may have melded with the group not only because he was a child at odds with the world, but also because he was like a Jew in his preoccupation with Nazis and his conflicted, even neurotic, feelings toward Germany.

As former roommate (and Ramones lighting director) Arturo Vega observes, Dee Dee's father was part of the occupying force in Germany and had something of a conquering warrior's attitude toward that country that extended to his wife and son.

"Dee Dee's mother definitely resented Dee Dee's father's oppressive control of her life, not to mention his drunken rampages. And Dee Dee was the same," Vega says. "He began collecting Iron Crosses and swastikas as a way of rebelling. Of course, his father beat the shit out of him when he did that, but Dee Dee didn't care. He seemed to feel that he was at least getting some attention. All of that hatred to him was like love."

Like some victims of Nazi horror, Dee Dee seemed to suffer from a form of masochism, asking to be hurt by the oppressor as a way of being acknowledged. Many who lived through the Holocaust experienced a similar impulse to deny themselves pleasure as a way of appeasing their guilt at surviving. Perhaps the attitude is best expressed in an exaggerated version of the old Groucho Marx joke, "I don't want to belong to any club that will accept me as a member." Made to feel worthless for centuries, but perhaps never more so than since World War II, they internalize this hatred and turn it against themselves, sacrificing love, success, or simple pleasure in the process.

Ironically, when Dee Dee's mother finally left his father, Dee Dee found that he was suddenly living on the flipside of this dichotomous experience. As a German-raised kid in a Jewish American neighborhood, he was like Alice through the looking-glass—much closer to where he began than it seemed. As Tommy says, though no one ever heard Dee Dee utter an anti-Semitic remark, they were aware of his obsession with Nazi Germany—and they didn't consider this exactly out of place.

"The neighborhood was almost entirely Jewish," Tommy says. "We were aware of the Holocaust. We knew what had happened."

Dee Dee wasn't the only one to have conflicted feelings about Nazis and Germany in his new surroundings. Tommy himself expressed mixed feelings without even realizing it. Though he stresses that he hates jokes about the war and doesn't believe Nazi references are funny, he now thinks, looking back on it, that the reason he may have been attracted to Dee Dee and Johnny in those days is that they represented something so opposite to what he'd grown up with. In other words, Johnny wasn't just physical and Dee Dee wasn't just odd. In their attraction to Nazi imagery, they were both dangerous. Just like rock 'n' roll.

"It's hard for me being a European Jew to say what American kids [like Johnny and Dee Dee] were thinking [when they did things like buy mini-statues of Hitler in Argentina], but part of my attraction to them was fascination in their danger, like hanging with Hell's Angels . . . Growing up with fear of Holocaust, being with them was like living with danger . . . It could have been that I was rebelling by hanging with them."

Whether Tommy was rebelling by joining Dee Dee and Johnny or delving ever deeper into their shared past of exile is impossible to say, just as it's impossible to say whether Dee Dee and Johnny were the ultimate anti-Semites or the ultimate non-Jewish Jews. One thing's for sure. All three considered themselves separate from the upbeat, smiley-face world of their time. And all three felt that there was a need to bring some darker, angrier truths to the surface. They wanted to create a band that would combat the rose-colored notions of the hippies and the sentimental Have a Nice Day hypocrisies of the 1970s. They wanted to create a band that would look at the other side and embrace the unhappy outsiders. They wanted a band that would be for kids like them, kids without illusions. To do that, they needed a lead singer.

*   *   *

How Jeffry Hyman (Joey Ramone) came to be the lead singer in Tommy Erdelyi's dream band is one of those coincidences that seem preordained in the heavens. Six-foot-six to Tommy's five-foot-five, withdrawn and silent where Tommy was driven and direct, Joey was nonetheless, like Tommy, descended from oppressed European Jewry. And his later alienation seemed to have as much to do with this as with his other problems.

As his mother, Charlotte Lesher (she took her second husband's name after divorcing Joey's father), says, "[My father's] father was an artist. And my father could draw, he was talented . . . and [he] could have probably been onstage. He was a funny man, and a good storyteller in the tradition of Sam Levinson or Myron Cohen. He was that way. He was a ham. And my brother and I were both hams . . . and later I had an art gallery, so I guess all of that—humor, performance, and art—is in our family. And maybe that part of me really enjoys vicariously that my kids have great poise onstage."

Joey's brother Mickey adds that his maternal grandmother was also musical. He says, "A story that my brother liked to tell . . . is that in the days before [there was technology], there were like listening booths, and you'd go into a listening booth in a music store and someone would play from the sheet music [so you could decide whether you wanted to buy] the songs. And supposedly she did that."

Charlotte points out that Joey's paternal grandparents were quite different. "They embodied another kind of immigrant's story," she says. "They were determined to make it financially while retaining their old ways and customs."

Soon after arriving in America, Joey's paternal grandparents set out to establish themselves in business, ending up eventually in the trucking industry. By the time Joey's father was born, they had made enough money to move to Brooklyn—a major step up in those days—there opening a transport company that helped take goods from the still predominantly Jewish Lower East Side to the growing sweatshop-and-child-labor-ridden Garment District uptown.

"They were very successful," Charlotte says. "When my first husband, Noel, was a teenager, the company was doing well enough for him to drop out of school and begin working there as the heir apparent."

The future father of Joey Ramone—the Jew incongruously named Noel—began at the very base of operations to learn his business from the bottom up. Hauling pants and fabrics back and forth between uptown and downtown each day, he also occasionally headed out on the open road, riding the nation's highways like some Jewish version of Elvis before stardom struck, his muscular arm hanging out the window, his curled lips whistling into the wind.

Indeed, when the seventeen-year-old Charlotte first spied the twenty-five-year-old Noel at one of those summer resorts in the Catskills (think *Dirty Dancing* meets *The Apprenticeship of Duddy Kravitz*), she was so impressed by his good looks and sophistication that she sensed almost immediately they would marry. She was right, for despite her parents' objections, they did so within the year, setting up a life together—only for Charlotte to realize almost as immediately their deep incompatibility. First insisting that she give up her dreams of becoming an artist—dreams that her father had encouraged by insisting she enroll in the Pratt Institute after she won a scholarship there—Noel soon began telling Charlotte that they were moving to the Upper West Side of Manhattan, and that they were doing so as soon as possible regardless of what she wanted.

"I had been hanging around in Greenwich Village while I was in school, and I'd loved it," Charlotte says. "But Noel hated it. It was too 'weird' for him.

He had that fantasy of living on the Upper West Side with all the 'successful' people. I was so bored there. I would go out walking while pregnant with Joey, and all the young mothers my age would be talking about where to send their children to school and where to shop and what they were going to serve for dinner that night. I couldn't believe it."

As if that weren't enough, just as Charlotte was beginning to adjust to their new neighborhood, Noel began announcing that their unborn child should grow up amidst trees and grass. Once more without asking, he moved them to a new home, this one even farther from the Village. To Charlotte's deep chagrin, she suddenly found herself mere blocks from the very spot in Brooklyn where she'd been raised, from which she'd fled when she went to college. "It seemed," she says, "as if we were rapidly going backwards, retreating ever further into an Old World style of life."

Upsetting as these moves were, they were nothing compared to the shock Charlotte received when Jeffry (whom even she now refers to as Joey) was born. Because Joey, as she says, "faced certain problems right from the beginning; and Noel seemed to regard these as weaknesses that needed to be eradicated from him—through force."

Charlotte doesn't like to speak about Joey's "problems" in detail except to say that he had to wear a full-length leg cast for the first eight months of his life, and that he emerged with some sort of growth on his back that had to be immediately removed. She will say, however, that these problems led to all manner of difficulties for Joey later, causing him to—among other things—grow at an extremely exaggerated rate (by third grade, he was five feet tall), be lanky to the point of emaciation, and have weak, easily damaged bones and muscles that kept him in the hospital as often as not.

"The other kids teased him mercilessly and often beat him up," says Joey's brother Mickey (initially head roadie with the Ramones, later guitarist with such bands as Lester Bangs's Birdland).* "Joey just took it in silence. Just as he did with my father. It was sad to watch. I have to admit, at that time I found it embarrassing."

---

*Often called the father of rock journalism, few realize Bangs was also a patient of Joey Ramone's second stepfather, the respected psychiatrist Phillip Sapienza. Indeed, Bangs often accompanied the entire Hyman/Sapienza family to their summer house in the Berkshire Mountains near Northampton, Massachusetts.

Aggressive and passive, artistic and practical, dreamy and action-oriented: these were the twin poles of Joey's life. Watching his parents, the cultivated, gallery-owning Charlotte, and the truck-driving, hard-bitten Noel, he must have felt somewhat divided even if he seemed outwardly to pursue his mother's path. When his father insisted, against his mother's wishes, that he have a Bar Mitzvah, Joey went through with the event, in essence giving his first public performance.

Is it possible that from his cultivated, secular, artistically inclined mother, Joey found the ability to transform his pain into art? And if so, was it from his practical, money-oriented, tradition-bound father that he found the ability to get his art out to the public and sell it? Was Joey in fact divided between these twin poles of the Jewish American experience, which demands, on the one hand, allegiance to patriarchal tradition and, on the other, the kind of cultivation and learning that often leads to a secular career in the arts?

It's impossible to say, but one thing is clear. During his childhood and early teen years, Joey led an increasingly Kafkaesque existence, retreating like Gregor Samsa—that artistic child of a money-minded father and a sensitive, mother—into an ever more neurotic (and in some sense Jewish) form of life-lessness. He turned his light on and off repeatedly before going to bed; and according to his mother he checked himself into a mental institution for the preoccupations that tortured him (though Joey's first roommate, Arturo Vega, says that his parents had him committed against his wishes). Joey found the world increasingly alien and difficult, and appeared to be withdrawing at an alarming rate.

Even a brief escape to San Francisco in 1967 offered but a temporary respite. Joey was fleetingly accepted at the "Gathering of the Tribes" in Golden Gate Park, only to find himself further exiled upon his return to Forest Hills. Now free of the fifties-style duck's-ass haircut and skinny suits that had typified him in his youth, he was adorned in the long hair and wild colors that aligned him with the world of counterculture rock, yet his freakishness no longer protected him. He was an outcast, a loser, a member of a "lost tribe," a jerk.

He retreated to his room once again, letting the dirty plates and discarded wrappers and half-eaten meals rise up around him. It was as if he didn't even notice them. As if he never expected to rise again. As if, in fact, like Gregor Samsa, that man turned into a cockroach, he expected to die alone in his room like a bug.

*   *   *

After many nights of troubling dreams, Jeffry H. would awake to find himself transformed into a giant pop star. For at that very moment, a plan was being hatched that could only have come from a Jew more alienated than himself, a plan that was no less grandiose than Rabbi Loew's with his golem. A plan that led eventually to his—and his savior's—metamorphosis.

"We all knew Joey from the old neighborhood," Tommy says. "He was someone you couldn't help but notice. And Johnny was friends with his younger brother Mickey. We'd jammed together once or twice. He seemed right."

Though Johnny resisted bringing Joey into the group, saying that he was too odd-looking, Tommy persisted, explaining to his bandmate that this was the point.

"He was another one the colorful characters who I thought of when I envisioned putting together a band using my friends from Forest Hills," Tommy says. "He was the kind of guy people looked at twice when he walked down the street. He was like the perfect outsider for the Andy Warhol movie I had in mind."

So Jeffry Hyman was called back into service, virtually being raised from the dead. With Joey on board, Tommy really began throwing himself into creating the "art concept" he'd always wanted. Doing away with Joey's high heels and tinted glasses, Johnny's sparkly glam pants and sideburns, and Dee Dee's long hair and flares, he created a uniform for them all. Simple leather jackets with blue jeans and tennis shoes—the kind of clothes that they had worn as kids in Forest Hills. Tommy knew these clothes would mark them as outsiders in Manhattan. It was purposeful.

"Part of the whole point was that we looked like what we were, yet we were aware of doing so, of intentionally creating this image," Tommy says. "It was an ironic statement about where we were from. We became a group in a uniform that we claimed was natural. We became a band."

At the same time, Tommy says, this band became a figurative "band of brothers." Each member was forced to change his name, just as Tommy himself had already done. Each member was required to merge into the group identity, to become "a member of the tribe."

Though they claimed that they got their name from Paul McCartney's pseudonym (He used to check in as Paul Ramon while on the road, the

Cute One has said), their choice also made them sound like a Puerto Rican street gang—a group of angry *ethnic outsiders*, in other words. This was not accidental.

As Tommy says, "It sounded tough. Like the streets of the city. Yet it also sounded ridiculous, like a joke. It was like something absurd yet dangerous. It really struck you."

So did the music, that most singular of the Ramones' creations—again largely as a result of Tommy's machinations. First he took Joey from behind the drums so that he was out front, leading the band. Then he set up a beat that was relentless yet joyful, angry yet celebratory, violent yet contained. Tommy capped it all off by altering Dee Dee's Nazi-obsessed lyrics, changing "I'm a Nazi baby" to "I'm a Nazi *Schatze*" (kind of like "sweetie" in German) and "I'm a German soldier" to "I'm a shock trooper in a stupor," the result being that these possibly glorifying lyrics became parodic. Like Mel Brooks in *The Producers*, Tommy reduced his "Hotsy-Totsy Nazis" to caricatures who were more laughable than frightening. He simultaneously stole their thunder, passing it to the screaming Jew at the front of the band, that Kafkaesque stickman who seemed like a bug metamorphosing into a rock star.

By putting Joey out front of the band, Tommy not only made the representative of the Ramones an outsider like himself, he made him, again like himself, a Jew as well. As Tommy says, "I always thought that Joey looked Jewish . . . I mean, the caricature, or the stereotype—one of the stereotypes. There are all kinds of stereotypes. But yes, I suppose that would be one of them, right? Sort of the Fagin character from Dickens." Moreover, he chose a Jew who came from a secular family that had changed its name—a Jew who in fact later changed his name a second time.

Born Jeffry Hyman, during his brief stint as singer with the glam band Sniper (note the violent connotations), Joey had gone by the stage name Jeff Starship. Like David Bowie, a bisexual outsider at the tail end of the classic rock era, Jeffry-Joey, a bifurcated Jew growing up at the height of the post-Holocaust era, initially tried to reflect the sense of outsiderness that he felt by draping it in a freaky "starman's" clothing. Yet, it wasn't till Tommy came and anointed him anew that the real Jeffry—part sensitive artist in the tradition of his mother, part cynical fighter in the tradition of his father—was finally expressed. It wasn't until Tommy put Joey in front of the band as his emblem, his representative, that he was able to break free of his oppressed history and become a sneering, sarcastic punk.

In short, Tommy was re-creating himself again—and he was taking his friends along with him in the process. He was making himself into a stronger, scarier, more independent version of Tommy Erdelyi. At the same time, he was underscoring the sense of separateness he felt as Tamas Grunewald. This short, frizzy-haired Jew from Budapest, this weird secular yeshiva kid from Brooklyn, this weak, angry outsider's outsider from Forest Hills, was expressing what it felt like to live on the edge of society. He was getting across through artistic means what it was like to be a reject, a rebel. What it was like to spend your life as the world's forgotten boy. Or rather, the world's forgotten Jew-boy.

*   *   *

Sitting in the living room of Tommy Erdelyi's home today, these long-ago transformations seem strangely present—as present as the existence of the Rego Park Jewish Center around the corner and his neighbors' mezuzahs, which hang on the doors down the hall.

They are the reminders of just where the Ramones' style, attitude, and music originated and indicators of where the band's legacy will live on in the future.

"There aren't many people who even know that I'm Jewish," Tommy says. "It's not like I advertise it. I don't see the point."

And yet, many who carry the torch know about Tommy's integral role in the band—just as many already know about his figurehead, Jeffry Hyman.

"I love Tommy," says Jed Davis, a budding Jewish rocker whose musical tribute to Joey Ramone, "The Bowery Electric," was recorded by Tommy, Marky, CJ (the Ramones' last bassist), and Daniel Rey in 2002. "When I saw him last August he asked me what I was doing for Yom Kippur. He's a good guy. And an inspiration to all us little Jewish kids who thought we couldn't be rock stars."

An inspiration. Even if his oppressed background in Eastern Europe seems to get the better of him sometimes, leading him to ask nervously, "Are you trying to out Jews with this book?"

Safe in America, surrounded by Jewish and non-Jewish neighbors, Tommy still feels uncertain. He might say that he has never commented on his Jewishness because no one's bothered to ask, but it's clear that it's an issue for him—one that makes him alternately proud and ill at ease.

Of course, considering that he was all but forced from his band three years after the Ramones recorded their first album, perhaps this isn't surprising. It wasn't for nothing that Tommy felt he was losing his mind cooped up in that bus with Johnny, Dee Dee, and Joey. Physically threatened by Johnny, treated with contempt by Dee Dee, and all but ignored by Joey, he felt he had to get away—to go back behind the scenes and help produce their records, just as he had originally intended when he put the band together like a performance piece.

Did he know that Johnny regularly tormented his friend Monte Melnick, and even the former Jeffry Hyman, with anti-Semitic remarks? Did he know that Johnny was recruiting Dee Dee to go on shopping expeditions for Nazi paraphernalia with him, especially when they were in infamously exile-friendly countries, such as Argentina and Brazil? Did he know that Johnny would one day have a large, autographed photo of Adolf Hitler hanging prominently above the fireplace of his LA home, apparently placing it there without irony? He must have sensed it, must have known that there was something beneath the surface, something that was roiling there all along.

As he says looking back on it, his face filling with a mixture of justification and regret: "Growing up with fear of Holocaust, being with Johnny and Dee Dee was like living with danger. There might have been an element of that—just as there was in my attraction to rock 'n' roll. It could have been that I was rebelling by hanging with them."

* * *

Tommy can take satisfaction in at least one thing. By putting his proxy, Jeffry Hyman, at the front of his band, he freed a Kafkaesque character living in his own personal concentration camp of isolation. He made it possible for Joey to stand up for himself, sing loudly, and, by the mid-1980s, speak out against his nemesis, denouncing Johnny's beloved President Reagan for visiting, of all things, a cemetery honoring not just German soldiers, but members of Hitler's highest order, the true believers of the elite corps known as the SS ("Bonzo Goes to Bitburg," *Animal Boy*, 1986).

Then again, hadn't Tommy already struck back far earlier when he undermined horror with humor and made the Nazis laughable in song? It wasn't only the storm troopers of "Today Your Love, Tomorrow the World" that he'd transformed into drunken idiots in a stupor. It was also the militaristic types of Dee Dee's "Commando," a song made up of rules like "First . . . the laws of Germany / Second . . . be nice to mommy / Third . . . don't talk to commies," and—Tommy's own contribution and personal favorite—"Fourth . . . eat kosher salami."

What better way to put the anti-Semites and Nazi fucks in their place than to hit them over the head with the absurdity of their views? Or, to put it otherwise, what better subversion of fascism than to involve it in a game of hide the kosher salami in which it gets screwed?

10

DER ÜBERMENSCH!!!

Comic Books, Golems, and Super-Jews
Christen PUNK

I think there is very much a case for a lot of the EC Comics material being post-Holocaust. You had a bunch of Jewish creators who
were very aware of the fragility of life. Because there were themes
that ran through these things and anti-prejudice was one of them.
Not taking people at face value, trying to look underneath . . . and
not just talking about the fragility of life, but of the status quo.

—Neil Gaiman, 2005

While the East Village rock movement now had the perfect band and the
perfect club, it still didn't have a name. Known variously as "street rock,"
"New York rock," and "downtown rock," it was like a two-headed newborn
whose parents are reluctant to legitimize it.

As it turned out, that job fell to one of the least bohemian—and Jewish—members of the still-forming downtown community, a guy from
Cheshire, Connecticut, with a name that sounds straight out of Scandinavia
(or a porn film): John Holmstrom.

"I'd moved to the East Village in the early '70s because I wanted to create comic books," says *PUNK* magazine's cofounder. "Not only were the rents
cheap, it was close to where Harvey Kurtzman, Jack Kirby, and Will Eisner
had been when they created the genre's golden age back in the 1940s."

Growing up in suburban Connecticut in the 1950s, Holmstrom had
fallen in love with the still sometimes brilliant products of that rapidly wan-

ing golden age. He'd faithfully collected titles in various series like *Tales from the Crypt* and *Batman* and *Superman*. Later in the 1960s, when others like *X-Men* and *The Fantastic Four* appeared, he not only collected them, he also began thinking about studying comic books seriously.

"This was also the era when Robert Crumb and others in the so-called new underground were creating revolutionary comics like *Zap* and *Despair*," Holmstrom says. "These series were more daring, touching not only the drug culture, but on racism, the war, sexual deviancy, and American imperialism."

At the same time, Holmstrom saw that old masters of the genre, Will Eisner in particular, were taking the form to new levels, creating book-length comic strips with serious stories aimed at adults. Though at the time the term "graphic novel" had yet to come into existence, Holmstrom wasn't alone in recognizing that something new and exciting was taking place.

"Eisner's book *A Contract with God* was one of the first examples, and it is still one of the most startling," says Holmstrom, who saw embryonic versions of the 1978 novel as early as 1972. "It's the one that everything from *Ghost World* to *Maus* has sprung from."

The story of a Jewish immigrant who makes a contract with God that he will be ensured a bright future if he engages in good works, Eisner's "novel" is pitched in the same terrain as Arthur Miller's *Death of a Salesman* and Bernard Malamud's *The Magic Barrel*, both classics of Jewish American literature that deal with the betrayal of the American dream. In *A Contract with God*, Frimm Hersh becomes disillusioned with religion after his daughter's death, then equally disillusioned with the materialism that he uses to replace it, ultimately bribing his rabbi to draw up a new, supposedly binding, legal document with God.

"This time you will not violate our contract," Hersh screams at the heavens.

But the storm Eisner depicts raging above him is chillingly evocative of Hersh's fate.

"I knew I had to study with him," Holmstrom says. "His work was revolutionary. It broke all the rules."

Heading off for New York at the age of nineteen, Holmstrom enrolled in the School of Visual Arts and convinced Eisner to take him on as his protégé. Studying with the then fifty-five-year-old comic book legend by day and dreaming about creating his own comic-based magazine by night, Holmstrom became increasingly aware that he was working within a kind of tradition, one that was passed down from artisans (the practitioners would have thought it pretentious to call themselves "artists") to apprentices who were expected to pass it down to the next generation to keep it alive.

In being accepted as a member of this order, this guild without a name, Holmstrom also became familiar with the economic and cultural circumstances that played a role in its development. He learned that Eisner and others like him had ended up in what was disparagingly referred to as "the funnies" because they had been denied entrée into the "higher" realms of artistic expression, such as painting, which were then taught almost exclusively in "restricted" universities.

"Jews couldn't go to college except in rare instances, and they had to have money to do so," Eisner explained (ironically enough, at an academic conference on graphic novels at which he was the keynote speaker). "I didn't come from that kind of background, so I ended up going into comics instead. I was like a lot of Jewish kids in the business. We had greater ambitions. As a result, we ended up expressing them in our work—and expanding the limits of the genre in the process."

In expanding comics, Holmstrom saw Eisner and his fellow Jewish artists change not merely the style of the genre but the subject matter as well. Working closely with innovative artist/writer-editors like Harvey Kurtzman and Jack Kirby (Jacob Kurtzberg), they created scenarios in which their superheroes fought not only supernatural villains, but evildoers of a more worldly sort, including Nazis, fascists, and racists (though, interestingly, never overt anti-Semites).

Of course, even if Holmstrom hadn't known this history, he could have learned as much a generation later when a novel by a Jewish American writer explored the golden era of comic books and won the Pulitzer Prize for 2002. In Michael Chabon's *The Amazing Adventures of Kavalier and Clay*, the story of the rise of comics as an art form is interwoven with the stories of both a real (at least in terms of the novel) and an imaginary Jewish avenger. The "real" avenger is none other than the golem, that legendary Frankenstein-like figure created from clay by the sixteenth-century kabbalist, Rabbi Loew; the imaginary one is Superman, that mythic creature from a dying planet who comes to our own to protect it from evil.

As Chabon makes clear, and as academics had long ago observed, the story of Superman is suspiciously similar to that of the golem, both in the details of its creation and the ultimate form it took. Penned and inked on the eve of the Holocaust by two nerdy-looking Jewish kids from Cleveland, the Man of Steel seemed to embody all the dreams and wishes not only of powerless teenage boys, but of a persecuted people on the brink of destruction—just as the golem had done for generations of Jews in Europe after he was created in response to yet another threat of annihilation.

In fact, the story of Superman could basically be seen as the golem's story given a Jewish American context. Come to a brash new land (Earth/America) from a dying old world imploding on itself (Krypton/Europe), Superman is to a great degree the archetypal immigrant. As he grows up in an *echt* American landscape of midwestern cornfields and blue skies, he soon reveals his special strengths despite himself, only to be coached by his adoptive American parents to hide these beneath a mask of ineffectualness (a schnook's mask, they might have said, had they known the term) so as not to be viewed as a freak by his "countrymen." At the same time, however, his adoptive parents advise him to use his powers for good, sending him off to that Jew-York-in-goy's-clothing, Metropolis, where he will fight crime, injustice, and international Nazi spies while attempting to win the heart—yet never the body—of the All-American Girl.

It's an absurd, yet absurdly moving story and one that has come in many ways to symbolize the American dream. For we all want to believe that beneath our Clark Kent exteriors there lurks the heart of a Superman, a man of steel who is invincible in the face of fear and always focused on the safety of the country—and, perhaps even more dearly, the woman—that he loves.

It's a dream that seems to have had a special resonance for Holmstrom, for as he continued working with Eisner and thinking about starting his own magazine, he became increasingly obsessed with the idea of creating a mythic figure that would embody his longings for strength while also being complicated. He didn't have a clear idea of how this man would look or act or think, but he knew that, in the tradition of the superheroes, he would be bigger than life, while in the tradition of Eisner, he would also be, at least in terms of his feelings, as vulnerable as Holmstrom or any other jerk on the street.

Holmstrom probably didn't know that New York Jewish intellectual Irving Howe had dreamed of much the same thing back in the 1950s, when he became interested in the disparaged or at least neglected world of Yiddish literature, even then written in a language as dead as Krypton. In its focus on *dos kleyne menshele*, or "the little man," Howe saw his own desire to illustrate "the virtue of powerlessness . . . the sanctity of the insulted and the ignored."

No, Holmstrom probably didn't know that. But when he encountered figures who seemed to fit his vulnerable-valiant template, individuals who first entered his room through his record player, then confronted him, bold as superheroes, on the stage of CBGB, he knew he'd found what he wanted. Even if he didn't know what to call it. Not, that is, until his young buddy, Eddie ("Legs") McNeil, whispered its name in his ear one drunken night. "Punk," McNeil said. "We'll call it Punk."

"We'll call it what?" Holmstrom said, wide-eyed.

As much as he loved McNeil, this kid who seemed to embody the spirit of the new movement (no, that was too strong; not the movement, the moment), he knew that his youthful sidekick was often more interested in the sound of his own voice than in what he said. Eddie used beer like a verbal lubricant. That's why Holmstrom and his other buddy, Ged (George E. Dunn, future *PUNK* publisher), had been friends with him in high school despite being four years older. And that's why they were hanging with him while back home from college this summer, doing things like filming parodies of the Three (Jewish) Stooges together. Eddie was entertaining, always getting into drunken adventures, just as they hoped his Alfred E. Neuman–like character Legs would as the magazine's mascot. Still, Eddie's—er, Legs's idea was growing on Holmstrom as he tossed it back and forth between his ears.

"You know, like punk kids, losers, smart asses," McNeil said. "Besides, it's eye-catching."

It's definitely that, Holmstrom thought. And considering that he wanted his new magazine to be noticed, to be more than noticed, to be like something exploding from the newsstands, an assault on the senses almost, he began to like the name all the more. The simplicity of it, like a curse word, like a fuck you to the establishment, made it a bit like old Americana, an expression from the days of Eisner and his minions.

"OK," he said. "Punk it is. We'll have to make up signs for it."

"PUNK IS COMING," McNeil said.

"Yes, PUNK IS COMING," agreed Holmstrom.

Of course, now that meant Holmstrom had to come up with what *PUNK* would look like.

*   *   *

As it turned out, creating the image of *PUNK* wasn't as difficult as Holmstrom at first imagined. That image had been forming in his mind ever since he'd first moved to New York; ever since he'd begun working for Eisner; ever since he'd begun reading comic books, in fact. Almost from the beginning, Holmstrom had wanted to create a comic that reflected his special circumstances— circumstances that he felt he shared with a generation of like-minded disaffected youth. He wanted something that embodied the mixture of anger and hopelessness, of boredom and restlessness, of humor and ironic detachment that they felt. Something that revealed their disgust with the lies and hypocrisy of the ridiculous hippie movement even as it forced a whole new satiric approach down the reader's throat. It would be a magazine that was as shocking as it was funny, that brought back the joy of being a kid in the fifties and sixties, when rock 'n' roll, comic books, and the spread of trash movies made the future seem exciting and fun.

Like a *MAD* magazine for an older crowd, he thought, something satirical yet goofy and unpretentious. Yes, like that glorified comic book born of the whoopee-cushion branch of socialist-flavored Jewish-American thought—that massive fart in the sacred halls of Nixon, suburbia, fraternity-minded traditional schlock. His new magazine would be brash and unavoidable and abrasive, modern and disturbing and unique. It would be like . . . like . . .

What?

And then Holmstrom remembered the Dictators.

* * *

All during that summer in Connecticut, he'd been playing their record for Legs and Ged. And all during the following months in New York, he'd continued to do the same. From the moment the three woke up in the afternoon, to the moment they went to bed near morning, that record seemed to be on the stereo, blaring out its message of beer and fun and sex. *The Dictators Go Girl Crazy* it was called, and it was just that term, *girl crazy*, like something your parents would say, that it evoked.

Like a comedy skit about backward suburbanites who don't understand their suddenly wacky teenagers, *The Dictators Go Girl Crazy* made a madly amusing racket around the Tenth Street "Punk Dump," filling the rickety windows and poorly sealed brackets with the sound of six smartasses backing themselves with a crunching basic form of rock that seemed at once comic yet brilliant in its deliberate simplicity and strength.

Holmstrom and Legs especially liked the songs "Master Race Rock" and "Back to Africa," which mocked taboo subjects in a manner worthy of underground comics legend Robert Crumb. At the same time, they loved the rants of Handsome Dick Manitoba that preceded the songs, not to mention the sound of his and lead guitarist Andy Shernoff's voices when they shouted down all the old hag women in Miami and stupid guys in Dallas who liked the band because "they didn't know we were Jews." The very mention of the word "Jew" on the album was almost as exciting as those songs about anti-Semitism and racism. It was all part and parcel of defiance of accepted convention. Perhaps even more important, it was funny. Most important of all, it rocked.

For all the jokes and breaking of taboos, one of the greatest things about the Dictators' album was that it sounded like something out of a 1960s car radio or garage. It had some of the sloppiness of the New York Dolls, that one-time-wonder band now petering out on its own raggedness, but it was alive in a way that the Dolls (at least on vinyl) never were, building up its simple songs into faux big moments that seemed to be as tongue-in-cheek as they were thrilling. It was like glam rock wearing dirty boots and a big Afro wig. Or, more exact, garage rock wearing your mother's combat boots and a late 1960s Jewfro à la Abbie Hoffman.

This music drew on everything from mocking Yippie politics to smirking Fugs-based social critiques to the sneering yet romanticized anger of late VU Lou Reed. It was threatening and exciting, but not in a violent way. You felt stupid if you didn't get it, and pretty damn superior and clever if you did.

"It was the end of glam and the beginning of punk," Holmstrom says now.

At the time, though, all he knew was that it was a harbinger of something new, something that he loved. Legs had given it a name, but it didn't seem to have a context. That quickly changed. As Holmstrom and McNeil went about putting together their magazine and hanging up their posters announcing "PUNK is Coming," they found themselves spending ever more time at CBGB, seeing there—both on the stage and in the audience—not only the Dictators, but other bands rapidly popping up, such as the Talking Heads, Television, and the Ramones.

Many of these bands had a cartoonish quality—Richard Hell's (Richard Meyers's) evil genius contribution to Television, David Byrne's Clark Kent nerd sensibility in the Talking Heads, Gene Simmons's (Chaim Witz's) golem-like character in the CBGB rarity KISS (he wanted to create a band of super-heroes that could have protected his mother's family during the Holocaust, the Israeli-born, Brooklyn-bred Simmons has said). Still, it was the Ramones who most appealed to Holmstrom and most embodied the outrageous quality that he aspired to.

Dressed in their matching leather jackets and sporting Beatles-cum-lobotomy-patients haircuts, the Ramones took the comic-rough image of the Dictators to its logically absurd next step. They looked like four living, breathing, pogoing comic book characters as they bopped around the stage in various attitudes of lunatic attack.

There was Dee Dee, a kind of Legs McNeil on acid, all childish psycho-killer expressions and innocent lust. Beside him was Johnny, his mulish, ape-like mug working overtime as he struggled to play his cheap, absurdly low-slung guitar in a masturbation-fast blur. Meanwhile, behind them, perched up on the drum stool, was Tommy, a little guy with an intense focus that would have seemed disturbing if it hadn't been for his ridiculously shrunken T-shirt and large sunglasses.

Best of all was the freakish stickman at the center of the proceedings, the one who seemed to be hunching over his microphone while simultaneously lurching at the crowd, the shy, hair-in-his-face, also sunglasses-clad, superpale, supertall, superthin-looking human.

A superhuman perhaps?

A superman?

A super-mensch?

An *Übermensch*?

Naw. More likely, a super-extenuated, Kafkaesque antihero in the tradition of *The Metamorphosis*. A super-antihero of the old Will Eisner golem school, epitomizing the weak, the disaffected, and the lost.

*   *   *

When the first issue of *PUNK* appeared, Lou Reed, another antiheroic stickman, was featured on the cover: the patron saint of angry misfits for an earlier era and spiritual godfather to the new punks (even then, many claimed Iggy "Osterberg" Pop should have been the true winner in the godfather sweepstakes), Lou was there pretty much as the result of an accident. The new *PUNK* trio of Holmstrom, Legs, and Mary Harron (the future director of *I Shot Andy Warhol* and *American Psycho*) had all but tripped over him one night as he sat in the audience at CBGB, then plopped themselves down at his table, uninvited, to tell him they'd put him on their cover if he'd agree to an interview.

"Oh, your circulation must be enormous," the *alter kocker* rocker sneered. Yet he played along, putting on his bilious, sardonic guy act for over two hours, even inviting the group that had all but ambushed him to join him for dinner afterward so that he could continue to berate them over burgers and beers.

He was funny and depressing and embarrassing. His presence on the first cover forever associated him with the new movement as a kind of angrily avuncular figurehead. But it was really that other figure that had first seized the imaginations of Holmstrom and Legs who appeared most often in the pages of *PUNK* over the years. That stick-like, Kafkaesque, super-antihero lead singer of the band Holmstrom found almost synonymous with *PUNK*. Joey Ramone.

Joey appeared in almost every issue of the magazine, figuring prominently in such classic punk/comic collaborations as "Mutant Monster Beach Party" and "Nick Detroit." Perhaps even more important, he was represented in both drawings and photos, Holmstrom's classic rendering of Joey as a rail-thin yet elegant cross between Dracula and a homeless duke making him the perfect punk noir figure for this romantic dark hour of the city.

Considering the fact that Tommy conceived the Ramones with angry Queens-based avengers in mind, and that all of the band members had been raised on a steady diet of comic books, it isn't that surprising that Joey and *PUNK* should become so closely aligned. *PUNK* fit perfectly with the DIY ethos of punk in a JD DUI (Juvenile Delinquents Driving Under the Influence) kind of way that was completely in keeping with the spirit of comic books.

Both comics and punk appealed to the unacceptable yet real feelings submerged in their audiences. Both used their lowbrow content to create excitement, fun, and laughs. Both took more than a small degree of pleasure in being seen as dangerous, corrupt, and verboten by the morality police of their eras, and both were eventually crushed for varying periods of time as a result. No wonder Holmstrom looked to both comics and punk, to the great graphic artists and to the Ramones, Eisner and Joey in particular, as heroic figures as inspiring as Superman. No wonder that the Ramones, and others like them, returned the compliment, incorporating not only the style of comics into their image, but in many cases, the actual comics themselves.

For the Ramones the connection was direct. Holmstrom provided the cover art for their third and, according to many critics, best album, *Rocket to Russia* (1977). For numerous other bands, the influence, though not as explicit, was there. Just look at the covers of early albums by Suicide, the Cramps, or the Neon Boys (the embryonic version of Television), or at any of the posters advertising bands from the period or even today. The vast majority draw on that early comic book influence, at once innocent yet evocative of Marilyn Monroe–era decadence. Comics reverberate with rebellion and juvenile delinquency and pure visual excitement like the most basic form of rock 'n' roll pleasure. Just like punk.

As Will Eisner himself points out, "I always thought that John [Holmstrom] was doing something wonderful with what he'd learned. He was taking it and giving it back to the kids, bringing rock music and comics together. After all, there was always something very visceral about comics, just as there is about rock 'n' roll. Both sprang from the streets, the lower classes—rock from the black ghettos; comics from the Lower East Side tenements of my youth."

*   *   *

Or to put it another way:

> Faster than a blitzkrieg air force!
> More powerful than a jackboot kick-step!
> Look up on the stage!
> It's a nerd!
> It's a brain!
> No, it's . . .
> JOEY RAMONE!!!

Lenny Bruce: The patron saint of punk delivers the news. PHOTO COURTESY OF
KITTY BRUCE

Lou Reed and Nico, the night porters: "I cannot make love to Jews
anymore." PHOTO COURTESY OF LISA LAW

Danny Fields: Bar Mitzvah boy, 1954. Photo courtesy of the collection of Danny Fields

The echt Americans, 1968. From left to right: Steve Paul (owner of The Scene), Danny Fields, Ron Asheton. Photo courtesy of the collection of Danny Fields

Vega and Rev: Suicide in front of Schwartz's Funeral Home, 2nd Avenue, 1976 (home to *New York Rocker* publisher Andy Schwartz). Photo courtesy of Roberta Bayley

The Modern Lovers before the fall. *From left to right:* Richman, Brooks, Robinson, Felice, and Harrison. Photo courtesy of Thomas Consilvio

Lenny Kaye and Patti Smith: Pre–Patti Smith Group, Le Jardin at the Roosevelt Hotel, 1973.

Photo courtesy of Danny Fields

Hilly Kristal: The fiddler under his roof, CBGBs, 1970s. Photo courtesy of Stephanie Chernikowski

Benjamin Brown (far right) baling hay on his farm near the Jersey Homestead, 1932. PHOTO COURTESY OF THE COLLECTION OF DANIEL BROWN

The Dictators in lampshades: too kitsch? PHOTO COURTESY OF STEPHANIE CHERNIKOWSKI

The Dictators in "de streets": too tough? Photo courtesy of Bob Gruen/Star File

Where Joey Ramone became a man: Yeshivat Binat Chaim, Forest Hills. Photo courtesy of Steven Lee Beeber

Tommy Ramone at 13. Prospect Park, Brooklyn, 1962. Photo courtesy of the collection of Tommy Erdelyi

Joey's brother Mickey at the Rego Park Jewish Community Center, where the Tangerine Puppets performed.

Joey Ramone: white bread enough for ya?

We're a happy family? *From left to right:* Joey, Tommy, Dee Dee, Johnny.

Joey Ramone: the other thin white duke. PHOTO COURTESY OF JOHN HOLMSTROM

PUNK creator John Holmstrom interviews *MAD* genius Harvey Kurtzman.

The Voidoids: we are the blank generation. *From left to right:* Richard Hell, Ivan Julian, Marc Bell (Marky Ramone), Robert Quine, 1977.

Richard Hell: writer. *Above desk, clockwise:* Hell's father, the Neon Boys, Hell with Susan Sontag, Rimbaud, and Theresa Stern. PHOTO COURTESY OF MARCIA RESNICK/RETNA LTD

Chris Stein and Debbie
Harry: the lovers. PHOTO COUR-
TESY OF JANETTE BECKMAN/RETNA LTD

Chris Stein: The dark Jew, 1972. PHOTO
COURTESY OF DENNIS McGUIRE

Joey Ramone, Linda Stein, Seymour Stein, and Dee Dee Ramone.
PHOTO COURTESY OF DANNY FIELDS

Debbie Harry: the shiksa goddess, 1978. PHOTO COURTESY OF RON POWNALL/STAR FILE

Genya Ravan: the Holocaust survivor as punk. PHOTO COURTESY OF STUDIO STU

Helen Wheels: not exactly demure. PHOTO COURTESY OF MICHAEL ALAGO

Young, loud, and smartass: Dead Boys' bassist Frank Secich joins lead signer Stiv Bators for a goosestep duck walk. PHOTO COURTESY OF THERESA KEREAKES

Johnny Thunders: Nu York doll? PHOTO COURTESY OF MARCIA RESNICK/RETNA LTD

The New York Dolls in regalia. *From left to right:* Arthur Kane, Sylvain Sylvain, David Johansen, Jerry Nolan, Johnny Thunders (sans *peyes,* con the swastika). Photo courtesy of Bob Gruen/Star File

Sid and Nancy: Such a *sheyne punim.* Photo courtesy of Lech Kowalski

John Zorn in the studio: May the force be with you. New York City, 1994. Photo courtesy of the collection of John Zorn

Malcolm McLaren: no
future? PHOTO COURTESY OF THE
COLLECTION OF STUART EDWARDS

Malcolm McLaren and mother at his
Bar Mitzvah. PHOTO COURTESY OF THE COLLECTION OF
STUART EDWARDS

McLaren and Pistols: Fagin
and his artful dodgers.
PHOTO COURTESY OF BOB GRUEN/STAR FILE

Gary Lucas performs his live soundtrack to *Der Golem*.
PHOTO COURTESY OF ARJEN VELDT

Lou Reed: the *alter kocker* indie rocker at the Downtown Seder, 2004. PHOTO COURTESY OF MELANIE EINZIG

Danny Fields at home, 2003.
PHOTO COURTESY OF STEVEN LEE BEEBER

Yo or Oy? Handsome Dick Manitoba cops a nosh at the 2nd Avenue Deli, 2003.
PHOTO COURTESY OF MIKE EDISON

11

A JEWISH HELL

Richard Meyers Creates a Jewish Mother's Worst Nightmare

My father was born a Jew, but he didn't believe in any of that . . . [he] raised me as a communist and atheist.

—Richard "Hell" Meyers

Richie Hell struck me, my Richard Hell, he struck me as much a Jew as anybody I ever knew in New York. . . . Just every nuance, every facial tick, every giggle. I mean, in whatever way these things are cellular, culturally cellular, he was a Jew.

—Richard Meltzer

If Joey Ramone was a nice Jewish boy, the prodigal son returned to do good, what then was Richard "Hell" Meyers, that tortured half-Jew from Lexington, Kentucky? He created an image of punk that became dominant—at least visually—in England, but was he a *mensch*? No one has ever referred to him as that. Hell is either reluctantly respected or resented, a friend to some, but to most a complicated, thin-skinned character better known for his volatile temper and tendency to take offense than for his generosity and compassion.

It might be better to describe him as a Jewish mother's worst nightmare. Like the son who goes off to college with inflamed notions of literary success in his head, rather than settling down and coming to his senses, Hell went off the rails, falling in with a bad crowd, so to speak, a bunch of bohemians, beatniks, and rock 'n' roll musicians. Yet he always displayed some allegiance to liberal thought and commitment to the word of God as embodied by the people of the book. He treated writing as sacred. Many Jewish mothers might have felt shocked by his forays into the world of punk rock, but just as many would have been somewhat comforted to see him using his experiences later in life to attempt a career as a journalist and novelist.

Born in Kentucky in 1949, Richard Meyers was the son of Ernest Meyers and Carolyn Hodgson, two kids from Jewish and Methodist backgrounds, respectively, who met in New York while Ernest was attending Columbia University and Carolyn, Hunter College. Though neither seemed too bothered by the difference in their backgrounds, there is some question as to whether their parents felt the same. In a series of letters that Richard's mother sent him in the 1990s so that he could better know his father, who died when he was eight, Richard's maternal grandmother refers to an earlier discussion in which she and Richard's mother addressed "the questions I have about your future happiness." While not exactly a Romeo-and-Juliet story, with Montagues and Capulets keeping the star-crossed lovers apart, there may have been some concern (at least on Richard's grandmother's part) regarding the difference in their backgrounds. This is not at all surprising. In the 1940s, mixed marriages were about as rare and as traumatic as divorces. Today, of course, divorce is common, and at least half of Jews marry "outside the faith," as rabbis who bemoan the trend refer to it, raising alarm bells of "assimilation to the point of disappearance"—or, as a cynic might see it, fears of rabbinical obsolescence.

Clearly both Ernest and Carolyn came from forward-thinking backgrounds. They were both college graduates who went on to graduate school, becoming academics. Ernest taught psychology at the University of Kentucky following the Second World War, and after his death in 1958, Carolyn taught women's studies at Old Dominion University in Norfolk, Virginia, where she arranged for Richard to give a poetry reading in the early 1990s.

Both Ernest and Carolyn relished books—primarily, literature of the unconventional, even taboo sort. Examining the letters in the Fales Library, one is struck again and again by the number of times one of Richard's parents mentions to the other that he or she is reading a certain book the other has suggested, or is just discovering a new one that the other must read. They read a wide array of subjects, including psychology, philosophy, and fiction. But, in terms of Richard's later literary interests, perhaps the most telling are those that fall towards the outré, even erotic end of the spectrum, like D. H. Lawrence's *Lady Chatterley's Lover* and Henry Miller's *Tropic of Cancer*.

When we look at Richard's own literary output—poems and songs with titles like "Wanna Go Out" and "Love Comes in Spurts"—we can't help but see a sort of family tradition being carried on. While perhaps not conscious or intentional, Richard clearly shares many of the interests of his parents. So much so that we have to ask whether, in fact, he wasn't greatly influenced by them. If so, to what degree might that influence be related to Jewishness?

Unfortunately, Richard refused to be interviewed or provide information for this book, insisting that he did not consider himself "defined" by Jewishness. He continued to do so even as I tried to explain that I wasn't saying that he was—merely that he perhaps shared some partial connection to the culture, given that his father was descended from it. I tried to explain that identity is constructed from a vast array of experiences, and that, as in a palimpsest, these layers of meaning create who we are. But Richard continued to resist volubly, saying, "I resent the attempt by groups to appropriate me for their means. I don't like that kind of thing and I want no part of it."

In all honesty, Richard's resistance disturbed me. It made me go back and reexamine my intentions in writing this book. Was I merely trying to lay claim to a group of individuals who had no similarities other than a superficial cultural link? Was I using the worst sort of reductionist thinking and flattening them to two-dimensional representations of one thing and not another? Was my complicated argument based at bottom on a dichotomistic, black-and-white, overly simple division between "Jew" and "Gentile"?

In short, was I committing the sin I saw unintentionally perpetrated all too often by many of my fellow Jews, the ones who rattled off the names of famous individuals with Jewish names—Einstein, Freud, Marx, Kafka, Mahler—in an effort to prove their own special place in history?

An argument could be made for this. I don't think it would hold. I am focusing on what I consider the "Jewishness" of certain individuals, but in doing that I'm not saying that Jewishness is everything. I'm only saying that it plays, to varying degrees, a part. While Tommy Ramone, Richard Meltzer, Lenny Kaye, and Handsome Dick Manitoba might find their connection to Jewishness essential, others such as Richard Hell, Chris Stein, and Joey Ramone might find it tangential. Yet elements that seem to stem largely from a shared Jewish history and culture can be found in each performer's work. These are worth examining, even if no definitive picture can ever be drawn.

To put it another way, there is no way to fully understand these musicians without exploring the Jewish part of them, whatever that may consist of. They all display something in common that is otherwise incomprehensible.

Embedded in the first words Richard ever exchanged with me was a comment that convinced me his story was worth pursuing. At the opening of a one-man show by punk-era artist Richard Hambleton—best known for his "shadow paintings," life-size silhouettes haunting the basement of former D-Generation singer Jessie Malin's East Village club Niagara—I introduced myself and said, "Since I was told you were Jewish, I wondered if you might be interested in speaking to me for my book." His smile turned to a frown. Richard replied, "My father was born a Jew but he didn't believe in that. He didn't have anything to do with religion."

I tried to explain, as I had to others, that I did not mean Jewish in the religious sense, but in the cultural. For much of Jewish American history, withdrawal from religious Judaism had been a striking feature of the culture. I went on to say that Jews were Jewish in the same way that Italians were Italian or Germans were German, and that if they had a common religion of any sort it was secular humanism, a belief that human-based ethics and not an invisible deistic-based one should morally guide us in life. Jews should be talking about these issues, I said. Hadn't the mistake of letting others answer the Jewish Question been made before?

"But I wasn't raised Jewish at all," Richard said, exasperated. "I was born in Lexington, Kentucky, and my father raised me as a communist and an atheist." I laughed and tried to explain that this proved my point all the more, that many Jews had become communists and atheists as a part of their flight from religion, and that to be raised as such in the 1950s, and in Lexington, Kentucky, made Richard in this respect all the more Jewish. But he wasn't buying it. He moved on to look at another of Richard Hambelton's shadow paintings, his face acquiring a punk-era darkness that I'd previously missed.

Richard's new, young wife Pauline (full name, Sheelagh Pauline Bevan), encouraged me throughout the evening to speak to him again, so I tried at least two more times over the course of a year to convince him to meet with me. On both occasions Richard resisted, the last time accusing me of trying to "appropriate" him for my culture.

And yet, during this period, I saw a posting on his Web site in which he replied to a fan's question, a girl identified as Alexandra. She wrote: "I'm extremely bored today, I was wondering. Are you Jewish Richard? Meyers is a Jewish name. I don't think you are. If not how are you going to spend the Holidays" ("R. Hell Site Forum," November, 30, 2000). Richard replied that very day, under the subject heading "If you say so": "Or, 'Who's asking?' (Don't answer that, please, bored Alexandra, I just mean it figuratively.) I definitely am a Jew to an anti-Semite. My father was a (German) Jew from Pittsburgh, my mother a Southern Methodist from Birmingham (Welsh and English). My father's family were liberal intellectuals who didn't really practice any religion—though they certainly identified themselves as Jews—and he died when I was seven [sic]. I don't know anything about the religion/culture to speak of. Someday I'm going to do something about that."

This message is extremely revealing. Richard repeats that he is not Jewish except as defined by the outside world, especially "anti-Semites." He says he is descended from northern, nonreligious, liberal German Jews who clearly identified with that culture. What could be closer to my point of view? Especially considering Richard's final comment, "I don't know anything about the religion/culture to speak of. Someday I'm going to do something about that." Despite his claims to the contrary, he was interested in his heritage.

A few months later, Richard's friend Roberta Bayley told me that Richard wanted to "kill" me because I had been speaking to others associated with him. I had told him I would be doing this when I encouraged him to go on the record himself to avoid being "defined" by others. Then Roberta said something I had been thinking all along. "What's the big deal?" she said. "Why does he care so much unless he feels like he's got something to hide?"

Richard's disavowals of his Jewishness were so intense, so deliberate, so angrily insistent and complete that I couldn't help but say to myself, in imitation of Hamlet's mother, Gertrude, "The gentleman doth protest too much, methinks." Richard Meyers could not stand the idea that anyone would associate him with his Jewishness. Perhaps this is not such a surprising reaction from someone who was raised in the South of the 1950s. I well know, being a Jew from Atlanta, that Jews were not taken for granted there the way they were in New York—and Atlanta, "the New York of the South," is far more cosmopolitan than Meyers's Lexington, Kentucky. Being blond-haired and "Aryan"-looking (or so I've been told), I heard numerous anti-Semitic remarks to which I otherwise would not have been privy. (To the credit of those making them, they were almost always embarrassed when I pointed out I was "of the tribe.") I knew I was an outsider. Every southerner knows the joke about the KKK. The letters actually stand for Koons, Kikes, and Katholics—the South's three most hated groups, in descending order. (One has to hand it to those Klansmen. At least they got the derogatory name for the Jews spelled right). In short, I knew what Television biographer Tim Mitchell confirmed in his own research into Hell's background. Lexington was a place with few Jews and such would have been noticed. With that in mind, let's move now to the Richard that is revealed in his archives, for there we see a truly complex man, a poet, writer, and musician as well as a southerner, a New Yorker, and a Jew.

* * *

Most of the Hell archive relates to his career as an artist. There are drafts of his poems; different versions of posters he designed for his bands the Neon Boys, Television, the Heartbreakers, and the Voidoids; manuscripts for books, screenplays for films, and aging videos. There is evidence that he wrote and rewrote not only his literary outpourings, but also the image of himself that he presented onstage and to the world.

In examining this with Leif Sorensen, the graduate student assigned to catalog Hell's materials, I found that my own ideas were not as far off the mark as Richard had led me to believe. For if there is one subject that Richard returns to again and again in his archives, one subject that he has revisited from the beginning of his career to this day, it is the life of a woman he created with his friend Tom Verlaine (Tom Miller) back in the early 1970s, the story of a fictional poet named Theresa Stern.

Little known to today's Television and Voidoid fans, Theresa Stern cast a dark silhouette over New York's mid-1970s rock scene, almost as if she were a CBGB star in her own right. Her collection, *Wanna Go Out?* (1973), was available through Richard Hell's publishing house Dot Books, while interviews with her could be seen in *PUNK* magazine, which also published occasional reviews "by" her of Richard's shows. Her words were there to see, as was her picture, one that gave a fright. A heavily made-up, big-haired "woman" who seemed to love getting in your face, she had some of the same qualities as another figure soon to top the charts—Frank Zappa's "Jewish Princess" (*Sheik Yerbuti*, 1976):

> I want a darling little Jewish Princess
> Who don't know shit about cooking and is arrogant looking

A vicious little Jewish Princess
To specifically happen with a pee-pee that's snappin'
All up inside
I just want a princess to ride

When Zappa sang this, there was laughter mixed with protests. But when Theresa Stern emerged on the scene, her biography clearly stating that she was a half–Puerto Rican, half-Jewish prostitute who "like Groucho Marx with clubs . . . wouldn't want to know any guy who would like [her]" (*PUNK*, 1976), there was no negative response. Why? Because like those other crypto-Latino Jews then so popular—Juan Epstein, Alan Vega, and the Dictators—Theresa Stern was part of a larger tradition dating back to Chico Marx and continuing beyond punk to the figure of Andrew "Dice" Clay, a Jewish comic playing a leather-jacketed "Italian" who wouldn't have looked out of place in the Ramones. Theresa was the Jew as Gypsy tough-gal exotic. The Jew as Other, not quite white, but more virile. The Jew as sexual threat and intoxicant.

This Jewish "Other" was not merely a stereotype created by Gentiles. In many cases it was an intentional depiction of Jewishness projected by Jews to the world. These Latino-acting—in many cases half-Jewish—Jews were different from studious, proper, intellectually controlled people of the book. They were a type of Jew that is indeed part Latin—the Jews originally from Spain and Portugal, known as the Sephardim. Not nearly so numerous as the Eastern European Jews who mostly populate New York, they still retain a presence there. A group of Sephardim immigrated to the city in 1654 and were soon counted among its most successful citizens. Now part of a larger New York Jewish culture, these "Latin" Sephardim still think of themselves as unique and to a certain extent separate.

Whether the Sephardim retain any significant link to Latin culture is debatable, and in fact beside the point. For it is not an actual link that mattered in the minds of performers who focused on, and in most cases created, Jewish Latin characters. It is what they represented to the Jewish imagination. They were a projection of desire, a wish-fulfillment fantasy, a created image even more important to the Jewish world than to the non-Jewish one.

When the Dictators spoke using certain Italian constructions and the *bruddahs* from Forest Hills decided to go with a name that brought to mind a Puerto Rican street gang, the Latin associations may not have been exactly conscious, but they sprang from the same source. Like Joey Ramone (Jeffry Hyman) and Ross the Boss Funichello (Ross Friedman), Richard Meyers was but another attempting not so much to hide his Jewishness as to transform it into a more interesting ethnicity. He revealed an aspect of Jewishness that was more threatening and encoded—one that represented the badass rather than the nice Jewish boy; one that was embodied by the Jewish gangsters who blended so seamlessly with their Italian cousins; one that made Jews suddenly sexy, glamorous, and tough.

As Alan Sacks, the Brooklyn-raised Hollywood producer instrumental in creating *Welcome Back, Kotter*, made plain when we spoke, the character of Juan Epstein arose from a very similar desire: "I created the show with Gabe Kaplan, who played Kotter, based on a stand-up routine he'd been developing about his old neighborhood. In this routine, he'd do a bit about a kid named Epstein the Animal. This kid was so tough that all the mothers in his neighborhood would get their kids off the streets for an hour each day so that he could have the streets to himself. We were determined to have him in the show, but Michael Eisner, who was head of programming, insisted that we make him half–Puerto Rican because, he said, it would be funnier."

In other words, a genuine tough Jew would be too threatening, too scary, too unbelievable. He would have to be combined with a Latin. *Kotter*'s remaining two Jewish characters—Arnold Horshack, a parody of an ineffectual Eastern European Jew who borders on a *feygele*; and Kotter, a New York Jewish street kid (Sweathog) who grows up to become a responsible member of the community (a teacher, the literal translation of rabbi), together with Epstein create a triptych of sorts. Horshack is the opposite of Epstein, and Kotter, in the middle, is a melding of the two. Epstein is the id, Horshack the (very weak) ego, and Kotter the superego. Epstein-Horshack-Kotter—like Chico-Harpo-Groucho and Dino-Jerry-the Nutty Professor—represent a gradual Americanizing of the sexy Jewish other, a New Yorkizing that results in a smartass (emphasis on "smart") kid from the streets who grows up to be a basically good boy, an upholder of the pride of the people if not the general social order.

As Richard Hell has stated again and again over the years, Theresa Stern, the half–Puerto Rican, half-Jewish mythic creation he came up with in conjunction with his fully non-Jewish friend Tom Miller, provided him with one of the most essential breakthroughs of his life. "She" gave him a mask through which he could write his poetry, and in doing so she brought him back to his "true voice."

* * *

Let me repeat that. Richard Meyers Hell has said repeatedly over the years, in interviews, catalogues, book bios, and elsewhere, that Theresa Stern—the half-Jew, half–Puerto Rican woman that he created as a young man—allowed him to find "his true voice." The essence of who he was as a writer. The essence of who he was, period.

Theresa Stern was pivotally important to Richard "Hell" Meyers as a young man, and she has remained so ever since. According to archivist Leif Sorensen, "Theresa Stern is a bit of an obsession for Richard. He has repeatedly gone back to her over the years, and in fact has wanted to make a movie about her for decades. He seems to find something very essential in her. You're definitely onto something very important by looking at her."

In a career that has seen many things fall away—music, poetry, movies, a wife, lovers—one thing has remained consistent: Richard's obsession—and that doesn't seem to be too strong a word—with Theresa Stern. From his early twenties to his early fifties, he has continued to be fascinated by this character. In France, in 1999, for instance, he gave a reading of Theresa Stern's poetry at the Club La Maroquinerie. That night Hell not only sacrificed reading other poetry more directly associated with his name, he depicted himself as Stern on the program's cover. Moreover, he used the photograph of himself in drag that he'd superimposed over Miller's so many years before. Only he—or rather Theresa—was there for public view. It is she with whom he chose to be identified that night, she whom he put forward as a projection of himself. Of all the poetry that Hell has written, almost half has been published under the name Theresa Stern.

* * *

But there is more to Hell's Jewishness than Theresa Stern. In addition to his "communist atheist upbringing," his engagement of intellectuals such as Susan Sontag, and his emphasis on words over music, there is the following: his approach to performance, which put him increasingly at odds with his old friend Tom Miller; his use of guitarist Bob Quine, an "immigrant" Jew who like him was born outside New York; and his smartass, angry stage presence. This last carries over into his daily life, much as it did for that other punk writer and rebel, Lou Reed. Indeed, it ultimately led him to work in film when he became disenchanted with music.

Let's look first at the Tom Miller/Richard Meyer dynamic. The two created an alliance rooted in French symbolism, particularly their love affair with that movement's central figures, Verlaine and Rimbaud.* But they came from two distinct cultures, and this seems to figure largely in their eventual rift. Meyers, as noted, was part-Jewish. His father was raised in Pittsburgh, where he adopted the life of an intellectual, atheist, and political progressive, like many nonreligious but culturally informed Jews of the time. Miller was raised in the classic WASP setting, according to childhood friend and bandmate Billy Ficca. "He came from Delaware and seemed pretty reserved. He was not like Richard that way. That's for sure." When they met at the boarding school where Richard was sent after being bounced out of Lexington's public school system for truancy and misconduct, Miller was in his element and Meyers the odd man out. Yet, being a sensitive kid interested in music and literature, Miller was also an outsider in his own right. As Billy Ficca—and many others—commented, "We were all outsiders. Nerds. The kids who care about art and that sort of thing always are." If Tom secretly hated the boarding school system and wanted out, Richard knew deep down that the hatred and sense of otherness he felt there cut two ways. Richard ran away from school first, and Tom followed later after Richard encouraged him to do so repeatedly in letters. Richard moved first to New York to be a writer, and Tom came up later, again at his friend's insistence.

Still, the most telling elements of the friendship did not appear until the two went from being poets in the making to musicians starting a band. The Theresa Stern experiment may have allowed certain revelations. Though it was Tom who had the idea for the character, Richard seized upon it and ended up writing the poems in *Wanna Go Out?* But it wasn't until their first band, the Neon Boys, transformed itself into Television that significant differences in their characters began to emerge. Chief among these was a take

---

*While Miller's link to the famous lovers is direct via his stage name, Meyers's is indirect, and stems from his explanation of his hairstyle, the one that became so associated with punk. "I wanted something that looked like that famous photograph of Rimbaud." This is not to imply that there was any homoerotic element to the relationship—more that it was a dual identity the two could share. This dual identity found its final realization in the photograph of Theresa Stern. The image was created by superimposing two identically posed photos of Miller and Meyers in drag.

on music and performance style that seemed as much temperamental as philosophical in origin.

As many have noted, the Neon Boys were a more identifiably punk band than Television. Their music was edgier, faster, and angrier, the lyrics more in your face and comical, expressing an urban, streetwise sexuality in puns and other clever linguistic devices that were adolescent in the spirit of *MAD* and other comics. Consider this line from the Richard Hell–penned, Neon Boys–era version of "Love Comes in Spurts," for instance: "I held her waist and her wrist and I kissed her in the hair / Forgotten love started pumpin' like a fountain inside there." While doing so, bear in mind that the music Hell created to accompany his songs was more in the spirit of what was rapidly becoming known as punk than anything Miller/Verlaine was devising for his own tunes.

As Tim Mitchell says in his recently issued biography, *Sonic Transmission: Richard Hell, Tom Verlaine, Television*:

> In April 1973, the Neon Boys went into a four-track recording studio in a basement in Brooklyn, where they recorded six songs, three of Miller's and three cowritten with Meyers . . . Miller's songs here were "Tramp", soon to be discarded, and two titles that were to survive into Television's early sets, "Hot Dog" and "Poor Circulation." The cowritten songs were "That's All I Know (Right Now)," "Love Comes in Spurts" and "High-Heeled Wheels"— each a lively mixture of sixties garage bands, the Rolling Stones and the New York Dolls, with a dash of The Velvet Underground. Meyers sings these songs like a truly alienated Mick Jagger, or a more anguished David Johansen, sneering and yelping, youthful and declamatory, but effortlessly reaching the high notes and folding his voice around the songs' melodies—and sounds like a true star in the making. His songs take the traditional rock and roll subjects of love, sex and drugs, but look at them through a filter of French Decadence and Surrealism, giving them a defiantly original twist. Miller's musical structures for them are essentially built on primal punk, but also sometimes climb upwards unexpectedly—sometimes climactically, sometimes hysterically— before being brought back down to earth again.

Miller's music for his own songs at this session was not without adventure, such as the unexpectedly slow, clunking intro to "High Heeled Wheels" and an equally unexpected chord progression in its bridge, but essentially it was commercial music. Meyers, on the other hand, was pushing the lyrical and musical limits of the pop song. Following the trajectory of the two Neon Boys as they go their separate ways, we can see how their increasingly different musical and lyrical styles illustrate the basic divisions that always lay between them. The Neon Boys were in your face; Television was a more stately affair, a largely introspective instrumental exploration of inner space that earned the band comparisons to the Grateful Dead. Television—while containing songs with fine lyrics such as "Venus De Milo"—was primarily a proficient instrumentalists' band, anything but DIY, that most cherished aspect of punk. When Tom finally forced Richard out of the band, it was supposedly over Richard's "lack of seriousness" about learning the bass. Ivan Julian, of Hell's later *very* punk band the Voidoids, points out, "Richard might not have been technically proficient in that sense of the classically trained, but he definitely had his own very interesting style. If it weren't for that, the music of the Voidoids would not have had the unique angular quality that it did."

But there was more to it than Richard's lack of instrumental skill. As Billy Ficca observes, "Richard would leap about onstage and look like Pete Townsend, putting on a show and going all out. Tom rarely looked up from the floor while he was playing. To him it was all about the music, while for Richard it was also a show." As Danny Fields commented when discussing the unique quality that he saw in the Ramones, "There's that Jewish showbiz tradition, that whole idea of putting on a show." Does this desire to perform mask a compulsion to be loved and in control? It's a claim commonly made about comics—and everyone knows about the high percentage of Jewish comics. An outsider like Richard might have wanted to exert his personality all the more strongly, whether to be recognized as a player or to solidify an identity before an audience. Richard's voluminous journal entries and letters in the archives that he sold to NYU in 2003 reveal a near-obsession with creating an identity. So do his novels and poems. Whether as Theresa Stern, Richard Hell, or Eric, the punk in Susan Seidelman's examination of the East Village scene, *Smithereens*, Meyers clearly was looking for a way to present himself, a way to be seen, through music, literature, or film.

Tom wanted something else. The child of WASP restraint and privilege, he ultimately found that Richard's outrageousness was the antithesis of what he wished to present through Television. He wanted something more serious, more impressive, and more interior. He didn't want a vaudevillian performance along the lines of Milton Berle in drag. He wanted a quartet that could present serious jazz-punk-rock to the critics and be embraced for its dedication, proficiency, and grace.

If Meyer's relationship with Miller—especially in its breakdown—symbolized a deeper rift with the WASP mainstream of his youth than he understood (or perhaps would like to admit), then what did his next two ventures mean? He first formed a band with the flamboyant "Gypsy" Italian guitarist Johnny Thunders. That didn't work ("because the songs were too stupid," Hell explained, saying he could never sing "Pirate Love" again). Then he did the same with the Jewish-nerd genius Robert Quine, a character straight out of Kafka via Woody Allen, a Manhattan-bound Jew with a fear of tall buildings and speeding bullets, if not locomotives.

Quine, like Meyers, was not a New York Jew, but an "immigrant" from Akron, where his family owned a profitable rubber company. Raised in a "very secular, intellectual Jewish home," according to fellow bandmate Ivan Julian, Quine had been pressured by his family to pursue a safe career like law, and though he had always loved music, he indulged his parents by attending law school at nearby Washington University in St. Louis. He passed the Missouri bar before bagging it all and heading first to San Francisco, where he taped hours of live VU shows that he eventually released as a boxed set. After failing the California bar repeatedly, he headed for New York. There, it was as if he had come home, Julian says, recalling how the guitarist told him on a number of occasions that he could never live anywhere else. "I remember he told me that when he first arrived he had found a cheap spot in Brooklyn, but that he couldn't even survive there. 'Only Manhattan,' he said."

In this cauldron of ethnicity, diversity, and immigration, the eccentricities that made Quine an outcast in Akron were perhaps still noticed, but they were tolerated. Indeed, they became part of his charm. And of his music. At a memorial for Quine held at CBGB's Gallery not long after his death in 2004, one speaker after another marveled at his complicated and sometimes strange nature—just as they marveled, to perhaps an even greater degree, at his intellect and guitar pyrotechnics. Possessed of a truly encyclopedic wealth of information about music (he could name the specific release dates, chart positions, and even serial numbers of records at will), he was a genius who could have excelled at any number of professions, a genius who brought forth a series of strangled, nervous-sounding, staccato notes that seemed as if they were about to fall apart at any moment, yet cohered in intricate webs. As Ivan Julian points out, Bob's uncle Willard Van Orman Quine held the Edgar Pierce Chair of Philosophy at Harvard University from 1956 to 2000, an intellect on "the Einstein level." Learning, absorbing, and producing was clearly in Quine's upbringing and perhaps his blood.

Ultimately, it was his attitude that earned him his punk credentials—that and his place in Richard Hell's band the Voidoids. "Bob could have played guitar straight, but he chose to make deliberate 'mistakes' if he thought they sounded better," says Julian. "He was less interested in proficiency for proficiency's sake than he was in effect." This is exactly how Hell approached playing the bass. Both men were continuing a certain Jewish American tradition in which "debased" art forms or styles are treated with respect. Like comic book artists who used the much maligned pulps to create their artworks or classicists, such as Bernstein, Bartók, and Bloch, who had drawn on folk and pop styles to broaden their palettes, or folk masters like Dylan and Ochs who'd borrowed from rock though it earned them cries of "Judas" (need we comment on the Christ-killing, "rhymes with" qualities of that name?), Quine, like Hell, was interested in unheard, unconventional, outsider sounds, just as he was interested in bringing these sounds to *dos kleyne menshele* on the street. Both were carrying on a Jewish tradition that extended beyond the Americas. It earned Quine a place on the trio of albums that Lou Reed completed after getting clean from drugs (and by his own admission, coming clean regarding his past). It earned Hell a place outside the classicism of Television. His combative *fuck you before you fuck me* stance drew comparisons to Reed himself.

Richard Meyers is less a rock musician than a kind of half-Jewish male Madonna. From southern rebel to New York poet to punk musician to actor to writer once again, he's gone through multiple guises in his time. Like Madonna, who for all her costume and career changes has maintained the allure of taboo breaker so essential to her appeal, Richard has kept the intellectual, thinker, writer at the core of everything he's done. Writer-musician, writer-actor, writer-intellectual, writer-movie critic, and writer-punk, he always gets back to the word, that thing that was there in the beginning, that led so many of the early critics-turned-musicians into punk. Like Lenny Kaye, Richard Meltzer, Sandy Pearlman, and Andy Shernoff, Richard Hell followed the word to form a band. He fell in with the great plan of Jewish mothers and fathers throughout history—he kept faithful to the word and the intellect. The people of the book never stray too far.

*   *   *

In putting the final touches on this chapter, I went to Richard Hell's Web site to make sure that I had accurately transcribed the exchange that took place between him and "Bored Alexandra," the Forum correspondent who had asked whether he was Jewish. What I found both did and did not surprise me. Typing the word "Jew" into the Web page's search engine, I found suddenly numerous references. The most prominent concerned an audio recording of a lecture on Nathaniel West that Richard had given in 2000. As the writer noted, Hell's talk on West—a Jewish writer (né Weinstein) from the 1930s who penned the classic novella *Miss Lonelyhearts* (the dark tale of a Dear Abby–like advice columnist) and the even more classic (and dark) Hollywood satire *The Day of the Locust*—was "interesting [because] it includes Richard trying to decide whether he himself is a Jew or not." Clearly, the topic had occurred to Meyers long before I introduced it. Perhaps he was upset by the reaction he received at his talk. Or perhaps he is only willing to speak on the subject if it's in a forum he deems worthy of his efforts. Or then again, maybe Richard is just contrary. As John Zorn says later in this book, "Jews are contrary by definition. If you say black, they say white. You know the old joke, if you have two Jews you have a debate, three an argument, four a revolution—with splinter groups."

12
THE SHIKSA GODDESS

Chris Stein Creates the First Punk Princess

With Debbie it was like . . . when I saw the Lenny [Bruce] movie . . .
I was definitely always reminded of that [Shiksa Goddess thing].
Because, you know, it was certainly kind of that. She didn't have
blonde hair when I met her. She just had short, dark hair. It wasn't so
blatant. But still—I remember [Lenny] was so stricken by Honey, you
know, by her shiksaness. So, I mean, that was a major element in it.

—Chris Stein, 2004

Chris always knew exactly who he was. And I never knew who I
was. So probably that's why we sort of fit together.

—Debbie Harry, 2004

If Richard Meyers is some sort of Jewish—and non-Jewish—nightmare, what do we make of Blondie? They stand accused of selling out by the
punk community, ostensibly because they softened their image (in fact
because they made a lot of money). Blondie may have had a sexual edge that
kept viewers from thinking of the girl next door, but there's no denying that
this was an act a mother could tolerate and a father—perhaps in a not entirely
wholesome way—could love.

From her early smeared lipstick 'n' ripped T-shirt phase to her later glamorous disco-rock style, Blondie lead singer Debbie Harry was the punk who
was ready for pop. Possessed of certain qualities that allowed her to sneak the
new music in like a Trojan horse, she had an air of aggressive—yet not too

aggressive—female sexuality, a whiff of decadent surrender to the promise of the city, and a knowledge of tight Brill-Buildingesque arrangements that had been missing for too long from rock songcraft.

But what of Harry's partner in both the romantic and the musical/business sense, Chris Stein? Was the public ready for him? What underlay the music he helped create with Harry? Was the public ready for his dark take on romance, his rebellion against authority, his embrace of historical horror, and, perhaps worst of all, his possession of the woman he had helped dub Blondie?

The general public saw only the lead singer onstage, but those within the inner circle knew that Stein was at least as important as Harry in the creation of the band. In fact, embedded within their knowledge was an even deeper understanding, a riddle wrapped in an enigma. Stein was a relatively short, downcast, depressive Jew, and yet he had won this beautiful woman, this dream of a woman, this cool, smart, sexy chick who had at one time been a Playboy bunny. He had won the ultimate Shiksa Goddess—pert nose, pearly skin, icy manner, and blonde—OK, dyed, but so what?—hair.

Was Stein aware of this at the time? No, but it occurred to him later, when he was watching the man he had been deeply affected by as a teenager, that patron saint of New York cool, New York Jews, and New York punk, Lenny Bruce.

"With Debbie it was like . . . when I saw the Lenny [Bruce] movie . . . I was definitely always reminded of that [Shiksa Goddess thing]. Because, you know, it was certainly kind of that. [Debbie] didn't have blonde hair when I met her. She just had short, dark hair. It wasn't so blatant. But still—I remember Lenny was so stricken by Honey, you know, by her shiksaness. So, I mean, that was a major element in it."

While Debbie chooses to leave Stein's comment unaddressed—when I ask her about it by phone, she simply laughs for a couple of seconds and says, "A girl's got to have something"—she does admit that one of the main things that attracted her to him was that he was both intelligent and not threatened by her intelligence. In fact, she adds, she sees this as being a Jewish characteristic. "[Chris] might not appear to be that way, but he's very self-confident, and his sexuality is totally male, yet he loves women, and he's not afraid of their intellects at all, and it's a wonderful combination, and quite rare, when you come right down to it . . . I don't think a lot of men get that kind of training. I think that they're really taught in a much different way. But in that respect, the Jews got it all, and more power. That's all I can say."

Even if Debbie and Chris were oblivious to their situation at the time, others who observed their relationship were not. Tish and Snooky Bellomo—later better known as punk clothiers, but then still part of an embryonic version of Blondie—recall, "Chris was a dark, brooding Jewish guy and Debbie was light." Adds Snooky, "Sure, there was something there between the Jewish boy and the Shiksa. . . . We're both Italian girls who dated Jewish guys almost exclusively and I'm married to one today. We always said that we were possessed of 'shiksappeal.' It's an old story in New York. Absolutely."

Yes, there was something there, an old dynamic, one we've seen already in relation to the Dictators and the Jewish gangsters, not to mention Richard Hell/Theresa Stern and Harpo/Chico Marx. There's that old tug between the good white Jew and the forbidding dark Latinate one. A tug between respectability and freedom, soulfulness and threat.

*   *   *

But let's back up and look at the beginnings of Blondie through the prism of Stein and Harry. For while the others in the band were definitely important to the development of the music, it is these two who perfected the image and the original songs that launched the group. Chris was the musical craftsman carrying on the tradition of Brill Building pop, and Harry was the lyricist and singer he inspired to express the intelligence that boyfriends before him had forced her to keep secret.

We'll begin with Chris, for it is in his corner that we see the more direct influence of New York, especially Jewish New York, on the band. Born in 1950 and raised in Brooklyn, Stein was the son of an Eastern European immigrant father who wanted to be a writer, and a first-generation Eastern European mother who wanted to be an artist. He had something of a classic Jewish bohemian childhood, the "Woody Allen cliché," as he calls it, "with the Ben Shawn prints on the wall and everything." He goes on to say that his parents were both "Reds" who met at a meeting of underground communists. His father later became a labor organizer who wrote for radical papers similar to John Reed's *The Masses*, and his mother long harbored intense feelings for the oppressed underclass.

Despite their political sympathies, however, Stein's parents were mismatched. His "neurotic, somewhat controlling" mother became preoccupied with economic security as his bohemian father drifted further from the home until he'd moved out completely and taken up with a much younger female "beatnik."

"I remember we'd go to the Catskills and my mother would basically lock herself in a cabin and paint the entire time," says Stein. "Not that my father was the easiest person to get along with," he adds. "He had a very sarcastic, Yiddish sense of humor, one that I've inherited. One that is very New York."

Stein remembers hanging out on the streets of his neighborhood and using that same sense of humor on his equally sarcastic Jewish friends. "It wasn't very wholesome really. We'd talk about each other's mothers and everything. It was very cutting. Very punk."

Not that the Yiddish-styled dozens were the only thing Stein was experiencing on the streets. While he and his friends were regularly dissing each other's *mamales*, certain social convulsions could be felt trembling beneath the sidewalks, the period of transition between 1950s gang culture and the rapidly rising counterculture creating tension for him and his group.

"We would pass by the pool hall and these gangster types would beat up anyone with long hair," says Stein. "I remember this pair, the Sirico brothers [later famous as 1970s mobsters], would call us faggots and try to do us damage."

Of course, it wasn't only the greasers who were out to get Stein and his mostly Jewish neighbors. In 1965, when he was fifteen, he and a group of his friends were kicked out of Midwood High (the same Brooklyn school where Woody Allen had been a student ten years earlier) because they refused to get haircuts. Stein ended up going from the school that had produced Alvy Singer and Fielding Mellish to one that coughed out Patty Duke and Johnny Thunders. Johnny was actually a student in Stein's class.

"It was a school for fuck-ups who couldn't fit into the system," says Stein. "I was always a little off center . . . and when my father died in 1965, I began to become more withdrawn and sullen."

Never exactly a happy-go-lucky kid, Stein became depressed in a way later associates such as Tish and Snooky saw as particularly Jewish. He brooded and read and became increasingly interested in the occult and religion, studying everything from H. P. Lovecraft to the Jewish mystical tradition known as Kabbalah. Around his seventeenth birthday in 1967, Stein went to San Francisco for "the gathering of the tribes" (much as had Joey Ramone), returning from there to first spend some time in the "bughouse" (again like Joey and numerous other acid casualties), then to intentionally flunk his army induction exam ("I told them to check off everything, that I was a drug addict, gay, whatever") before heading straight to Woodstock.

By the time he returned, Stein was ready to move to Manhattan for good, and like many others, he went to the Lower East Side, where rents were cheap, kids plentiful, and new music was in the air. Two groups proved especially influential—The Velvet Underground of Lou Reed and Tuli Kupferberg's the Fugs.

"We loved the Fugs, they were so funny. I'd go see them all the time," Stein says. "My friends and I had already been singing their songs back in Brooklyn. You know, '*Clara June, Clara June . . .*'"

The Velvet Underground was even more beloved. "They were just such a big deal then, everyone knew them. In fact, one of the high points of my life was getting to open for them. I'd been in this band . . . and we were asked if we wanted to open for the Underground. Of course we did. It was amazing."

As he settled into the Lower East Side, however, Stein, no longer with the band, drifted into reclusiveness. By his own admission, he began considering starting a new band simply to get out of this state, seeing in it a way to "put on an identity, like a comic strip character," much as Lenny Kaye had done when he'd adopted the "cape" of the glamorous faux Brit rocker, Link Cromwell.

To get to this point, Stein (a certifiable genius whose IQ easily qualified him for Mensa) went, like so many others, through the back door first. He became friendly with both the Warhol crowd and Andy via a high school friend who'd already moved downtown, then hooked up with Factory regular and local glam-psychedelic singer Eric Emerson, a legendary figure who many believe would have gone on to great things had he not died in 1975 as the result of a bicycle accident.

Though Emerson never gained the fame for which he seemed destined, he did become an important footnote to punk in at least one regard. For when Emerson introduced Stein to his girlfriend Elda Gentile (yes, her real name), and she in turn invited Stein to come watch her new band the Stilettos, only one degree of separation remained between the future Blondie co-conspirator and Debbie, the future figurehead of the band, the girl across the room, the Ultimate Shiksa Goddess.

* * *

But how did Harry come to be so close to Stein? Though they came from different worlds, in a psychic sense they grew up much closer than they thought.

While Stein was in Brooklyn dealing with his father's death and the taunts of goombahs at the pool hall, across the river in New Jersey, Harry was doing something similar in a photo-negative kind of way. The adopted daughter of a salesman (who worked for decades in the largely Jewish garment district) and a college-educated housewife, Debbie, like many adopted children, imagined that her biological parents were famous. Her fantasy mother was Marilyn Monroe. At the same time, she found herself trapped in a suburban area that was rapidly changing from predominantly WASP (or at least Dutch, like her parents) to Italian, as newly prosperous families emigrated from Brooklyn. Debbie knew what it was like to be different, both within the home and outside it. "I don't want to go into details, but [my parents] definitely weren't happy about the change in the neighborhood," Debbie says. "They didn't encourage me to be with my new friends. They were pretty intolerant, really."

Equally troubling to Debbie was the fact that her parents, her father in particular, were constantly berating her for not acting like a traditional girl. "I was 'too independent' is how he always put it. What he meant is that I did what I wanted. I wasn't passive like girls were supposed to be." Interestingly, Debbie says that the same was true to an even greater degree for the Italian girls she knew. She was friendly with the rebels from that group, as well as with two of the three Jewish girls who attended her school. She says, "I had Jewish friends and I knew Jewish families and I was well aware of that sort of pride in intellectualism . . . I guess it was just more interesting. And I guess I was sort of depressed and I really wanted to have a life, get a life, and I guess that was all part of it. It's all your fault. The Jews."

Debbie laughs when she says this, but it's clear that her alienation from her background and her search for something new still resonate.

When Debbie reached eighteen, she decided she'd had enough. Throughout high school she'd been thinking of escape, and since the only practical destination was New York ("I couldn't afford a ticket to Paris"), she headed there straight after graduation. Working first at the Playboy Club, where one can only assume she used the demure, passive sexuality that she had been raised to project (Debbie refuses to comment on this period, and seems to resent its being introduced), she soon moved on to waiting tables at the center of the downtown *hipoisie*, the club that functioned as the CBGB and more of the late 1960s and early '70s, Max's Kansas City.

Founded in 1965 by another Jewish bohemian, Mickey Ruskin, Max's had long been the home of the Warhol Factory and its contingents. Everyone from Lou Reed to Terry Southern to Warhol himself passed through its doors each night to check out the scene and be seen. Debbie went about establishing herself as a member of the downtown community, much as Chris, her lover-to-be, was doing in his own way somewhere nearby. She went to Warhol movies, occasionally visited the Factory, and regularly saw the New York Dolls. Eventually she decided to start a band, one that was as much camp, Warhol-inspired performance art as it was a musical force: the pre-Blondie, all-female group the Stilettos. (Harry had briefly been in a hippie band called The Wind in the Willows, but she had little to do with its makeup and was never happy with its image or sound.)

To say that Debbie started the band is open to debate. Though she was one of its founders, it seems that fellow Stiletto Elda Gentile had the initial idea and the drive to follow through on it. A longtime denizen of the Warhol scene, Elda then was a much more important figure than Debbie. She had been in a couple of Warhol-related productions; she had been involved with Factory member Eric Emerson (at this point Chris Stein's roommate), and most important, she and Emerson had conceived a child together, a lovely blond-haired boy born in 1971.

Emerson's influence on the downtown scene—and particularly Blondie—cannot be overstressed. A star of Warhol films such as *Chelsea Girls* and *Lonesome Cowboys*, he was also an integral member of The Exploding Plastic Inevitable, the Warhol entourage that traveled with The Velvet Underground in its early days as part of a "multimedia" experience. While Warhol associates did their thing as the band performed—Gerard Malanga snapping his whip, Barbara Rubin accosting audience members with a microphone and asking if they were happy with the smallness/firmness/largeness of their butts/tits/dicks—Emerson did a kind of crystal-meth-persuasion interpretative dance of his combined acid and speed trips, flailing his arms about and laughing maniacally from behind his glitter-covered teeth. Later, he became as famous for holding up the first VU album by demanding royalties for use of his image on the cover, as he did for founding the band the Magic Tramps, in which Chris Stein played guitar before joining the Stilettos. But he is most important to this story as the conduit that brought Chris to Debbie.

Here's what happened. When The Stilettos were practicing their act one day, Elda invited Chris over to the apartment, where he saw Debbie and fell immediately in love. Or wait, that's what Elda says. According to Chris, he and Debbie didn't meet until Elda's friend, and his girlfriend, invited him to the Stilettos first gig, where he saw Debbie and became immediately infatuated. Debbie concurs: "I really couldn't even see his face clearly [from the stage] because he was sitting in such a way that his head was backwards . . . All I could see was this sort of glow, and I don't know if it was [fate] or it was just sort of apparent that we were supposed to connect up. I know that sounds kind of ridiculous, but I delivered the whole show to him. I couldn't look anywhere else."

In any case, Chris and Debbie met, and though they differ in the particulars (Debbie says, for instance, that she was immensely attracted to Stein from the stage, then contradicts this by saying that she only grew attracted to him over time after they became friends), they both agree that there was an immediate bond of some sort, and that they became friends if not lovers, gradually getting to know each other while waiting to see what would happen.

They also began working together. Chris joined the Stilettos as their first permanent guitarist. Elda had invited him over in the first place because she was sick to death of having to find backup musicians every night. So Chris saw Debbie on a regular basis and became increasingly taken with her. She meanwhile grew to "trust him," as Elda puts it. "Debbie was always shy and insecure, while I don't think Chris has ever had a shy day in his life."

This combination of fragile beauty and cocky chutzpah seemed to work for the two, not to mention for the band in general. With Chris on guitar and Debbie becoming increasingly confident on vocals, the Stilettos began to cohere. Initially, the act had been Debbie, Elda, and Amanda Jones, a kind of rainbow coalition of New York womanhood, with Debbie the blonde all-American, Elda the self-described "flamboyant Italian," and Amanda the "beautiful black woman," as Elda refers to her. Now, the three were still in place, but Debbie was stepping more to the fore. As pictures reveal, she was always at the center of the three once Chris came on board, and as she began to learn the hand gestures and movements that help to get across a performer's mood, she gained more control over the audience and the band.

Whether this was primarily due to Elda's influence (Elda thinks so) or to the way Chris began working with Debbie behind the scenes, success began to seem imminent for the band. And as it did, a separate bond began to form between Chris and Debbie.

"It was only natural," Elda says. "By this time they were definitely a couple and in love. They were bound to rely on each other and feel joined in most every way."

A record deal forced the break. After a show at the 82 Club in 1973, Elda was approached by Paul Fishkin of Bearsville Records, who expressed interest in signing the band. "He said that he loved our act and that he wanted to produce us, but he said that he only wanted the girls, not Chris or the other musicians."

Here Elda becomes a little hesitant in the telling, choosing her words carefully. The memory still rankles to some degree.

"I thought I had to at least bring this information to Debbie, that we had to address it. But as soon as Debbie went home, she must have told Chris, because not long after there was a coup d'état."

While Chris says "I never heard the story of signing a record deal 'without the musicians' till now," and believes that "there was just too much jealousy between the girls," whatever was the reason, the end result was the same. The Stilettos broke up and Blondie was set in motion.

Though initially it seemed that Elda might go on to fame and fortune regardless, she soon fell by the wayside while Chris and Debbie charged ahead. It seemed an odd state of affairs at the time, especially considering how Chris and Debbie went about developing their new act. For as they transformed themselves from the campy Stilettos to the more pointedly ironic Blondie (Chris's Jewish take on things coming to the surface), they also went about changing their venue. From this point on, until they hit it big, their base of operations was CBGB, that sticky-floored shit-hole where black-clad bands like the Ramones and Television performed for bikers and hobos while trying to avoid stepping in the droppings of owner Hilly Kristal's dogs.

In the sweaty crucible of CBGB, surrounded by the smell of dogshit and stale beer, Chris and Debbie created a new band. It was somewhere between a racket and a mess at first, a pale imitation of the Stilettos and the Warhol scene, rechristened as Blondie and the Banzai Babies with two backup singers, the Italian-American sisters Tish and Snooky providing a camp Warhol vibe that helped fill out Debbie's voice.

As Debbie continued to develop confidence and Chris began to create a new sound that drew as much on Brill Building pop as Iggy Pop, things began to change. First Tish and Snooky stopped receiving calls about rehearsals. Debbie and Chris bumped into them one day and pretended not to have realized that they hadn't told them about one planned for that night.

Then Chris, Debbie, and fellow bandmates Jimmy Destri, Clem Burke, and Gary Valentine received a shock when Patti Smith, reigning queen of the scene, "stole" their bass player Fred Smith (né Fred Lefkowitz), and "gave" him to boyfriend Tom Verlaine as a replacement for his own half-Jewish bass player Richard Hell. This rattled the group, but it had the effect of heightening its competitive spirit and so bringing the members closer together. Burke's inventive drum work (he filled in on a Ramones tour between Marky and Richie), Valentine's jagged guitar playing, and Destri's fluid keyboarding joined Stein's new songs and Harry's new lyrics to create a new tightness and synergy. The unique qualities that Blondie later brought to the scene emerged in embryonic form for the first time.

No longer was Blondie a camp take on Warhol and his trashing of straight culture. Now it was a kind of post-modern kabuki in which Debbie's coy, Marilyn Monroesque innocence did battle each night onstage with her ironic post-feminist wink-wink, nudge-nudge. Long before Madonna began her path from Material Girl to Kabbalah-obsessed Esther, beneath the shadow of the Lower East Side tenements where Harry and the band lived and from which Stein's family had long emigrated, a Jewish son of Brooklyn and a Gentile daughter of the suburbs came together in the classic New York pairing: Marilyn Monroe as Shiksa Goddess with her Arthur Miller boyfriend, the brooding heeb. From this point on, the template of Blondie—both the band and its figurehead—was set.

*　　*　　*

And yet the story is not quite over. It was only when Blondie was discovered at CB's by the Jewish trio of Craig Leon (producer of the Ramones, Suicide and others), Marty Thau (manager of The New York Dolls, owner of the label that released Suicide's debut, etc.), and, most importantly, Richard Gottehrer (a former Brill Building songwriter) that it really found the sound that propelled it to the top of the charts. As Leon recalls, "Ritchie said she looked good and Marty said 'Yeah let's go ahead' and so we did . . . but nobody would touch [Blondie]. I mean we would actually get kicked out of offices [with people] saying 'who needs this old crap!' . . . We went everywhere trying to hustle people. Ritchie was using all his old contacts . . . [and] the last resort was to go to . . . Larry Uttal who did a lot of stuff in the '50s on the old Bell label. He sold it, it became Arista, and then he went on to Private Stock. So Larry gave a minor league budget to go ahead and do this."

With the old school Uttal holding the purse strings, and the combination of Leon and Gottehrer as coproducers, Blondie had the best of both worlds. While Leon was thoroughly in touch with the new sound, Gottehrer, with the support of Uttal, knew how to combine that sound with the old. Like many others already discussed, Gottehrer was a Jew who loved music yet made his name as a writer rather than a performer. Joining the Brill Building staff in 1961 at the age of twenty, he was responsible for such hits as "My Boyfriend's Back" and "I Want Candy." And yet Gottehrer was an avatar of sorts, for he was one of the first to step from behind the curtain and actually go onstage. In 1965, he and two fellow Jews, Bob Feldman and Jerry Goldstein, formed the Strangeloves, a truly strange band that combined subterfuge and revolution to produce two major hits.

Billing themselves as either Aussies from down under or aliens from outer space, the Strangeloves, like the Ramones, were as much a joke band as a serious outfit. Also like the Ramones, they produced seriously great songs. The best of these, "I Want Candy," drew intensely on the stylings of black music (in this case, Bo Diddley's) and attests to the Jewish-black connection that was then so much a part of pop music. Hundreds of similar songs were written by Jews at the time, including the Juvenile Delinquent comedy "Charlie Brown" (Jerry Leiber and Mike Stoller), the existential blues number "Lonely Avenue" (Doc Pomus), and perhaps most famous, that doo-wopish take on a Zulu folk song, "The Lion Sleeps Tonight (Wimoweh)" by Neil Sedaka's former band the Tokens. Brill Building legend Jerry Leiber once commented, "I felt black. I *was*, as far as I was concerned." Gottehrer echoed these sentiments: "Jewish culture is very soulful. It's got a richness in spirit. You find the same thing in African American culture. Somewhere ingrained in us is the concept of slavery. We were enslaved in Egypt, and then of course, we were kicked out of the east as Jews, and we were kicked somewhere else. And African Americans were forcibly brought here, and weren't even integrated into this society. They sort of worked their way in through music. So we both have that—that soul." For a darker take on this, consider the following diary entry by Doc Pomus (Jerome Felder), the Brill Building writer who'd lost the use of his legs as a child due to polio: "To the world, a fat crippled Jewish kid is a nigger—a thing—the invisible man—like Ralph Ellison says."

Combining this soul with expertise in studio wizardry and the art of songcraft, Gottehrer helped Blondie achieve the sound and style of Brill Building pop. More, as producer he encouraged Chris to pursue his interest in comic lyrics filled with innuendo and Debbie to emphasize her ironic take on sexuality and innocence. He had a habit of writing and producing songs that presented women as worthy of acknowledgment and respect. For instance, Ellie Greenwich contributed directly to early Blondie albums, even singing backup on their first Australian hit, "In the Flesh."

It was a habit that Gottehrer shared with other composers and producers of his era, like Phil Spector, Doc Pomus (whose daughter Rachel Felder was Joey Ramone's "soul mate" in the final years of his life), and later Lenny Kaye. These men sparked the rise of the great girl groups of the 1960s and later the queen of punk—and to a certain degree female rock—Patti Smith. As Lawrence Epstein says in his book *The Haunted Smile*, discussing how Jewish comics like George Burns transformed the traditional—and mean-spirited—"Dumb Dora" (think Dumb Blonde) acts into something more respectful and gentle, "Burns kept the form of the Dumb Dora act, but—drawing on the idealization of the *Yiddische* mama—he dignified the woman by making her the center of the act. If the straight man didn't understand this new Dumb Dora, he never got angry . . . Burns took the social observations that had been important to Yiddish life, and filtered them not through a shrewd con artist but through a seemingly naïve partner."

Gottehrer helped give birth to the ironic feminine power of Debbie Harry.* The musical movement Debbie helped to spearhead gave birth nationwide to a whole new attitude among women that opened the doors to female rock.

---

*Gottehrer also gave birth to the bad boy Richard Hell, when he produced his *Blank Generation* debut, just as he did for that rockabilly star reborn as a Jew, Robert "Ira" Gordon (formerly of the pop-punk Tuff Darts), when he produced his debut, *Robert Gordon with Link Wray*. Gottehrer went on to carry the mantle of Brill Building pop beyond the CBGB scene, helping to create and produce the post-punk girl band, the Go Gos, and, most recently, the Raveonettes, a girl-guy duo that's like a cross between the Shangri-Las, the Jesus and Mary Chain, and Phil Spector's Wall of Sound.

As William Ruhlmann says in the *All Music Guide*, "If new wave was about reconfiguring and recontextualizing simple pop/rock forms of the '50s and '60s in new, ironic and aggressive ways, then Blondie, which took the girl group style of the early and mid-'60s and added a '70s archness, fit right in . . . Blondie's secret weapon, which was deployed increasingly over their career, was a canny pop straddle—they sent the music up and celebrated it at the same time. So, for instance, songs like 'X Offender' (their first single) and 'In the Flesh' (their first hit, in Australia) had the tough-girl-with-a-tender-heart tone of The Shangri-Las . . . while going one step too far into hard-edged decadence—that is, if you chose to see that. (The tag line of 'Look Good in Blue,' for example, went, 'I could give you some head and shoulders to lie on.') The whole point was that you could take Blondie either way, and lead singer Deborah Harry's vocals, which combined rock fervor with a kiss-off quality, reinforced that, as did the band's energetic, trashy sound. . . . It provided a template for the future."

It was not by accident that Sex Pistols manager (and, to a great degree, creator) Malcolm McLaren later had a hit with Gottehrer's Strangeloves classic "I Want Candy." When McLaren made this a chart-topping single in 1982 with his follow-up to the Sex Pistols, Bow Wow Wow, it was clearly because he saw it as the perfect vehicle for the underage mouthpiece of the band, fifteen-year-old Annaebella Lwin (born Myant Myant Aye, Burmese for Cool Cool High), to get across her coy mix of innocence and experience, wink and blush, nudge and withdrawal. To get across, in other words, her veddy British (as in Empire) take on Debbie Harry. Combining a twangy Duane Eddy–like guitar with an African tribal drum corps, and creating a cartoon-like video where Annabella cavorted on the beach amidst bouncing balls and boys, McLaren merged Blondie's sensibility with Gotterher's while adding an even more provocative pederastic element. He was only exaggerating what each had brought to the table already. His beat was merely a blacker (as in African) version of Bo Diddley's, his female star a more international (as in European/Burmese) and exaggerated-beyond-recognition version of that all-American Shiksa Goddess, Blondie.

In other words, he created a further update on the irony latent in the Brill Building school, transforming Blondie's blonde goddess into a darker, more taboo idol that reeked of Bangkok and the porn trade, not America and the suburbs—much less Shiksa Goddesses.

13

HOTSTY-TOTSY NAZI SCHATZES

Nazi Imagery and the Final Solution to the Final Solution

We forgave the Germans
And we were friends
Though they murdered six million

> —Bob Dylan, "With God on Our Side"
> (*The Times They Are A-Changin'*, 1964)

The reason for the flourishing of the aristocratic [camp] posture among homosexuals also seems to parallel the Jewish case. For every sensibility is self-serving to the group that promotes it. Jewish liberalism is a gesture of self-legitimization. So is Camp taste, which definitely has something propagandistic about it. Needless to say, the propaganda operates in exactly the opposite direction. The Jews pinned their hopes for integrating into modern society on promoting the moral sense. Homosexuals have pinned their integration into society on promoting the aesthetic sense. Camp is a solvent of morality. It neutralizes moral indignation, sponsors playfulness.

> —Susan Sontag, "Notes on 'Camp'," 1964

Author's Note: *According to rumor, the following scene is true. While I can make no definitive statement as to its veracity, I heard it from at least two highly placed sources who prefer to remain nameless. Understandably.*

In a bedroom somewhere in the East Village, Chris Stein and Debbie Harry are making love, a Nazi flag beneath them, its red backdrop in perfect counterpoint to her blonde hair.

Meanwhile, in another apartment nearby, Dead Boys lead singer Stiv Bators and his Jewish girlfriend Cynthia Ross are doing the same, her equally blonde hair splayed out against the black swastika in the middle, its bent arms radiating around her face in *sieg heil*–like salutes.

And not far from there, Stiv's bandmate Cheetah Chrome is similarly engaged on his Nazi-flag bedspread with his half-Jewish girlfriend Gyda Gash, her dyed-blonde hair free from its vintage *Feldkommandant*'s cap that goes so well with her matching tattoos of a Jewish star and a the word *STIGMATA*.

Is it surprising to find so many punk principals involved in the same pursuit? Everyone knows that the punks were attracted to the dark side, and that they liked to shock their audiences both onstage and off. But what to make of the fact that in each of these instances, one of the participants is Jewish—at least in part? Both Chris Stein and Cynthia Ross had Jewish parents, and Gyda "Braverman" Gash had a Jewish father and Catholic mother.

Moreover, what to make of that other punk couple, Sid 'n' Nancy, he of the swastika T-shirts and she of the Jewish family in the Philly suburbs? Or of the five Jewish guys in the Dictators who played "Master Race Rock"? And don't forget early punk champion and child of Holocaust survivor, Genya Ravan, or Dictators press secretary and fellow child of a Holocaust survivor, Camilla Saly. Or Lou Reed and the iron crosses shaved into his hair, Jonathan Richman and his song about trains going through the Jewish suburbs of Scarsdale and New Rochelle, and Daniel Rey (Rabinowitz) and his band Shrapnel. Is there something sinister at work here? Something horrific? Something camp, perhaps? Say, concentration camp?

As we'll see, it's a mixture of all of these things. While the various punk responses to the Holocaust range from the mocking to the shocking to the world-rocking, as in the impulse to identify with the oppressors, each is in its own way an attempt to deal with this tragedy that affected the punks' lives whether they liked to admit it or not. No Holocaust, no punk. As many a Jewish parent has pointed out to his or her dismissive child, it didn't matter whether you were religiously Jewish, culturally so, or completely apathetic about the link—it didn't even matter whether you were Jewish at all: if you had one Jewish grandparent, that was enough to get you gassed in Nazi Germany. Christ, even one *great*-grandparent could do it sometimes. You could scream and cry all you wanted, but it made no difference. The field of red with the white circle surrounding the black swastika in the middle would get you. It would put the agony to your ecstasy. Its purifying fire would burn you to your very core.

*   *   *

Even if you weren't worried about what might have happened to you in Nazi Germany, the Holocaust had an impact on you as a Jewish punk. As Andy Shernoff observed, it made you embarrassed that you were descended from a people who had allowed themselves to be so victimized. That's why he and others were so proud when Israel beat the combined forces of four Arab nations in the Six-Day War, and why folks like Chris Stein collected Nazi memorabilia even after they made it as stars. It was not to glorify their oppressors but to show that, as Debbie Harry explained, "he had won, the Jews had won."

Of course, the thrill of breaking taboos did play a part. When Chris Stein and his best friend, Glenn O'Brien—editor of *Interview* magazine and for a number of years in the late 1970s cocreator and host with Chris of the local cable access show *TV Party*—were on their way home from the airport, where Chris had just picked up a specially delivered ceremonial sword of Himmler's, Chris suggested that they should stop at a synagogue to "see how everyone would react." O'Brien says, "He seemed to think that it would be funny to stop at a synagogue. He had a weird gleam in his eye."

This wasn't *The Night Porter*—a 1973 art-house film starring Dirk Bogarde and Charlotte Rampling about a concentration camp guard who is later reunited with one of his inmates and the sadomasochistic relationship that then ensues. Aside from the possible "revenge" element implicit here—both on the Nazis and on the gloom the tragedy imparted—there was something else at work: a reaffirmation, whether one wanted to think of it or not, of Jewish identity. As Richard Hell makes clear, it is the Holocaust and the Holocaust alone that defines him as a Jew. Consider the following remarks he made in an introduction to a 2002 talk on Jewish American novelist Nathaniel West (who changed his name from Weinstein in an attempt to disown his Jewishness). Decrying how others label him a Jew despite his objections, Hell said, "What is a Jew? Well, I concluded that a Jew is anyone who anyone else calls a Jew . . . Put plainly, Hitler was not an isolated phenomenon. We know what happened in Germany in our parents' lifetimes to many Jews who regarded themselves first as Germans, but the most cursory knowledge—even the history in this lecture about Nathaniel West—makes it clear that it can happen at anytime, anywhere. That's what being a Jew means to me, because that's what I know about Jewishness. That Jews are those that other Jews can claim and that bigots can reject and attack and seek to harm. So I realize that I qualify."

While it is a bit disconcerting to hear Hell implying that attempts by contemporary Jews to "claim" him are equivalent to what the Nazis were doing ("Hitler was not an isolated phenomenon"), his essential point is well made, in fact it's the same one made in *Anti-Semite and Jew* by Sartre. Jews are not only those whom identify themselves as Jewish, but those whom others identify as such. Indeed, as Television biographer Tim Mitchell notes, this was true for Richard Hell even when he was little Richard Meyers growing up in Lexington, Kentucky. "Lexington's Jewish community had built up since the early 1900s, when émigrés from Eastern Europe had begun to arrive there. By the fifties [when Richard was a young boy], although that community was well established, it still had to deal with the kind of anti-Semitism that excluded Jews from club memberships—as well as with the constant shadow of the Ku Klux Klan."

While this sort of anti-Semitism barely existed in New York, in part because it was a city of immigrants, perhaps in larger part because it was a city with so many Jews, it still lurked in the background as historical fact. For each of the children who were raised by parents who had experienced the Holocaust directly, there were thousands of others who grew up close enough to its horrors to understand its significance. If it didn't necessarily traumatize or paralyze them, it did have an effect, an unmeasurable one perhaps, one that varied in degree from individual to individual, but made itself insidiously known.

Among the Jewish punks who were interviewed for this book, a surprising number recalled meeting a certain neighborhood figure as a child, a man or woman with the tattooed numbers of the concentration camp inmate on his or her arm. This might not seem surprising, considering the number of refugees (or, as they were originally known, displaced persons) who ended up in the city, but what leads one to view these memories as embodying a horrific New York urban myth is that in nearly every instance, the man or woman (it is usually a woman) is employed smack-dab in the center of the young punk's universe, right there in that kidcentric location, the neighborhood candy store. It's as if every ice-cream truck in the country were driven by a double amputee from the Iraq War (excuse me, Operation Iraqi Freedom), or every birthday clown a recent parolee from an asylum for child abductors and molesters. It's the ultimate irony, in other words, the intersection of the bitterest individual with the sweetest innocent memory of childhood. It's like the salt-water and bitter herbs of the Passover seder, taken together just before the apple-cinnamon-nut mixture of the Hillel Sandwich to remind the participants of the bitter times during slavery in Egypt and how they should identify with other oppressed groups on this special night in which they celebrate the sweetness of family.

To put it otherwise, the Holocaust survivor terrifying the children as she hands them caramels and pixie sticks symbolizes a certain kind of New York experience. She's the Jewish madwoman in the attic, the dark skeleton in the closet. She lies in wait in Candyland like a black figure at the bottom of a well of sweets. She's a contestant in a freak show about the world's horrors, a flipside to the fun in the Ramones' blitzkrieg bop. A punk rock nightmare. We accept you. One of us.

*   *   *

The horror of the camps spread down the candy store aisles as well, to the magazine racks where those same owners displayed their comic books. Whether it was the "mutant," genetically inferior X-Men, doing noble battle against an oppressive police state, or the horror comics of EC, pitting "monsters" against frightened "good folk" who failed to look below the surface, or *MAD* magazine, skewering the lies and hypocrisies of postwar America like a Junior League Lenny Bruce, the products of a post-Holocaust mentality were there on display. It was no accident.

Neil Gaiman, the English creator of the award-winning *Darkman* graphic novel series and the Jewish creator of a 1970s English punk band, Chaos, says, "[In EC comics,] you had a bunch of Jewish creators who were very aware of the fragility of life. Because there were themes that ran through these things, and anti-prejudice was one of them, even through the horror comics: not taking people at face value, trying to look underneath . . . talking about the fragility of the status quo." Gaiman, whose family's German Jewish side was wiped out in the war, goes on to say that horror—as well as comedy— are by their very nature always an attack on the status quo. "Either the world is not the world you think it is, or safe people are not safe, or strange things will come back to haunt or destroy you, whatever . . . *MAD* especially created a very anti-authoritarian equation . . . The original *MAD* comics were considered practically communist, because they were taking 1950s American sacred cows and skewering them and slicing them."

The combined elements of horror and satire that undermined the social order were as Jewish as they were New York as they were punk. They were the same elements that Lenny Bruce referred to when he said that it didn't matter if you were Catholic—if you were from New York, you were Jewish. The Englishman Gaiman noticed them when he came to the city from London and found the quintessential New York experience. "I'm standing in a deli and this guy orders a tuna sandwich, and it hasn't shown up within approximately thirty-five seconds, at which point, he starts this entire loud comedy routine based around the theory that 'If I wanted a tuna sandwich tomorrow, I would have said *hey dude, can I have a tuna sandwich tomorrow?* But no, I wanted it today. I've been standing here how long?' And I'm just standing there thinking . . . if you told anyone in London, 'You can either make a scene in a deli and everyone will be staring at you, or you can shoot yourself,' they would have said, 'Good, just give me the gun and I'll just go behind the wall so as to not bother anybody.' Whereas the entire New York thing was get out there, get irritated, and get funny."

In both *MAD* magazine and the comedy of Lenny Bruce—not to mention to a lesser degree in the spiels of contemporary Jewish "humorists" such as Mort Sahl and Shelly Berman—this loud, irritated funniness that satirized social proprieties and institutions was fed by a larger distrust of governments, legal systems, and even history. Bruce attacked everything from the Catholic Church to the liberal Democrats of the Kennedy administration to the "authorized" purveyors of the story of the Holocaust in an effort to make his audience look below the surface, because he felt that civilization was drowning in hypocrisy. Whether he was simply attempting to make light of the *Shoa* so as to ease its horror, or attacking those who had just begun to use it to promote a political agenda (chiefly in Israel), Bruce employed humor to undermine the accepted norms, a Jewish response throughout millennia of living on the fringes of society that was exaggerated all the more in the period following the Holocaust.

As distance in time provided the psychological and political safety to address the Holocaust more directly, it, like any other historical event, was interpreted variously, sometimes for competing purposes. Intellectuals such as Hannah Arendt saw in it an example of the "banality of evil"—the ability of shallow bureaucratic humans to commit murder dispassionately whether they were Jewish or not. Zionists saw in it a rationale for the establishment and defense of Israel, a Jewish state that would put the safety and interests of Jews first. Bruce saw the Holocaust as merely another in a long line of crimes against humanity perpetrated by humans of every stripe. In one of his most controversial bits he makes an analogy between (1) the Holocaust, (2) the Allies' fire-bombing of Dresden, and (3) America's use of atomic bombs in Japan. As he says, affecting an exaggerated accent in the spirit of Dr. Strangelove: "My name is Adolf Eichmann. And the Jews came every day to what they thought would be fun in the showers. People say I should have been hung. *Nein.* Do you recognize the whore in the middle of you— that you would have done the same if you were there yourselves? . . . Do you people think yourselves better because you burned your enemies at long distance with missiles without ever seeing what you had done to them? Hiroshima *auf wiedersehen.*"

Clearly not everyone's cup of methadone, but for a generation that was increasingly hearing—in after-school Hebrew classes, synagogue sermons, and movies such as *The Pawnbroker* (1965)—about the evils done to its people at the hands of others, it was a message that was felt, absorbed, and to a certain degree openly acknowledged. For if one is raised to see the Nazis as the enemy and the Jews as the good guys (not to mention victims), when it comes time to rebel, who are you going to side with? Especially when it is the nature of your people to examine the position of the outsider, the maligned other rejected by the status quo, the enemy of the state? If you're a Jew, and the Jewish and non-Jewish powers-that-be tell you the Nazis are bad, then aren't you going to want to mess with that dynamic a bit? Like Lenny Bruce, aren't you going to want to throw it in their faces for shock value at the very least? Aren't you going to want to upset them as much as you can—just as a generation made up of your older siblings had done by adopting the rhetoric and slogans of the communists so despised by all (including Jewish parents who were often embarrassed by their own parents' socialist pasts)? Furthermore, aren't you going to want something even stronger, considering that most of those former radicals were already becoming fine, upstanding New Age Yuppies? Where had all the Yippies gone with their self-righteousness, their revolution, their hopes for a brighter future? There was no future. And you, their younger siblings, were tired of hearing about the fascist state of Amerika. You were ready to attack *everything*, while perhaps buying bullet-proof vests for the cops. You were ready to adopt the look and attitudes of the fascists, no matter how complicated, simpleminded, or ill-guided your motivations might have been.

*   *   *

This trend emerged in the late 1960s, in England, the only place where a swastika might be as disturbing to non-Jewish parents as to Jewish ones. Here, with the Rolling Stones, the first widely circulated images of rock stars in Nazi uniform appear. Brian Jones and his German girlfriend, Anita Pallenberg, did it first, followed by Keith Richards, now the paramour of the lovely Anita, Keith Moon of The Who, and Ozzy Osbourne of Black Sabbath, to name just a few. All these bad boys of the British Invasion shared a historical background that had been turned upside down by the war. As any historian—or moviegoer (see John Boorman's *Hope and Glory*, 1987)— knows, before the Second World War the sun never set on the British Empire, vast swaths of the globe colored in that most royal of colors, pink. When the Germans finished off the job they had begun in the First World War, however, draining the British of their capital reserves and the will to fight uprisings across their domain, the empire all but crumbled overnight. Suddenly, England was reduced to a single, ration-hungry, bombed-out, gray island that throughout the 1950s was ruled by gangster youths and hooligans, many of whom, being Jewish, were not even "real" Brits (more on this to come). In reply to an upper-crust gent's indignant comment, "I fought the war for your sort," one of the original Brit invaders, Ringo Starr, said, "I bet you wish you hadn't won."

It isn't such a leap from here to Johnny Rotten's screaming "Belsen Was a Gas," while his loutish bassist Sid Vicious carves swastika's into his chest. With two hundred years of world domination destroyed by the Nazis, it's not surprising that the wild—and perhaps disappointed—children of those who "won the war but lost the peace" might rebel in the very way that would hurt their parents most—by identifying with the enemy and in many cases adopting the same enemy's philosophy.

The story elsewhere was a bit more complicated. In France, a country that had suffered occupation and guilt over varying degrees of collaboration, the first punk to appear was, as in New York, a Jew. National pop hero and bad boy Serge Gainsbourg (Lucien Ginzburg) was more than just Jewish, however. As a child during the occupation, he had been forced to wear a yellow star and fear for his life. While his family's flight from Paris ultimately saved him, the psychological effects went deep and later influenced his emergence as France's Grand Pierre de Punk. Gainsbourg made clear that he had absorbed his Nazi oppressors' lesson that he was genetically vile, and had come early in life to see his face as grotesque. An A-list celebrity Lothario who infamously recorded not just one, but two versions of what in essence is a musical take on simultaneous orgasm, "Je t'aime. Moi non plus" (the first with French sex goddess Brigitte Bardot, the second with her English counterpart Jane Birkin), Gainsbourg regularly referred to himself as the Beast who got the Beauties—a line the French media unfortunately seemed all too ready to accept.

Would Gainsbourg have been considered quite so grotesque in New York? Or for that matter Israel? Probably not. But such was the case in his native land. And such fed his lifelong urge—some would say compulsion—to scandalize. His role in the world had been clearly designated. He was the sexualized beast, the pop smoothie with a rock 'n' roll heart. So when in 1975 (the same year the Dictators released their debut), at the height of his career, he suddenly shocked his audience again by putting out a record of 1950s-style rock numbers dealing with the legacy of the Nazis and the Holocaust—*Rock Around the Bunker*—it was somehow perfectly in keeping with his image, and perfectly positioned to catapult him to status as the first French-styled punk. Not that this seemed calculated on Gainsbourg's part. It seemed to spring from his deepest nature, just as did other similarly troubling Gainsbourg masterpieces of this period, among them *The Man with the Cabbage Head* (a kind of prog rock symphony to despair) and *The Ballad of Melody Nelson* (a concept album mixing blues, psychedelia, and lounge music to create a portrait of the aging Casanova as the rapist of his own talent). Clearly American in its musical inspiration—including many American phrases in its lyrics—what is most telling about *Rock Around the Bunker* is the way it delivers each of its barbed comments on fascism in a clearly comedic manner:

> Put on your black stockings boys
> Adjust your clingy pantyhose just right . . .
> We're gonna dance the Nazi Rock.

The music, too, is satirical—upbeat, basic 1950s rock. Like the Ramones, the Dictators, and numerous other American punk bands that hearkened back to the simpler rock of the late 1950s and early '60s, Gainsbourg's music contradicts his lyrics, as if he is trying to shock his audience—or, more likely, trying to leaven the horror through camp so that it can be directly addressed.

Noted UK music journalist and Gainsbourg biographer (*A Fistful of Gitanes*) Sylvie Simmons says, "Gainsbourg . . . had considerable complexes as he grew up about his 'Jewish' body being so small, unmuscular, unhirsute, about being mistaken for a girl, getting rebuffed by prostitutes in his youth, etc. And yet, Serge displayed that Jewish irony/humour thing in his Nazi rock album *Rock Around the Bunker*. I think the fact that he bought himself a platinum Star of David to commemorate his first big hit, 'Je T'Aime'— notably, a duet with a beautiful, non-Jewish, young Englishwoman—is significant in a self-explanatory way."

Something was in the air. Gainsbourg was joined by both UK punks and experimental outsiders like Lou Reed, whose album *Berlin* dealt with the city's decadent legacy and drew parallels between it and New York; David Bowie, who, posing as a Nazi-saluting Thin White Duke, lived in Berlin around this time; and Iggy Pop, another early proponent of swastika chic whom Bowie brought with him to Berlin to record foreboding albums that were embraced by a punk audience. But it was in America, particularly in New York, that it all began. It was here that the Jewish children of the Holocaust had come together, ready to create a new rock.

* * *

Before we get into New York punk's connection to Nazi themes, let's look back just once more—this time at pre-punk America. The Rolling Stones, among the first to adopt Nazi regalia on a large scale, were here imitated by less well known yet ultimately equally influential bands such as the Stooges, adored by punk impresario Danny Fields, and later, the Blue Öyster Cult, so important to the burgeoning New York rock scene.

In the case of the Stooges, the impulses are closer to those that emerged in England—economic dissatisfaction at the closing of auto plants around their native Detroit. Like the Dead Boys of Ohio, another punk Rust Belt band, the Stooges came from largely Slavic and German communities devastated by the loss of economic stability. Think Michael Moore without a camera (or liberal education) to fall back on, and you might have some idea of the types who made up the Stooges and later the Dead Boys. These dead-end kids were the stooges (punks?) of industry, with nothing to look forward to in the post-industrial, postwar era. They were suddenly as obsolete as Henry Ford's Model T—and Ford itself was rapidly losing ground to that other Axis power, Japan. Meanwhile, they saw Jewish families in well-to-do suburbs around Detroit like Farmington Hills and West Bloomfield and their anger boiled over. As Ron Asheton says in the revised edition of *Please Kill Me* (1997) describing Iggy's—and later his—propensity to date Jewish girls, "He had this whole thing of hooking up with rich Jewish girls. He had this really rich Jewish girlfriend whose name was Alex. And Alex had a sidekick named Georgia. Iggy started bringing them over, and he'd be so fucked up that they started digging on me, because I had all the Nazi stuff. They became like psycho-Nazi-rich-Jewish-girls. So I usurped Iggy. That's when I got to understand Iggy a bit more—of how he was using these people . . . so I would end up using them and their limousines."

The Stooges' embrace of Nazi imagery was based on economic resentment and a simple desire to align themselves with the darkest, most frightening, and shocking forces imaginable, and the "psycho" Jewish rich girls who gave themselves to the Stooges shared the latter impulse. Something a bit more complicated was going on with the Blue Öyster Cult. Formed at SUNY Stony Brook by a Jew (Eric Bloom), a "Nazi wannabe" (Allen Lanier), and a couple of French Canadian brothers (Albert and Joe Bouchard), the BOC was—like its offshoot at SUNY New Paltz, the Dictators—basically the creation of its manager, Sandy Pearlman, a Jewish kid who saw "great potential" in the "fascistic possibilities" of the rock concert, according to BOC biographer Martin Popoff.

Pearlman combined this fascination with fascism and an equivalent fascination with the occult to create a dark, mysterious image for the BOC, a band that had previously been a psychedelic jam outfit named Soft White Underbelly. At the same time, Pearlman seemed to reclaim from Hitler the position of chief evildoer by placing himself at the head of an intricate and complicated counterplot. Pearlman's emphasis on the nefarious schemes of magicians, extraterrestrials, and alchemists—and his personal interest in Freemasons, the illuminati, and H. P. Lovecraft—seemed to mask an unconscious self-loathing for the alleged conspiracy-driven cabals of his own background. His genius lay in the nebulousness of his perpetrators. They could just as easily have been the governments of Hitler, Stalin, Mao, or Nixon. He had the typical modern sensibility that saw most governments and social institutions as potentially evil and worthy of distrust. Or rather, he had the typical modern *urban* sensibility embodied by "East Coast intellectuals," "liberal elitists," and any number of other groups whose names are at least in part code for "Jews."

That is, until the third—and what many consider best—BOC album, *Secret Treaties*. Here, Pearlman's Nazi obsessions came to the fore. With an album title that refers to alleged secret business dealings between the Axis and Allied powers during the Second World War, songs such as "Subhuman" ("Warm weather and a holocaust . . . Tears of God flow as I bleed") and a cover illustration of the band standing in front of a Messerschmidt 262, *Secret Treaties* couldn't have been any less secret in its intentions. As mentioned in an earlier chapter, it drew the attention of both the German government (which banned the album out of fear that it would incite neo-Nazi ideologists) and the Jewish Defense League (the New York City–based, baseball bat–wielding, anti-Semite–beating right-wing group), which threatened to stage protests at BOC concerts. It also featured "Career of Evil" ("I'm making a career of evil"), written by Patti Smith while she was still in a relationship with the group's resident "wannabe Nazi," Alan Lanier. The song segued directly into Pearlman's own "Subhuman," apparently to make clear the connection between the two.

Of course, it's possible that Pearlman was—as former Captain Beefheart-guitarist and *Der Golem* soundtrack creator Gary Lucas believes—merely staging an elaborate Jewish in-joke in which "provocation" was really anything but, and so-called Jewish self-loathing was indulged in as a kind of shtick. As we've already seen, this appeared to be the case in Pearlman's subsequent career, when he managed the jokey Dictators and produced the ultra-liberal Clash (*Give 'Em Enough Rope*). Many fans of BOC, especially Jews such as future Ramone Tommy Erdelyi, saw it as an ironic, humorous take on a heavy metal band, a kind of intellectual's parody that became almost pop art, far from a Spinal Tapesque naive acceptance of heavy metal conventions.

* * *

Whatever the case, Pearlman's preoccupations with Nazis were of the Jewish kind, just like the adoption of Nazi imagery by the Jewish punk bands soon to follow. And yet, where the BOC and other earlier bands were at least in part out to scare you with their ominous references to the Nazi past, there was something new in the attitude of the emerging punks. They took the frightening elements of history and turned them on their heads in the manner of Mel Brooks's *Springtime for Hitler* play in *The Producers*.

They were camp.

Susan Sontag, the New York Jewish feminist and intellectual of the 1970s with whom Richard Hell had a notable meeting (see Bockris's collection about the overlay between the Beats and the Punks, *Beat Punks*), explains in her essay "Notes on 'Camp'" (1964), "third among the great creative sensibilities [after tragic-or-comic seriousness and the seriousness of 'cruelty' such as that displayed in the work of Kafka] is Camp: the sensibility of failed seriousness, of the theatricalization of experience. Camp refuses both the harmonies of traditional seriousness, and the risks of fully identifying with extreme states of feeling."

So Nazi imagery in punk is anything but disrespectful—that is, it's anything but disrespectful to Jews because it is instead disrespectful to the Nazis. It is Jewish revenge incarnate, rooted in comedy. When the punk bands used swastikas in a camp way, they were making clear the "failed seriousness" of those symbols and the risks—in this case *extreme* risks—of "fully identifying with extreme states of feeling" like those of the ultra-patriotic National Socialists. Better to be ironic and detached than to trust unreliable emotions, pretending that they're inarguable truths to be acted on.

Of course, there was that element of rebellion discussed previously, just as there was an urge to shock for shock's sake. After all, what could be more rock 'n' roll—or theatrical—than to use shock techniques to grab the attention of the audience? Yet one cannot discount the element of camp "play" inherent in the performances of bands like the Dictators and the Ramones. Later, Shrapnel, the Daniel Rey/Rabinowitz band, featured a cardboard German tank as part of its stage act, and the Sic F*cks featured those Italians possessed of shiksappeal, Tish and Snooky, backing up bandleader Russell Wolinsky on songs such as "Spanish Bar Mitzvah" while wearing nun's habits adorned with swastikas. As much as they might have been intending to shock, as much as they may have enjoyed breaking taboos long established by their cultures, they were clearly also reveling in tearing down the symbols of oppression—and oppressive seriousness. In doing so, they were not only attacking the Nazis, but the moral imperative toward seriousness that the Nazi's Holocaust had seemed to demand—and not just from the Nazis, who were long dead, after all, but from their own Jewish community and parents with their self-righteousness and Never Again sloganeering a few decades too late.

As Sontag herself recognized, the relationship between camp and Jewishness—at least in twentieth-century America—is a close one, the two states emerging from similar origins. As she says in "Notes on 'Camp,'" "The peculiar relation between Camp taste and homosexuality has to be explained. While it's not true that Camp taste *is* homosexual taste, there is no doubt a peculiar affinity and overlap. Not all liberals are Jews, but Jews have shown a peculiar affinity for liberal and reformist causes. So, not all homosexuals have Camp taste. But homosexuals, by and large, constitute the vanguard—and the most articulate audience—of Camp. (The analogy is not frivolously chosen. Jews and homosexuals are the outstanding creative minorities in contemporary urban culture. Creative, that is, in the truest sense: they are creators of sensibilities. The two pioneering forces of modern sensibility are Jewish moral seriousness and homosexual aestheticism and irony.)"

Sontag, writing in 1964, apparently didn't foresee the inversion of "Jewish moral seriousness" that would soon take place in an emerging post-Holocaust Jewish generation—an inversion that would in fact lead to something we could almost call Jewish camp. Still, she seems to have anticipated it in her description of camp and Jewish sensibilities: "The reason for the flourishing of the aristocratic [camp] posture among homosexuals also seems to parallel the Jewish case. For every sensibility is self-serving to the group that promotes it. Jewish liberalism is a gesture of self-legitimization. So is Camp taste, which definitely has something propagandistic about it. Needless to say, the propaganda operates in exactly the opposite direction. The Jews pinned their hopes for integrating into modern society on promoting the moral sense. Homosexuals have pinned their integration into society on promoting the aesthetic sense. Camp is a solvent of morality. It neutralizes moral indignation, sponsors playfulness."

Again, Sontag is right on the mark—at least for the period in which she was writing. And yet, even as she spoke, a new generation of Jews was expressing a new sensibility and so heading in a new direction. This sensibility—less moral than comic—was in many ways a rebellion against the Jewish desire to be taken seriously by the predominant culture via the acquiring of a *Bildung*, just as to a certain degree it was a rebellion by the mostly Eastern European Jews who made up the punk movement against the German Jews who largely embodied that desire. Unlike their older *brothers* and *sisters*, the punk Jews no longer wanted to work toward the betterment of the world in the most earnest of ways. They wanted to enjoy that world and show their comfort in it. They wanted to be able to make a joke, even a bad, unsophisticated one. Hence, the Dictators' self-proclaimed worship of cars and White Castle burgers and the Ramones' self-professed love of trash TV and slasher films. Hence, too, these bands' comic songs of questionable taste, such as "Master Race Rock" (Dictators) and "Blitzkrieg Bop" (Ramones). If you weren't going to laugh, what were you going to do?

Both these bands—and others later, such as the Angry Samoans ("They Saved Hitler's Cock"), embraced the aestheticism and irony of camp. As did many who helped create punk from behind the scenes, such as Danny Fields, Howie Klein, and Seymour Stein, all of whom also happened to be homosexual. As Legs McNeil and Gillian McCain make clear in their oral history of New York punk, *Please Kill Me*, the breakdown, or rather, reconfiguration, of gender roles was integral to the scene, which was not only highly focused on new definitions of what it meant to be Jewish, but also on what it meant to be a man or a woman, especially in a traditional, heterosexual sense.

In keeping with this is one final aspect of Sontag's take on camp, where she states that "the experiences of Camp are based on the great discovery that the sensibility of high culture has no monopoly upon refinement. Camp asserts that good taste is not simply good taste; that there exists, indeed, a good taste of bad taste." While this is clearly relevant to punk's embrace of previously maligned three-chord rock (not to mention Jewish American culture's embrace of so-called debased forms, such as blues and jazz, as expressed in low-high-culture landmarks, such as *Rhapsody in Blue*, *Appalachian Spring*, and *West Side Story*), what is also implicit here is camp's discovery that the sensibility of high culture can do much more than exclude—it can also malign. If camp sees the "good taste of bad taste," it also sees the bad taste of the so-called good. Hence, Jewish camp's mocking use of Nazi symbols such as swastikas. Once the height of Kultur in wartime Germany, these symbols of the Third Reich were that no longer. Indeed, when associated with governmentally approved culture of all sorts—including Nixon's Vietnam-era Amerika—they provided a dark kind of beauty. That is, if one equates beauty with revelation. Or truth.

It was almost enough to make Dylan stop frowning while singing "With God on Our Side," and Lenny Bruce stop grinning while holding up a tabloid rag's absurd headline "Six Million Found in Argentina." It was as if they could both stop trying so hard to make it all go away through earnestness or absurdity.

After all, hadn't it been enough to make Chris Stein and Debbie Harry roll over on their flag of mass graves and kiss each other goodnight before drifting off to sleep?

14

THE NEW JAPS (JEWISH AMERICAN PUNKS)

Jewish American Women and the Birth of Female Punk

To be a German Jew is to feel entitled and endangered. She was born Kathy Alexander, the kind of German Jew that is known by real New Yorkers as "Our Crowd"—her family, the Alexanders, along with the Lehmans, Loebs, Ochs, etc., were the best educated, wealthiest, and most sophisticated Jews in the world. It was at Brandeis, the Jewish university, that she studied Latin and Greek, found her Jewish husband, Bob Acker, dated John Landau (another wealthy German Jew who eventually produced the film *Titanic*), and her roommate was Tamar Deisendruck, another German Jew who became a respected composer. She came from a small ethnic group, German Jews, who were responsible for originating the most influential theories of the 20th century: Marxism, Psychoanalysis, the theory of relativity, Holocaust theory, and post modernism.

—"Sarah Schulman Discusses Kathy Acker," *Pavement* magazine, 2003

Onstage at the Peppermint Lounge, a group of women are attacking their instruments, the drummer flailing away in an aggressive rhythm, the bassist a still presence of fury and snarl, the rhythm guitarist bobbing her blonde hair as she looks down at the stage, frowning—the boys in the audience gazing at them with a mixture of shock and awe.

But it's the lead singer who's the real focus of the boys' attention, the girl with the unusual name and sexy-tough image, her enticing smile and piercing eyes making them excited yet nervous, as if they'd be scared to meet her in a dark alley—much less a low-lit bedroom.

For those aware of rock trivia, these girls are more than just an oddity that will entertain this audience tonight and then disappear. They, especially their lead singer, are a link to a later movement in which women will appear in record numbers for the first time as leaders of their own groups.

This is the earliest women-only rock band to be signed to a major label. All but forgotten today, it's far more important than that other group so often cited as the progenitor of female rock. The Runaways, like the Monkees, was artificially created by a group of male writers and producers intent on cashing in on a rock novelty. This band, Goldie and the Gingerbreads, is the all-real *female* thing.

Goldie and the Gingerbreads! What kind of name is that? you ask. That doesn't sound very tough! Or badass!! Or punk!!!

But consider. Not only were Goldie and the Gingerbreads a kind of female Beatles months before the Fab Four (the real ones, as opposed to the pre-fab four Monkees) hit their first American stage; they were led by a girl who was a badass's badass, a punk in the truest sense of the word; a punk who—as we should no longer be surprised to find—was also very Jewish.

"Goldie" of Goldie and the Gingerbreads was in fact Goldie Zelkowitz, rebel child of the Lower East Side. She was the first woman in rock to get up onstage with an electric guitar and others of her sex to create a sound that focused on women's issues and women's desires. It wasn't exactly the sort of thing you'd expect to see at CBGB—anymore than you would have expected to see the Beatles there in their heyday, despite their beginnings in the similarly seedy Cavern. Goldie, like the Jewish men in rock before her, was more important behind the scenes than onstage. Under the name Genya Ravan—a slightly less Americanized version of her real name, Genyusha Zelkowitz—she put out solo recordings (*Urban Desire*, 1978, *And I Mean It*, 1979) and did guest vocalist spots (Lou Reed's *Street Hassle*, 1978, Blue Öyster Cult's *Mirrors*, 1979), but she was best known as a producer (The Dead Boys' *Young Loud and Snotty*, 1977). In fact, she was billed as "Rock's *Only* Woman

Producer," an honorary title that revealed as much about what she wasn't as what she was.

Though the Runaways might have been the first to adopt leather jackets, and Patti Smith the first to make a name for herself in the East Village, Lower East Side native Genya Ravan was there before them, assuming real power both onstage and off. She was in many ways the mother of Riot Grrrl, creating a kind of template for the New York female rocker that continues into the present. Yet, by the punk era, she had been all but silenced. She was a force, but not a presence; a factor, but not a visible figure. As the woman who wasn't there, she was emblematic of other Jewish women in punk.

*　　*　　*

Genya's beginnings in the Old World seem to have pushed her down the rock 'n' roll path. Born in Lodz, Poland, near the outset of the Holocaust, her story is too dark for Hollywood, an adventure film with a bitter ending that tops anything that later occurred at CBGB for grittiness or depth.

Rockers such as Patti Smith and Debbie Harry remember their early years as driven by suburban boredom, class anger, or the demands of fathers who were threatened by female independence. Genya's were filled with life-and-death decisions as people of various nations sought to wipe her and her family off the face of the earth. In one of Genya's earliest memories, she clings to her mother's back while her mother clings to her father, who himself is clinging to the side of a train crossing a deep, dark ravine. Her father calls out, "I can't hold you any longer!" and Genya pictures them all plummeting hundreds of feet to their deaths. Her grandparents, aunts, uncles, and two brothers had already died in the concentration camps by that point. Like Tommy Ramone, she was a DP before moving to America. There her parents rarely left their Lower East Side apartment out of fear of what might happen to them—or her—outside on the city's streets.

Perhaps her past made Genya far tougher than those other heroines of punk, her vision darker and her rebellion more intense. As a child and teenager she sought out just the dangers her parents warned her against, taking up with bikers and gang members and bad boys of all varieties, just so long as they upset her mother and were nothing like her father, who hid from life in the house.

Other women who later played an integral role at CBGB were from similar backgrounds. Donna Gaines, a New School academic who wrote about disaffected youth and became one of Joey Ramone's best friends, was very like Ravan in her rejection of Jewish "weakness" ("the vigor and vitality lost in centuries of Europe's killing fields") and her lust for bad—mostly Irish—boys from the wrong side of the tracks. As she says, while growing up in Rockaway Beach in the 1950s, she was attracted to these boys because they seemed "bigger and wilder. They played harder and sometimes they were dirty . . . Perpetually *farbiseneh* [pissed off], they never smiled, except right before they slammed you in the ear . . . they were *other*, and that meant desire."

The same was true for Jewish CBGB performer Helen Wheels (Helen Robbins), who, like Patti Smith, began her career as a semi-member of The Blue Öyster Cult, designing their leather gear, cowriting songs, and involving herself with both Richard Meltzer and Albert Bouchard. Wheels ended up as a local act too hot for even New York to handle. Peter Robbins recalls of his sister, who died in 2000 from complications following neck surgery: "She loved rebels of every sort, misfits and miscreants . . . I remember an early boyfriend of hers who scared the shit out of me . . . she had written to him in prison. When he got out, she decided 'I'm going to [date] this guy, and do it a lot.' She had a photograph of his dick. It had the Rolling Stones mouth with the tongue sticking out . . . the wilder, the crazier, the more it would upset mom and dad, that's what she did, at least until she got really good at [performing]."

Many of the women in these audiences were the children of Holocaust survivors, among them Dictators fan and later press secretary Camilla Saly, who spent much of her late adolescence at CBGB, drawn by its mixture of comedy, rebellion, and darkness. It was not just the death camps of World War II, but the long history of similarly tragic events that led both performers and audiences to the world of tough guys and dolls dressed in leather and looking for kicks. Women on both sides of the stage shared this history and something more—their upbringing as Jewish girls in America.

Jewish parents of the 1950s and '60s tended to raise their daughters in one of two ways. They could either teach them to fear the outside world and remain sheltered from modernity and change inside the house, or they could encourage them to be tough, aggressive, and independent. New York Italian American parents faced the same choice—and so did their daughters. On the Italian side, rebellion against Old World restrictions and the strong female of matriarchal tradition created iconoclasts such as Holly "Vincent" Cernuto (of Holly and the Italians), Annie Golden (of the all-Italian—aside from her—Shirts), Tish and Snooky Bellomo (of Harry and Stein's Blondie and the Bonzai Babies and Russell Wolinsky's "Spanish Bar Mitzvah"–performing Sic F*cks), and Carmelita Rossanna "Lita" Ford (of the Runaways). These Alpha Gabba Females in turn helped create and lead the Chick Punk Rock Pack, and they owed their success as much to their backgrounds as to their individual talents.

Jewish culture mirrored those backgrounds, and Jewish girls knew it, though at first they were too timid to emulate the Italian chicks and confront an audience. Unlike their brothers, who pretended to be Italian toughs onstage, Jewish girls at first were content to drift across the backdrop, as quiet and out of sight as ghosts. That is why acts like Genya's were so explosive. When she made her name with Goldie and the Gingerbreads, she made the stage safe for Jewish female rockers like herself.

Then she moved on to another groundbreaking position as the first female leader of an all-male band. Unlike Janis Joplin, who had begun her career as the singer in front of a band already established by men—Big Brother and the Holding Company—Genya created a new band from scratch, the jazz-rock fusion hybrid she dubbed Ten Wheel Drive. This rhythm-driven band that regularly rocked fellow Holocaust survivor Bill Graham's Lower East Side club, the Fillmore East, was renowned for its musical proficiency—and the fact that Genya, perhaps reflecting Jewish culture's embrace of the sexual, occasionally performed topless. Why shouldn't a woman be sexual before thousands? Rock 'n' roll wasn't a Catholic mass. It was about rebellion. And drugs. And sex.

Of course, being a rebel, Genya was often at odds with her own best career interests. Though her record company wanted to stress her similarities to Janis, she was adamant in resisting, demanding that they emphasize that she was Genya and no one else. She did the same later, when she left Ten Wheel Drive to strike out as a solo artist, recording a number of albums in the early 1970s that were far from the prevailing trends of the time. Not a singer/songwriter, she was a ballsy rocker in the truest sense, belting out R&B-based songs that wouldn't have sounded out of place on the Chitlin' Circuit. And when, during punk, she took this act into almost heavy metal territory, she refused to camp it up or play it as ironic, because that just wasn't where she was at. Yet her natural punk attitude surfaced in spite of herself in her choice of lyrics and imagery, in songs such as "I Won't Sleep on the Wet Spot" and the Brill-Building-styled "Back in My Arms Again." Her album cover for *Urban Desire* (1978) pictured her perfectly poised in spirit between Patti Smith and Debbie Harry, her bared armpit and level stare a cross between come hither and fuck off.

This punk attitude wasn't enough to make her a hit with audiences, however. Genya was too much "a leader," she says, never a follower. She was beyond caring what others—even the audience—thought of her, and though she helped women break into rock, she was almost too much for rock herself. It was behind the scenes, away from the eyes of the audience, that she made her impact later in life. As second in command at Hilly Kristal's CBGB Records, she helped produce Hilly-signed bands such as the Dead Boys and the Shirts (led by Annie Golden). Here she became as famous for telling Stiv and Company to remove their swastikas as she did for helping the Shirts achieve some measure of fame. She understood the punk aesthetic even if her music didn't exactly sound like it. Like those bands—and her business partner Hilly—she had long been doing it for herself. Doing it herself had freed her to become a rocker in the first place, enabling her to transcend her parents' fear of the Old World and embrace a new one instead. Of course, that new world was New York.

* * *

The Holocaust drove Jewish women like Genya to be out front with their ambitions, but strangely enough, it drove Jewish men to silence these women, or to want to. Feminism pushed Jewish women forward, and male reaction yanked them back.

Strong, even defiant, women have always been a part of Jewish history. In the Bible, women like Eve, Rebecca, and Miriam defied male authority figures in their quest for greater independence. In the mid-nineteenth century, German Jewish female immigrants opened salons in New York to help foster the intellect and the arts. At the turn of the twentieth century, progressives like Emma Goldman and Emma Lazarus advocated for workers'—and women's—rights. Jewish women were always at the forefront of movements aimed at empowering the oppressed.

It wasn't until the first generation of punks was coming of age that the activities of Jewish women reached a true watershed, one that ended up affecting not only the citizens of Manhattan and the boroughs, but the country, and to some extent the world. Beginning with Betty Friedan's manifesto, *The Feminine Mystique*, and continuing through the efforts of Gloria Steinem (*Ms* magazine), Andrea Dworkin, and others such as New York congresswoman Bella Abzug, feminism was more than just aided by the efforts of Jewish women, it was largely led by them.

The history of New York is filled with examples of strong, nontraditional (at least in typically "American" ways) Jewish women. Whether they were in the theater (Fanny Brice), music (Scepter Records founder Florence Greenberg), or the arts (Lee Krasner), New York Jewish women were integral in creating a setting where feminism could later flourish. Aside from the godmothers of feminism, Mary Wollstonecraft and Simone de Beauvoir, almost everyone who helped create the movement was Jewish. There were literal leaders like Betty Friedan, Gloria Steinem, and Andrea Dworkin, and feminist-oriented poets and novelists such as Tillie Olsen, Marge Piercy, and Erica Jong. Proto-feminist English author Virginia Woolf (née Adeline Virginia Stephen) was married to Jewish publisher Leonard Woolf. Contemporary Jewish-American feminists such as Susan Faludi and Naomi Wolf have all but taken the Stein/Harry relationship as their demarcation point, shifting their attention from women to men so as to show how feminism will triumph only when men learn to be open and accepting of strong, intelligent women—the very attributes that Debbie Harry credited to Chris Stein and Jewish men in general in chapter twelve.

In the punk world, this tradition is best epitomized by the previously mentioned hell on wheels, Helen Wheels. Born 1949 in Queens and raised thirty miles east of the city in Nassau County's Rockville Centre, Wheels was part of that Jewish emigration away from Manhattan that others like Lou Reed experienced, yet because she was a woman, her youth was more affected by feminism than by regrets over loss of cosmopolitan roots.

Like feminist leaders Steinem and Friedan, Wheels (born Robbins, from the Ellis Island–abbreviated Robinovitch) grew up in a cultural subgroup that was relatively open to women. According to Wheels's brother Peter Robbins, the Reform Judaism observed by Wheels's parents made clear that daughters should be considered as worthy of success as sons. "Helen was a bookish, quiet child who became interested in oceanography," says her brother. "My parents encouraged her to go on to college as much as they did me, and she graduated from Stony Brook when that was still an experimental college, then went on to become a master seamstress at the French Fashion Institute."

All the while, Wheels was caught up in the same changes that affected so many punks-to-be. Life-altering exposure to drugs and Bob Dylan led her to abandon both science and fashion for the more poetic realms of music. Throwing herself into the orbit of the Blue Öyster Cult and gradually building a base for her transformation into a rocker in her own right, she went from being the bookish, quiet child to the loud hell-raiser known as Helen Wheels. But again, the foundation for both possibilities had already clearly been set in her childhood.

"The men in my family were wonderful, not remotely macho or withdrawn, which is clearly part of Jewish culture," Peter Robbins says. "They were gentle and soft-spoken and showed real kindness, and there was always a special bond between my father and Helen. He let her know that she could achieve anything she wanted."

Perhaps even more important was the example set by Wheels's mother. A classic 1950s housewife who raised children by the Dr. Spock method, during the 1960s and '70s, she not only followed the progress of feminism passionately, she gradually rose from a secretarial position at Nikon to become one of its most powerful female executives.

"It was amazing and so wonderful and clearly an example to Helen," says Peter. "My mother loved and followed the careers of Bella Abzug and other tough-talking and -acting Jewish women like her, and she would get so excited when another would get elected to office, and Helen was like that too, one hundred and ten percent. They would talk about those things all the time."

Perhaps it isn't surprising that while her mother was breaking the glass-ceiling, Helen was throwing *mazel tov* cocktails at the glasshouses of the punks. Though she had long hair and a baby face and little musical skill to begin with, she more than made up for these "drawbacks" by putting on one of the rawest and most aggressive rock shows of the time—one that her sometimes resistant male cohorts couldn't easily ignore. Dressed in short leather skirt, high leather boots, and an Iron Cross necklace, Wheels would jump onto tables in the audience and plunge her switchblade into them while kicking over drinks. She was almost literally kicking the ass of the audience as she performed stage moves that were the next best thing to martial arts. Feminine and demure, she was not.

The male audience couldn't ignore Wheels's act, but segments of it did try. On more than one occasion, she received jeers and catcalls. As Wheels's contemporary and fellow Jewish rocker (Flaming Youth) Deborah Frost recalls, "Men were threatened by strong Jewish women, particularly Jewish men. I saw it myself on more than one occasion—especially at the higher levels of the industry where the deals were made." Frost—today a rock critic married to Wheels's former flame, Blue Öyster Cult drummer (and convert to Judaism) Albert Bouchard—goes on to say that Jewish women faced yet another obstacle in their paths: "If a Jewish guy like Eric Bloom [from BOC] was considered exotic outside of New York, he sure wasn't back there. And the same was true for Jewish women. Debbie Harry was exotic. A Jewish woman like Helen Wheels was more like your cousin or your sister. It's a genetic thing probably—otherwise you get all those inbred deformities."

Like Genya Ravan, Wheels reacted to these put-offs in pure punk fashion, accentuating just those things that had alienated her audience in the first place. First she went from shouting her lyrics to shrieking them. Then she added muscle to her act, working out to the point that she became an award-winning bodybuilder in New York. Jewophile Robert Crumb, renowned for dating almost exclusively Jewish women, such as his classically Jewish New York comic book artist wife Aline Kominsky, was ready for Wheels, drawing the cover for what eventually became her "best of" album (*Archetype*, 1998) while the two were still an item. Others, many of them Jewish, were not. Wheels embodied those so-called Jewish characteristics that Crumb so loved to exaggerate—the aggressive, in-your-face, ballsy, tell-it-like-it-is attitude that naysayers called obnoxious, even if those naysayers, ironically, praised the exact same behaviors in men as punk.

The individuals who most resisted Wheels's overtly "Jewish" characteristics were her Jewish punk cohorts, almost all of them men. "The Dictators were among her biggest fans, but I guess there were those Jewish guys who might have felt differently," says Peter Robbins. Adds Wheels's great friend Mariah Aguiar, "I just don't think that they could handle a tough woman like Helen. She was like her mom, a trailblazer, and there will always be resistance to that."

During the same period in the late 1970s that Jewish women were trying to enter punk, other Jewish women were trying to break into comedy, with equally mixed results. Lawrence J. Epstein observes in *The Haunted Smile*: "Women who did stand-up comedy . . . were not supposed to exert a comparable amount of power [as men]. Such women were branded as aggressive, a term of profound disapproval . . . Jewish women . . . were the 'new' Jews, the unaccepted minority, the people seeking power who were not allowed to gain entrance into society, in this case the society of comedians." Jewish men didn't want Jewish women coming in and fucking it up for them, competing with them for the niches that, with so much effort, they had carved out for themselves. So they called them "too Jewish," "too aggressive." What they meant was, "too good at what they did."

The worst of it was saved for Jewish women in Israel. There, in advertisements for everything from lingerie to soft drinks, violence against women was prevalent—even violence in the guise of Holocaust S&M in which Jewish men substituted for Nazis and Jewish women were their victims. In an infamous sequence of ads from the early 1980s in the left-leaning, mainstream magazine *Monitin*, for instance, Jewish women were seen running from a freight train, dressed only in their skivvies as threatening military types lurked in the background. Why?

Perhaps male Israeli Jews needed to be reassured that they were not victims themselves, and so they imagined victimizing women to establish their strength. Or perhaps it was a bit more complicated, and like the punks, who used Nazi imagery to overcome their terror of the Holocaust, men in Israel wanted to frighten the fear, so to speak, turning the Holocaust into something almost humorous. After all, the other images in the *Monitin* advertising sequence were not simply horrific—they were attempting to be clever, picturing, for instance, women posed between fire extinguishers and blazing ovens. The result is a joke far sicker than anything by Lenny Bruce. But with a sick legacy such as the Holocaust and the sickening prospect of threatening Arab neighbors all around them, would it be so surprising to find Israeli men looking for a sick way out?

Similarly, while the psychological ravages of the Holocaust were not as intense for American Jews, "aggressive" female performers such as Genya Ravan and Helen Wheels still proved an irritant to their male Jewish cohorts. They got under their skins, and Ravan especially was silenced as a result. This outcome was doubly ironic.

Besides her memory of her father calling out "I can't hold on any longer!" as the family clung to him on the side of a train, Ravan remembers only one other thing from her experiences in the Holocaust. When she and her mother escaped from the camp where they had been held, she became frightened to the point that her mother had to cover her mouth to silence her whimpering—had to cover it for so long, in fact, that Genya almost suffocated before the danger passed. Nearly thirty years later, little Goldie Zelkowitz was almost suffocated again, artistically speaking, by those who didn't want to hear the fear and anger and tension in her voice. She was silenced by men who didn't want to be seen as scared or terrified. Men who wanted to be seen as punks—and anything but weak.

*   *   *

Helen Wheels and Genya Ravan didn't make it as performers in the punk era, but they proved deeply influential on a later era of female rockers, just as did their almost exclusively Jewish female contemporaries in the fields of performance art and literature. Annie Sprinkle (Ellen Steinberg) later worked with No Wave artist Lydia Lunch. Contemporary performance artists Meredith Monk and Aviva Rahmani were also from Jewish backgrounds. So were photographer Cindy Sherman, who was just becoming known for the images in which she "performed" various female stereotypes, and painter Judy Chicago, who between 1974 and 1979 created her famous pictorial history of women titled *The Dinner Party* by incorporating the work of hundreds of women artists. "Post-punk author" Kathy Acker cut an album with British punk band the Mekons ("Pussy, King of the Pirates," *Quarter Stick*, 1996), and downtown writer Lynne Tillman, who dated John Cale during his VU years, was part of the first Radical Jewish Culture music festival organized by John Zorn (more on this in the last chapter). Still, it wasn't until the emergence of Riot Grrrl in the late 1980s and early '90s that women, particularly Jewish women, really broke into punk.

From the ultimate Italian/Jewish performer Madonna "Esther" Ciccone, a New York émigré born of the downtown new wave/disco scene, straight through to Carrie Brownstein and Janet Weiss of Sleater Kinney and Kathleen Hanna of Bikini Kill, women in rock after the punk era continued to gain power onstage as well as off. Madonna—who, since converting to Judaism in the 1990s, has gone by the name Esther—began on the same label as the Ramones and the Talking Heads, Seymour Stein's downtown punk pioneer Sire. Stein is fond of telling how he signed Madonna in part because she forced her way into the hospital room where he was recovering from open heart surgery (such chutzpah). He knew that she would make it because she had this hard-nosed quality about her that could also be described as deeply Jewish. Stein's then-wife Linda was instrumental in encouraging him to sign Madonna, just as she had been in getting him to sign the Talking Heads (with their female bassist Tina Weymouth), the Pretenders (led by Ohio native Chrissie Hynde), and the Ramones (whom she comanaged with Danny Fields). As Linda said, assessing the influence of Jewish culture on her role as the first midwife of punk, "It's like I'm in Alcoholics Anonymous and I can say what's been true all along. I'm a New Yorker, I'm a Jew, and I'm a Puuuunk." By the end of her speech, Stein had risen to her feet and was screaming, shaking her fists.

Later, tougher post-punk archetypes in the 1990s were as often as not Jewish and emblematic of such. Chief among these was Courtney Love (Courtney Michelle Harrison), who, while on the fringes of the actual Riot Grrrl scene, was associated with it in the public mind through both her band Hole and her relationship with grunge avatar Kurt Cobain. Born of a Jewish mother and Catholic father, Love identified increasingly with her Jewish background in the wake of Cobain's death, saying at one point: "I have a weird Michael Douglas fetish. I love Michael Douglas. He's older. Jewish. Hot. I really want a Jewish prince. . . . [Kurt] had a lot of German in him. Some Irish. But no Jew. I think that if had a little Jew he would have fucking stuck it out. But he didn't."

While Love's words should be taken with a large dose of kosher salt, her image was a kind of funhouse exaggeration of a female Jewish punk along the lines of Nancy Spungen. Not only was Love attacked in the media for many of the same behaviors attributed to Jewish-American Princesses—including obnoxiousness, abrasiveness, and lack of grace—*megushemdikeyt*—she was so close to Spungen in spirit that she campaigned ernestly to play her part in Alex Cox's 1986 film *Sid and Nancy*. Ultimately she lost the role to Chloe Webb, but it is telling that she was shifted to a bit part as Spungen's friend Gretchen in New York—just as it is that in making a last-ditch effort to get the main role back she cried, "But I *am* Nancy Spungen!"

Love was the most visible Riot Grrrl to the mainstream, and the one who was most visibly Jewish, but others, such as Kathleen Hanna (who some allege is Jewish though she denies it), Carrie Brownstein, and Janet Weiss, arguably played more important roles. While none of these three made an issue of her Jewish background—and Hanna may in fact not be Jewish—all were at the center of the Riot Grrrl movement and helped bring it to a wider audience, particularly Brownstein and Weiss, who along with Corin Tucker have crossed over to mainstream success with albums such as *All Hands on the Bad One* (2000) and *The Woods* (2005).

The members of Sleater-Kinney have had wider success on a purely musical level, but Kathleen Hanna, today leader of Le Tigre, is in many ways the essence of the Riot Grrrl and the one who defined it for the faithful. Embodying a fuck-you, feminist attitude onstage—grabbing her breasts and challenging the boys to objectify them—Hanna drew up an actual manifesto for the movement in the best tradition of anarchists like Emma Goldman. Among its main proclamation is the wonderfully Jeffersonian first line: "I believe with my whole-heart-mind-body that girls constitute a revolutionary soul force that can, and will change the world for real."

Riot Grrrl was more than simply a music movement. It was political in both the personal and cultural sense, an organized attempt to change things for both performers and audience. Like punk, it hoped to create a community for the disaffected, and like punk it spread its message in part through comic means via zines with names like *Bust* and *On Our Backs* (both today glossies available at newsstands). A special Jewish-oriented Riot Grrrl zine— *Mazel Tov Cocktail*—appealed to this subgroup within the larger movement, and eventually morphed, through its creator Jennifer Bleyer, into *Heeb* magazine, the mouthpiece of the so-called Cool Jew movement currently spreading to urban centers like LA and San Francisco from New York.

Kathleen Hanna, currently living with Adam Horovitz of the all-Jewish hip-hop trio the Beastie Boys, is but one of a growing number of female bandleaders who now call Jew York their home. Karen O (Orzolek) of the Yeah Yeah Yeahs, Brett Anderson of the Ramones/Runaways crossbreed the Donnas, and Candace Kucsulain of Walls of Jericho are only the most visible faces to emerge in the wake of Riot Grrrl. None of them is Jewish, perhaps a sign that the changes wrought by that subgroup have finally filtered out to the populace in general. Now any girl/grrrl can take a mike and a guitar and fuck up the preconceived notions of her place. Demure? Screw that! It doesn't matter if we're Mayflower descendants or half-Koreans (like Orzolek). We can do what we goddamn please!

Or to quote another outsider female punk, the half-black vocalist for X Ray Specs, Poly "Marion Elliot" Styrene, "Oh Bondage, Up Yours!"

15

WRITE YIDDISH, CAST BRITISH

How England Stole Jewish Punk

[When the Sex Pistols found out I was Jewish, they called] me lots of nicknames . . . He's an old Fagin . . . Or the Svengali, the press would say. These were all the names of mythic Jews in literature . . . and I knew them all. . . . Having watched *Expresso Bongo* at the age of fourteen, I had a kinship with all of those things, and I understood the background through the life and times of my grandmother. So I could see all the networks. I could see how from *Expresso Bongo*, you could draw a line and take it all the way back to "the artful Dodger" and Fagin. No problem. So the Sex Pistols—they were my artful dodgers, as I was their Fagin. So what am I going to say, "No, I'm not"? Of course, I am. And I'm actually quite proud to be.

—Malcolm McLaren, Paris, 2004

In the back of the classroom, there's a little boy who's not exactly sure of his name. Is it Edwards? Is it McLaren? Is it something else altogether? As an adult looking back he won't be able to remember—all he'll know for sure is that there is this boy standing there oblivious as a voice shouts in the background. A voice that the boy suddenly realizes is directed at him.

"Hello, listen up, young man, Mr. . . . Pay attention!"

At the front of the room, the old woman with the gray hair tied up in a bun is looking directly at him, and as one of the boys at his side pokes him in the ribs, he realizes she is talking—no, screaming—in his direction.

Pardon, he thinks. But he doesn't answer. Instead, he remembers something his grandmother said before he left for school for the first time that morning. He remembers and he takes the cotton balls out of his pocket and stuffs them deep in his ears

The face of the woman up front is all the more twisted now, angry, purple.

But he doesn't care. He's smiling, surrounded by his muffled silence. He's smiling, remembering what his grandmother said: "If the teacher annoys you, look here in your hand. These are pieces of cotton wool. Put them in your ears, face the wall, don't face her. Don't listen to anything."

Especially, he thinks, when the teacher can't even seem to call him by a name that he recognizes. Or likes.

*   *   *

A week later this boy, Malcolm Edwards (a surname given him by his mother and stepfather because it was "English and proper"), Malcolm Levy (his stepfather's actual last name), Malcolm McLaren (his biological father's family name) is at home with his grandmother, far away from that classroom. After having been dragged by the ear from that class and put before the principal and told to give his home phone number, he found himself being carted off from that school altogether, his grandmother so angry that she wouldn't allow him to return. But not angry with him, as it turned out—angry at the school. "What do they know?" she had said. "I can teach you fine. I can make sure you know what's important."

Now he's sitting in the living room, staring out the window, waiting for the postman to arrive, viewing this as one of the high points of the day. He doesn't have much contact with the outside world now that he's at home all through the week. He can't really wander the streets, his grandmother says, because if does, he'll be picked up by the authorities and taken back to the school. Back there where the teacher will scream at him and the other kids will point and he'll be made to feel like a fool.

No, he must stay close to the house, in the living room, inside with her and the books she gives him to learn how to read. He must stay in here away from the world and learn about a different life, a different place, a different way of being.

*   *   *

For the next two years this young boy with the multiple names will find himself reading the same two books repeatedly as a way of discovering the mysteries of literacy. Both works of Charles Dickens, chosen by his grandmother, they will form his worldview later in life when he becomes far better known to the outside world than the faceless mass of classmates he's left behind at the school in Lordship Park. These two books—*A Christmas Carol* and *Oliver Twist*—will come in handy when he goes about creating his first big success, the original English punk band the Sex Pistols.

"My grandmother picked these books because they were her favorites and she thought they could teach me something about life," McLaren says today, sitting in the kitchen of his small flat near L'hôtel des invalides (site of Napoleon's tomb) in Paris. "Of course, her take on them was a little unconventional and probably quite different from what I would have been told about them had I read them back in that regular school."

McLaren's grandmother taught him that both Scrooge from *A Christmas Carol* and Fagin from *Oliver Twist* were heroes to be admired. In fact, according to her, Fagin was based on an actual person that Dickens knew from the Horseshoe Pub on Taunton Road, his model being Abraham Goldsmith, a nice Jewish man who made his money outside the law, then escaped to Australia where—unlike the poor, hanged Fagin—he became wealthy through real estate and lived a long, philanthropic life. That's her version, anyway.

"Everyone knows that Fagin was a Jew, and critics have long suspected Scrooge was the same," McLaren says. "While Dickens meant them to be anti-Semitic caricatures, my grandmother saw them as antiheroes who were the true focus of the story. She loved them because they reflected her own view of life. . . . 'Don't ever talk to a policeman,' was her motto. 'A Jew has nothing to do with the police.' And she wasn't the only one to think that way. Where I grew up, that was the attitude. We lived in a world that was separate, apart."

✻   ✻   ✻

The young Malcolm Edwards—abandoned by his father, a Scottish bounder, and his mother, a Jewish girl gone astray, and raised by his maternal grandmother under a fake name so as to blend into the English landscape more easily—was not so atypical in those times as one might expect. Like other characters in other novels featuring outlaws and antiheroes, he was a kind of

English version of a Bowery Boy. An East End rather than Lower East Side kid who lived his life on the outskirts of society; a Jewish kid who broke the law of the land to survive by a higher law, one that called for wit, charm, excitement, and, above all, entertainment.

To get the flavor of this world, one merely needs to read such novels of the period as Graham Greene's *Brighton Rock* (1938) or Muriel Spark's *The Girls of Slender Means* (1963). The first focuses on the netherworld of teenage gangs just before the war, and features the Jewish-Italian gang leader Colleoni. The second looks at the challenges faced by young women in postwar London. Then, too, there are movies such as *Expresso Bongo* (1959) and TV shows such as *Dixon of Dock Green* (1955–1976), the former an examination of early English rock 'n' roll, featuring Laurence Harvey as a conniving, Jewish agent, and the latter a kind of English *Dragnet* in which the friendly neighborhood bobby George Dixon works tirelessly to bring morality to London's largely Jewish East End. What all of these show, from different angles, is a period when London was run by hooligans, black marketers, and gang leaders—the vast majority of whom were Jewish teenagers. As McLaren says, it was "the only time since the Gordon Riots in the late eighteenth century that there was real anarchy in the country."

Or as he might have put it at the height of the Sex Pistols' fame, it was the only period during which there was true, youth-oriented—and Jewish— "Anarchy in the U.K."

"People in America are barely aware of it, and many in England have forgotten as well, but the period after World War II was an extremely dark one," says McLaren. "Though the country had ultimately triumphed over the Germans, it had been all but economically destroyed in doing so. Rationing was rife and housing short with many buildings remaining bombed-out for close to a decade and food and clothing largely available only on the black market."

In Spark's book, we see a story that would have been familiar to Malcolm's mother. A group of girls, forced into the city by the economic conditions of the time, become lodgers in what was then known as a "hotel," actually a home left untouched by the blitz and so legally bound to take in boarders. Left to run adrift of the strict morality of their time and forced to make a living in any way they can, they become involved not only with men of varying degrees of repute, but in some cases crime as well. Malcolm's mother might have most sympathized with the character Jane, a Jewish girl already feeling like an outcast in England who develops a strong intellect and a stronger will through a close study of literature and human behavior.

As bad as things were for girls like Malcolm's mother, more troubling was rationing and the way this fed into the black market. Like those gangs in Greene's *Brighton Rock*, but on a much larger scale, the black market was run by boys who were still in their teens, many of whom had grown up with Jewish backgrounds.

"When the war was at its height, many of the men leading the gangs had been drafted and forced to leave for the front," McLaren says. "While they were gone, these boys came in to take their places. They weren't ready to surrender them just because the older bosses had returned. They ruled the city during that period, and they were ruthless in dong so."

McLaren clearly remembers the atmosphere in the largely Jewish village of Islington where he grew up. "You had to be careful when you left the house. There were all of these bombed-out buildings where gangs of kids would gather. If you wandered into one of those, you could end up pushed into a twenty-foot pit before you knew it. They weren't playing around. Kids were being killed all the time. And it wasn't just kids. It was mad."

In this atmosphere, McLaren seemed to straddle two worlds. His grandmother, who had been something of a female "stage-door Johnny" (groupie) in her youth, then a diamond dealer later in life, schooled him, at least imaginatively, in the ways of Fagin's pickpockets and the need to avoid the police.

"It's not too hard to see the connection later in my career," he says. "When those boys [future Pistols Steve Jones and Paul Cook] were stealing clothing from my shop on Kings Row, I took them and made them my own. Those 'artful Dodgers' became my gang, my band, the Sex Pistols."

And yet, as in the 1970s, McLaren wasn't an outlaw himself. He didn't commit crimes or even consort with gangsters. He spent two years at home with his grandmother, then six years at a Jewish parochial school (Avigdor) in Islington, and then, when he and his grandmother moved to the suburbs, another four hanging out at the Jewish community center attached to his synagogue, dancing with the girls in the neighborhood. Naturally, it was expected that he would settle down with one.

*   *   *

McLaren's interest in the rock music that was played at those dances led him onto slightly more dangerous ground—the clubs and coffee shops that were beginning to emerge during this period, populated by what he refers to as "the demimonde." It was a slightly seedy underground world of gangsters, musicians, and artists in equal measure, not that different in essence from the one that McLaren later witnessed at Andy Warhol's Factory in New York.

There was one all-important difference, however. Like the neighborhood where he was raised, the English world of coffee shops and jukeboxes was also largely Jewish. In fact, it emerged in tandem with the gangs, a kind of transitional space where those outlaw leaders could go legitimate—or at least as legitimate as the authorities demanded.

"The gangs that ran London were in charge of many black-market items, from food to clothing to alcohol," says McLaren. "As it turned out, they also became responsible for importing these new machines from America that brought rock 'n' roll out to countries like our own. The Mansey family [whose famous fish restaurant still exists in Leicester Square] had particular control over jukeboxes, and used them to set up coffee houses and clubs where some of the first bands played. It's like in that movie *Expresso Bongo* where the Jewish agent played by Laurence Harvey [a South African Jew born in Lithuania] uses all the shady means at his disposal to create a career for the up-and-coming English version of Elvis played by Cliff Richard. That's pretty much how it was. Entertainment and crime were tied together quite literally in England. Just as they were to a great extent in America."

These two worlds were indeed tied together in America, with Italians and to a lesser extent Jews sharing the spoils. England was different primarily because Jews were dominant there. This fact owed a good deal to the more marginal place of Jews in English society.

McLaren and others have spoken about the way English Jews were taught to be, at best, subdued about their Jewishness, and, at worst, ashamed and dismissive. As A. Alvarez, a lauded English Jewish poet and novelist, notes in his review of *A Double Thread: Growing Up English and Jewish in London* and *The Jews of Britain, 1656 to 2000*:

> Many Americans claim to be proud of their roots and believe that ethnic differences make the stew rich. Not so in England, despite the tradition of tolerance that has made modern London as cosmopolitan and multiracial as New York. The immigrants arrive, speaking their old languages and following their old customs, and the great, slow-moving river of London churns

them together and turns them into something else. That something else includes British citizenship, the right to vote, and a British passport but, no matter how long they stay, it never quite washes away the sense of being foreign. . . . The only solution is disguise and impersonation, like spies in deep cover. Hence the spectacle that so baffled me as a child on the rare occasions when my parents, who were not religious people and went only to please my grandparents, took me to the synagogue: the crowds of English gents in Savile Row suits and bowler hats, looking as if they had just stepped out of a painting by Magritte, reciting prayers in a language I didn't understand printed in a script I couldn't read. Hence, too, the example of [Anglo-Jewish poet] Siegfried Sassoon, a lapsed Sephardic Jew with a Wagnerian first name, who called his autobiography *Memoirs of a Fox-Hunting Man*. Anglo-Jewry represents the Diaspora in its most extreme form: not assimilation, but worshiping as a Jew and behaving like a goy.

In other words, England tolerated the Jews, but it didn't embrace them. Whether this was due to their smaller numbers or, more likely, the strict English class system that made it clear that "Jews, apart from a few grandees, weren't gentlemen" (A. Alvarez) is open to debate. One thing is certain, however. As a result of their position in postwar England, Jews like Malcolm and his grandmother were—like Patti Smith's "rock 'n' roll nigger" of the song of the same name—"outside of society" along with the artists ("Jackson Pollack was a nigger"), seers ("Jesus Christ was a nigger too"), and rock musicians ("Jimi Hendrix was a nigger. Nigger nigger nigger nigger")—not to mention comics such as Lenny Bruce, whose bit about overusing words like "nigger" until they lose all meaning appears to have been the inspiration for Smith's song.

Was this a painful place to be? McLaren seems a bit unclear. Growing up with a fake name, red hair, and light skin (due as much to his Scottish father as to his Sephardic Jewish ancestry), Malcolm was able to "pass" and so avoid the more obvious negative effects of his Jewishness. Inside, he felt the imprint of having been raised in such a world—a fact he hardly could have avoided considering the cloistered nature of his upbringing.

"In the fifties, I never really met anyone who wasn't Jewish . . . It didn't matter, when we subsequently moved to the suburbs . . . and I went to an ordinary grammar school . . . I still somehow fell in with only the Jewish kids . . . [They] may have been no more than about ten percent [of the class], but they were the only people that I had a relationship with . . . On weekends, [I] went to the local synagogue, which in the recreation hall in the back of it, there would be this kind of Saturday night with all the Jewish girls and boys . . . That was my life, I remember distinctly, from the age of thirteen to the age of around fifteen. Then it was venturing out from the suburbs into the center of town with [the same] kind of curiosity, but still hanging together in a little gang."

* * *

According to Malcolm, that gang ended when he was sixteen. Encouraged by his mother (over his grandmother's objections) to become a sommelier ("she was so nouveau riche by then"), Malcolm quit high school and got a job at a wine merchant's in London, where, he says, he was closely exposed to non-Jews for the first time. The "[wine] world was full of really reactionary, hard-core, neo-conservative . . . ex-military boys who talked about wine merely from the point of view of sex. 'This wine is like a woman with too much fat under the arm. This wine, it's virginal, it's cute like a sixteen-year-old.' And I got no experience . . . There was nothing about blackberries or apricots, it was nothing about fruit, it was all sex. It was all these mad ex-generals on Civvy Street dealing in wine, because obviously it was something they enjoyed and something they must have drunk barrels of when they were in the army."

While McLaren does not attribute the wine merchants' behavior to their being non-Jews, he does say that they were entrenched in the ruling order of the day and, as the status quo, often fell back on the most mundane and uninspired of beliefs. In other words, they were far from living "outside of society," and as a result they seemed as foreign to McLaren as he evidently seemed to them.

As it turned out, an alternative "antisocial" world coexisted in the near vicinity, a school around the corner that quickly drew McLaren's attention. "I happened to eye and see a lot of girls going into this school, and I was curious enough to venture in, and my curiosity suggested this world was a good world, it was an interesting world. I came back to tell my grandmother about this world I discovered, this world called art school . . . I went to art school, and it changed my life completely."

* * *

A life-altering moment. Yet unlike those countless other English art school graduates turned rockers—among them John Lennon, Paul McCartney, and

Pete Townsend—McLaren's shift into the art world was not as dramatic as it might have been. As his grandmother later made clear, she may have thought "working with crayons" was ridiculous, but she definitely admired the element of *fakery* in art. In fact, McLaren says, she knew a man in the underworld who forged paintings that she later sold to estates throughout the country, using a *fake* English title—"and denying she was Jewish"—to do so.

"It was more of that Dickensian element," McLaren says. "I think my grandmother wanted me to step into the shoes of those great actors that she admired in her day." Indeed, McLaren's grandmother used to take him to one of the last remaining music halls when he was a boy, and have him wait outside "with the man selling newspapers on the corner" while she enjoyed the show. "She laughed with the vaudevillians who would tell filthy stories about England, and what it represented, the underbelly; the world that I suppose people like George Formby [sang about] . . . And she would come out and she would sing these songs, and she would teach me these songs."

McLaren is very aware that this beginning in life made him more than a little receptive to the world of rock 'n' roll and his ultimate role as a manager, producer, provocateur. Already schooled in the lowbrow, political school of music hall arts—a world that emerged over centuries from informal performances in pubs, many of which featured drunken songs against the royals—and raised on a steady diet of outlaw literature, including the previously mentioned duo by Dickens as well as later popular works like *Trilby* by Du Maurier (which featured the "tall . . . sinister" Polish-born Jew, Svengali), McLaren understood the connection between entertainment, the underworld, and art, not to mention the connection between these and Jews and crypto-Jews like Fagin, Svengali, and Scrooge. As he says, it was a connection that served him well later on during another life-altering phase of his career.

"There was no question that it was easy for me to find my artful dodgers, my Sex Pistols, [and] to behave like Fagin, to behave like Svengali. It all came naturally. This was my childhood. This is how I was brought up. This was my world, my anti-world if you like; not the real world outside, but the anti-world that my grandmother painted and . . . that she felt had virtues and feelings that I was going to continue."

* * *

Of course, before McLaren could create anarchy in the UK through his band of thieves known as the Sex Pistols, he first needed a stage on which to practice. What better place to do so than in America, specifically in New York City, that center of anarchy and entertainment and self-creation where Jews were as much a part of the landscape as the buildings—and where an inventive, ambitious character like McLaren assumed he might feel at home.

Following a brief visit to the city in 1972, during which he saw the infamous proto-punk band the New York Dolls and caught "a vision of the future of rock," McLaren returned the next year with a plan. He wanted to manage that band of ragamuffin, cross-dressing sex freaks. He wanted to have a hand in spreading their—and his—fame.

"They were like a bunch of artful dodgers themselves," he says. "They were literally like dolls bursting out of their clothing. That nice Egyptian Jew Sylvain Mizrahi with his rouged cheeks. He looked like a doll with too many hormones, one growing too fast. As did the others, though not as sweetly and sexily. But they all had something, and I thought that perhaps I could work with that."

In truth, McLaren had come too late to help the Dolls. Their moment was all but past by the time he arrived, the whims of fashion and the ravages of narcotics playing an equal part in their rapid downfall. Though he put them in new, taboo (or at least what he thought was taboo) Soviet communist gear, only to be attacked when this act proved disastrous (the New York audiences didn't want politics, they wanted fun), it didn't really matter. For what really counted was an idea he had in the process, an idea that he'd gotten in part from the band, but also in part from another member of New York's burgeoning downtown scene. While working with the Dolls, McLaren had been closely watching another outlaw outsider of mixed cultural background, another fashion-oriented pickpocket of both high and low culture from the wrong side of the tracks who was rebelling against the status quo. This lost child was Richard Hell, originally Richard Meyers.

"It was that attitude of nihilism that attracted me," McLaren says. "That sense that he felt nothing was worthwhile yet he embodied it with style and class and made it almost look attractive. It's like when the Sex Pistols sang 'No Future' later on, it was as if they drew on that. There was no future of the traditional sort—and Richard Hell seemed to indicate that."

*　*　*

At first McLaren didn't say anything to Hell. He was still too busy using his growing fashion connections to break into the downtown scene, putting on costume parties at his room in the Chelsea Hotel, trying to create an outlet for his talent beyond the Valley of the Dolls.

Known in New York as much for his "strangeness," his oddity as an Englishman, his "cuteness" as he refers to it, he thought he saw in the city a new spirit and dynamic that he wanted to embrace—even if he wasn't quite able to absorb it on its own terms. As he says, in New York everyone was so forward, so aggressive, so unselfconsciously seeking success and fortune and fame, things that in England you were not supposed to advertise even if you did want them. And while he loved this and felt more open to it because of his Jewishness, he was ultimately still an Englishman, and he needed to find a way to translate these feelings into his own context.

"I know that New York is a very Jewish place, but I never really consciously thought of many of the people I was meeting then as Jewish. They were just Americans to me. But looking back on it, I realize that the same qualities that I attributed to Jews, I also attributed to Americans. All Americans were Jewish to me. Or at least in New York they were. I saw later when I went south with the Dolls and when I traveled to other parts of the country as well that New York was a very unique place and that maybe there was more Jewishness in what I thought was Americanness to begin with."

Like a nationwide take on Lenny Bruce's dictum that it doesn't matter if you're Catholic, if you're from New York you're Jewish, McLaren initially saw the American character as a Jewish one, and he welcomed it and planned to export it back to the UK. As a first step in doing so, he decided to pursue another classically Jewish route—both in London and New York—and became a clothier, or as it's known in the UK, with not so subtle anti-Semitic connotations, "ragman."

Opening his infamous shop, Sex, on Kings Road in London, McLaren began to sell the kind of taboo gear in which he had originally clothed the New York Dolls—but this time he made the conscious decision to leave out the political element that had proved so disastrous. At Sex, the patent leather, whips, chains, corsets, and so on would signify exactly what the name of the store advertised. Not politics—unless maybe sexual politics—but fun.

Of course, as he was doing this he was also working on the idea that had originally so intrigued him, the idea of bringing Richard Hell and Sylvain Sylvain across the water with him and beginning—along with two other, lesser performers—a band that would capitalize on both Richard's and Syl's looks and attitudes. A band that would scream nihilism and sex, rebellion and outlawry, literacy and cleverness, and above all, anarchy against all that had come before. McLaren had been trying to talk the two into coming with him since before he left, again and again promising them that he could do great things and make them much bigger stars in the UK than they ever would be in their home country. "But they were scared," he says. "I think they couldn't see themselves beyond the safe womb of New York City. It was like New York was their Jewish mother and they couldn't abandon her. They understood the scene there and they knew they had a certain prestige and they weren't ready or willing to risk that by going too far. They weren't prodigals in that sense. But I was. I had gone away, and now that I was going back I knew what I wanted."

*　　*　　*

As it turned out, McLaren formed his band of artful dodgers all the same, using his own English version of outsiders while playing up his earlier role as the Svengali who'd pulled the new New York Dolls' hellish strings. Signing up two kids who hung around his store shoplifting clothes—Steve Jones and Paul Cook (they did the same elsewhere to get their instruments)—he went in search of more colorful characters, finding first the closest thing to a Jew in England, an Irish Catholic, John Lydon (Johnny Rotten), and later, a working-class lout, Lydon's friend and fellow outsider, John Ritchie (Sid Vicious).

McLaren molded these new additions to the band to fit the roles he had originally envisioned for Meyers and Mizrahi. First, he took Lydon's hippie-long hair and cut it into the "electroshock" look he so adored in Richard Hell (and which countless others later copied to create their own punk rock look). Second, he dressed Lydon in the same ripped clothing that Hell had originated (quite deliberately) in New York, while adding the violently provocative element of safety pins to hold them together (not to mention sex gear such as cock rings that looked like dog collars). Third, he let Ritchie play up his slightly goofy overgrown kid attitude, especially when Ritchie became enamored of heroin, thereby creating an approximation of the Dolls' decadent, boy-toy, messed-up grace. And fourth, he gave both new names that turned them into cartoon characters of vicious hellishness, Rotten 'n' Vicious, the perfect complement to Hell 'n' Punk.

While some would challenge the extent of his role in creating the Sex Pistols, there is no denying that McLaren capitalized on the New York image to a great degree and that he helped promote it to the point where it became not only hugely popular, but—at least in musical and cultural terms—a revolutionary force. Even more so than the Beatles' manager Brian Epstein, Malcolm McLaren helped *create* the premier band of his era. His influence spread even further via those he influenced.

McLaren's assistant at Sex, a screenprinter/artist named Bernard (better known as Bernie) Rhodes, did much the same with the Clash under McLaren's tutelage. "Bernard was very aware of what I was doing and he wanted to do something similar with another band," McLaren says. "If the Sex Pistols posed a revolutionary threat to the culture of the time, the Clash attempted to do so in a more political manner. This was in keeping with Bernard's beliefs and his attitudes, and I think it had a great deal to do with his own Jewishness. Unlike me, he was swarthy and had a nose and looked the part, and he was often angry about the sorts of things that were said and that he experienced. With his boys, among them that nice Jewish boy Mick Jones [author of the line 'He thinks it's not kosher!' in 'Rock the Casbah,' on an Arab grandee's consternation about Western culture, especially rock 'n' roll], he helped create the other great band of the era. And there's no denying that his role was pivotal."

Others agree, countering the contention that McLaren, with typical braggadocio, is overstating his and Bernie Rhodes's role in punk's creation. Vivien Goldman, a highly influential critic at the time (she first championed the Clash) and child of German refugees who barely survived the Holocaust (her aunts, uncles, and cousins were not so lucky), says, "Malcolm was always . . . like my mother used to say, a disgrace to the race. Because if you check out Malcolm's record, he was so appalling. . . He was very, very un-Jewish, very not what Jews should be doing at all." Goldman acknowledges, in terms of the Sex Pistols, "he did take those boys in, who otherwise would have had nothing, and he trained them in his skill, which was thieving . . . He and Bernie were the people who put the politics into punk. And then I guess I, to a large extent—other people maybe had better say this than me, it's embarrassing to come from me—but I know I had a large part to play in the politicization of the music press, or the politics, the level of politics in the music press, because I really pushed for it, and I was kind of—I was somewhat given hell for it."

To say the least. Goldman—one of the first to confront Siouxsie Sioux (Sue Dallion) about her alleged anti-Semitism (Sue regularly wore a Swastika while performing with her band the Banshees, and one of her earliest hits, "Love in a Void," contained the line "Too many Jews . . .")—was among the most vocal opponents of the fascistic National Front and was eventually driven from her job at *Sounds* when she objected to the magazine's increased, and positive, coverage of the NF's beloved Nazi "Oi" bands.

"I pushed it as much as I could. When I couldn't push it anymore, I left, in a big battle, which has become fairly known and written about," Goldman says. Nonetheless, she was hurt. The memory still brings tears to her eyes nearly three decades later when she recalls it. She'd experienced repeated incidents of anti-Semitism in England, and she'd thought, like so many others, that punk would be different. "Basically I was drawn to punk because of the ideology . . . punk is a very inclusionary movement . . . I mean, the English and the American experience is so different, but I would say that there are hardly any Jews in punk in England, and that the main role of Jews in punk in England was ideological, and in terms of formulating the identity of punk. It was not so much in the bands, although there was . . . Mick Jones . . . it's because of Mick, I think, that we have that line 'This is not kosher' [sic] which is the biggest Jewish line in punk, as far as I can see. . . . It was kind of radical, because it's so rare to hear any Jewish terminology used in England. It's not like here where everybody schleps. So I thought it was very bold to have the Jewish vibe out there in the punk mainstream."

Interestingly, Goldman sees not only English punk's emphasis on politics as stemming in part from Jewish outsiderness, but also its other, very un-American, aspect—the embrace of ska and reggae that so defined the sound of the Clash, the Beat, the Specials, and numerous other bands. And she's not alone. Deejay Don Letts, a non-Jew who was instrumental in championing and spreading reggae in the U.K. punk scene, and who recently discussed both in his new documentary *Punk: Attitude*, offers this opinion. "The 'children of Israel' theme that was so much a part of reggae was not an accident and definitely had resonances," he says. "All of the Old Testament metaphors in reggae referring to the Jews' flight from slavery in Egypt were well translated beyond Jamaica. If New York punk expressed a cry of dissatisfaction by those outside the status quo, then reggae-influenced punk in the UK did the same. Punk was about outsiders, and both groups had reasons to feel that way." In fact, both Letts and Goldman point out that English Jews figured far beyond their per-capita numbers in supporting reggae music and musicians, not only as fans, but as protestors at rallies opposing the National Front and its skinhead legions.

*　　*　　*

Of course, the influence of New York punk on its UK cousin goes well beyond the positive involvement of Jews in creating the look, lyrical content, and politics of the scene. It also includes a less discussed and perhaps destructive force, another very New York Jewish individual with whom Malcolm McLaren had all-too-personal contact: Nancy—of Sid 'n' Nancy—Spungen.

Today remembered as a kind of American Yoko to Sid's English Lennon, Nancy Spungen was both more and less than that. Part punk *naïve*, part punk decadent, a girl/woman who seemed as lost as anyone she supposedly corrupted, Nancy was, in one all-important respect, essential to the Sex Pistols' story. Like Ono, she began her career in New York. Like Ono, she brought her English lover artistically and literally into its orbit.

Born on February 27, 1958, and raised in the suburbs of Philadelphia, Spungen appears to have been both a victim of mental illness and a product of her time. As her mother points out in her memoir, *And I Don't Want to Live This Life*, Nancy's mental problems emerged almost from birth and seemed to stem from the fact that she had been born with her umbilical chord wrapped around her neck, depriving her of oxygen for her first crucial moments. At the same time, however, there's no denying that Spungen grew up in a classically Jewish middle-class home of the 1960s and early '70s, and that—like Lou Reed—she was taken to professionals and institutionalized when things became difficult.

Nancy's mother, Deborah, makes a convincing case for her daughter's being inherently troubled, depicting numerous scenes in which Nancy becomes subject to uncontrollable rages and crying fits even before she can walk. Referring to something she calls "the stare," Deborah points out that Nancy was often completely unaware of her behavior after the fact, and that in this she shared similarities with other children born under the same circumstances. Still, Deborah is largely concerned with explaining to an imagined reader of her own background how her daughter could have turned out the way she did. She's explaining, in other words, out of a sense of shame how she could have raised a girl who became . . . well, a punk. In Deborah's descriptions of the family home and its habits apart from Nancy, there's a hint of that desire for respectability that Lou Reed attacked in his song "Standing on Ceremony." It's as if she's primarily concerned with how her family's coming off, with saving face. As if in the end she views her daughter's death as an embarrassment more than anything.

Maybe this is unfair, considering the scenes of violence Deborah describes, wherein Nancy attacks either her siblings or her mother. But

Nancy's frequent cries—quoted by her mother—that Deborah is more concerned with appearances than her welfare, raise alarm bells, as does Nancy's attraction to punk above all, that music that would accept the broken and alienated despite appearances—that world that was created for the alienated, the outcasts, and the unwanted.

Is it possible that this middle-class Jewish background, based in respectability and material comfort, worshipful of order and stability, might have played a role in Nancy's rebelliousness? Certainly Malcolm McLaren thinks so. As he says, describing his feelings about Nancy's involvement with Sid, "I thought, oh my God, what is he doing with her?! She's the kind of girl I decided ever since childhood never to have anything to do with. She was like all those princesses who wanted their way and expected their men to bust their balls to get them what they wanted and what they thought they deserved." Or as Danny Fields might have put it, describing the allure of those *echt* Americans who were so unlike anything resembling Jewishness as he knew it, "They treated their women like shit. They didn't care what they said. In Jewish culture, my god, you could never get away with that. The woman is everything. You are supposed to constantly worship her. Everything centers around her. It would make you crazy."

According to McLaren, Nancy's presence was disruptive from the start, and it was bred of that classically Jewish-American middle-class attitude that Nancy was rebelling against even as she was ironically embodying it. "Like I said, Americans *all* seemed like Jews in that they were aggressive and driven and not embarrassed to be ambitious and confident. But she was in a whole different realm. She was amazing. I could never understand what Sid saw in her. Maybe it was the exotic." As McLaren points out, Spungen offered Vicious the combined allure of drugs and middle-class attitude. Spungen's mother notes, recalling the first time she met Sid at her suburban home, he was amazed at the way in which the Spungen family had created a sense of order and material wealth for themselves. At the same time, Deborah says, he saw how much they loved their daughter despite her protests to the contrary. While Sid might not have mentioned to Deborah that he saw how this love could prove suffocating, that is also a possibility. Who knows? With the conflicting testimony of Deborah and Malcolm, and the fact that the principals, who would know best, are dead, one can only conjecture.

Still, it's interesting to note that the chief symbol of English punk was not only attracted to, and molded by, the Jewish-American New York resident

Nancy Spungen, he was also molded by the equally Jewish Malcolm McLaren, who brought his own interpretation of Jewish New York back with him to England. It might even be safe to say that if Malcolm brought Sid the goofily decadent quality of Syl Sylvain, then Nancy finished him off by adding the self-destructive, obsessive quality of a rebel from the Jewish suburbs. After all, who thinks of Syl Sylvain as the chief Doll today? That honor goes to Johnny Thunders, the Italian rebel in the band who ultimately ODed, though only after briefly serving as backup for the solo Vicious. Who would remember Vicious today had he not ODed but instead gone on the Filthy Lucre reunion tour with his other thickening cohorts? Indeed, what if McLaren had done what those cohorts, chiefly the former Johnny Rotten, have said he should have done once Sid became addicted—that is, fire him from the band so that he would be forced to clean up. Like Alex Cox in the film *Sid 'n' Nancy* and many others, Rotten claimed that McLaren used Sid's self-destruction as entertainment, coldly allowing him to commit slow suicide onstage for the benefit of the crowd. If that's true, and if McLaren allowed Spungen to aid him in doing so, isn't it also possible that he just let them be who they were, loosing the chains of convention? He didn't start something so much as he didn't stop something, and in the process he made English punk what it is. No one ever said that punk was supposed to be pretty and have happy endings—better look somewhere else if that's what you're after. And no one—certainly not Rotten himself—ever claimed that compassion was a necessary virtue. Indeed, it was Rotten himself who raised high the banner of cold calculation as a new manifesto, crying instead that "anger is an energy" and love stupid. If McLaren lived that sentiment and helped give birth to punk in the process, should the so-called king of punk be attacking him for it? As Malcolm himself said, defending his artful dodgers to the press the day after their infamous swear fest on Bill Grundy's *Today* show, "Boys will be boys."

And where did he get that expression? From his grandmother, of course. The same one who had taken him out of the local grammar school so that she could raise him at home under the tutelage of Fagin, Scrooge, and Svengali. "Boys will be boys," she had told the principal who had chastised Malcolm for putting cotton wool in his ears to block out the words of his teacher. "Boys will be boys," she had told Malcolm later at home before adding, "A Jew never gets involved with the police. A Jew never talks. Don't deal with them. Say nothing." She repeated this again and again over the years, making sure he understood, making sure he saw his special place in the world, making sure that he knew the law of the government was against him. No, he couldn't trust them, and he would have to take care of himself and risk the consequences. It was what everyone did, after all, even if they claimed otherwise, even if they claimed they cared; all the altruists in the world were only altruistic as long as it suited them. No, she wouldn't allow her Malcolm to become another patsy, another *shmendrik*, another stooge. He would be her little Fagin in the making. Her little entertainer. Her little Svengali. Her little boy.

He would be the world's most glorious faker. Because life was all about entertainment. And after all, boys will be boys.

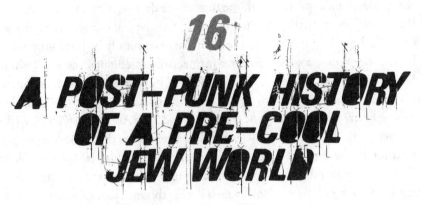

A POST-PUNK HISTORY OF A PRE-COOL JEW WORLD

*How the Radical Jewish Culture Movement
Took NY Punk Further Downtown*

I'd been reading a book that discussed the JDL [Jewish Defense League, both famous for its "radical," baseball bat–swinging responses to anti-Semitism and infamous for its terrorist attacks], and as much as I deplored their practices and attitudes, there was something about that word *radical* that I liked. I'd been thinking of calling the festival "New Jews" or "New Jewish Music," and Ribot had suggested the ironically comic "Loud and Obnoxious Music." But then I heard that word and I had it—"Radical Jewish Culture." That was it.

—John Zorn, 2004

It's another late night at CBGB, another round of bands with aggressively ironic names coming onstage to do their thing. Since the mid-1970s it's been like this, kids in their early twenties coming through with battered instruments and ripped T-shirts to create a music that's more in keeping with the original spirit of rock 'n' roll than with the pretentious noodlings of prog rock or the deadbeat monotone of disco funk. This club, which long ago saw bands as disparate as the Ramones, the Dictators, and the Neon Boys change the musical landscape, has, with the turn of the decade, seen a number of new bands carry even further the dual mantles of artiness and unpretentiousness. On right now, for instance, are the Sic F*cks, a comically inclined group that borders on punk-parody. It features former Stilettos/Blondie singers Tish 'n' Snooky providing backup on Russell Wolinsky compositions such as "Spanish Bar Mitzvah" ("We'll invite the Garcias and the Schwartzes / drinking Manischevitz and tequila by the quartzes") and "We Are Jerry's Kids" ("Rickles flies in, he drives us nuts / Richard Belzer tells jokes that make me *platz*"). And tomorrow night is X, a band from LA that's taking the sped-up, West Coast variant of punk known as hardcore in a more literary direction, writing songs such as "Los Angeles," which details the anti-Semitism of that scene ("she started to hate the niggers and Jews . . . she had to get out, get out") and could just as well be about any of the other equally anti-Semitic punk scenes in Boston ("I never heard the word kike until I moved there," says native New Yorker Eva Schlapick), San Francisco ("If I had a nickel for every time I heard someone badmouth kikes . . ." says fellow New York native Steven Blush), and England ("The neo-Nazi National Front had a serious following in the scene," says journalist Vivien Goldman). The irony of anti-Semitic punk becomes all the more apparent when tonight's headliners, the Dictators, come onstage. Still around, though putting less emphasis on jokes than machismo, the Dictators are trying to play up their aggressive side, which might have something to do with the fact that tomorrow night, England's the Stranglers will be on this same stage doing their best Clockwork Orange, Pistols-lite, No Future thing, courting the mayhem American audiences have come to expect from the music they think of as a four-letter word to shout in a crowded concert hall:

P-U-N-K

PUNK!!!!!

Of course, Sire Records president Seymour Stein has been encouraging his own charges to refer to this music as "new wave," sending the Ramones to Los Angeles to soften their sound with legendary producer Phil Spector, even as other bands like XTC and the Go Gos emerge at increasingly popular spots like Danceteria and the Mudd Club to play a jittery but less sonically aggressive version of punk that could more accurately be called new wave.

The scene is fracturing, going in different directions. One of the most interesting, yet seemingly doomed, arises in answer to the new wave compromise—No Wave. Emerging at both CBGB and the Kitchen, No Wave is a far cry from the punk churned out by the Ramones et al., yet it has a few things in common with the original. It's aggressive. Uncompromising. Revolutionary. It has done away with melody in favor of propulsive, almost industrial beats and hypnotic loops. And its vision is dark. One of the premier bands to emerge from this scene, Teenage Jesus and the Jerks, features the psychosexual shriekings of childhood rape/incest victim Lydia Lunch (Lydia Koch), a German-American beauty from Albany who is redefining female sexuality, along with a growing legion of almost exclusively Jewish female "performance artists" such as Meredith Monk and Annie Sprinkle (née Ellen Steinberg). Lunch will eventually join Jewish-American women writers like Kathy Acker and Lynne Tillman when she publishes not only an autobiography focusing on her struggles with her sexuality (*Paradoxia*), but also numerous poetry collections and a literary journal ("Blood and Guts," after Acker's *Blood and Guts in High School*) that address the topic on a broader level.

Perhaps most indicative of where the music is going, at least in the town where it was bred, is the sound that emerges somewhere in the intersection of all these trends. It combines comedy, parody, anti-melody, and even cartoon effects in a sound that is as cosmopolitan and Jewish as New York itself. It's created by musicians such as John Lurie and Marc Ribot of the Lounge Lizards (jazz parodists rapidly morphing into avant-garde bellwethers), Gary Lucas of Gods & Monsters (a punk/new wave/experimental group fond of songs about Jewish monsters like the man-from-clay golem), and Elliott Sharp (an instrument inventor, mathematician, "freelance avant-gardist," whose experiments in noise-collage combine everything from free jazz to Enoesque soundscapes). And yet it is perhaps best exemplified by the man who will end up being the musical and organizational center of this next wave about to hit New York, this wave that will take elements of punk and a dozen other musical styles—chief among them Jewish klezmer—to create the most challenging downtown music yet. It's a music so challenging, in fact, that, unlike punk, it will never really break out of New York, never be accepted on a wide scale, never be more than a cult music for a cult audience.

Who is this man? We can see him here in CBGB, standing behind one of the pillars tonight, his hair covering his face, his leather jacket zipped to his chin. His name is John Zorn, and at this point in New York music history, he is little more than a rumor, another face among many. Before long, however, he will be a figure of intense interest to those in the avant-garde "loft scene" rapidly rising up around Soho and the East Village. He will be the motor driving the engine of this music that will eventually be identified with the Downtown or Radical Jewish Culture movement. Joined by punk rockers, jazz musicians, and others, Zorn will establish a new and controversial offshoot of punk that redefines New York—and to a great extent Jewish-American—culture as we know it.

* * *

Ironically, Zorn wasn't conscious of his Jewishness until his early adolescence. Born in 1953 in Beth Israel Hospital near the East Village (First Avenue and 16th Street), Zorn was raised to disdain the conventions of organized religion and culture. Both his mother, a first-generation immigrant Jew raised in the Bronx, and his father, an Eastern European immigrant who may have been Jewish (Zorn notes that his name, which fittingly enough means "anger" in German, appears on many Jewish tombstones in Prague), felt that as "freethinkers" they were above the constraints of history. And they were intent on making sure that the same was true for their son, whom they saw as a kind of tabula rasa, a blank slate on which a new, idealistic vision could be written.

Zorn's parents were determined to keep him untainted by his Jewish background. Zorn remembers that while he was growing up in Flushing, Queens, they didn't celebrate any holidays and weren't particularly interested in things beyond the intellect. His mother, a professor of education at NYU, and his father, a hairdresser, encouraged him to approach the world rationally and to view it as puzzle one should be able to figure out.

For all their distance from cultural and religious Jewishness, Zorn's parents were strangely open to exposing him to the religions of other cultures if such proved "advantageous." Though he'd taught himself to read musical scores after hearing Bach in *The Phantom of the Opera* at age eight, and subsequently studied music at the UN School in Queens, when Zorn was eleven his parents insisted on sending him to a Protestant parochial school. There he was taught about Jesus and the resurrection—and teased by both his classmates and his Jewish neighbor.

"My parents said that going there would give me 'a way out,' but I was bullied and treated like 'the little Jew'," Zorn says. "Of course, my Jewish friends weren't much better. 'Who do you think you're fooling?' they'd say. It was difficult. And very confusing."

By fifteen, Zorn found himself increasingly alienated from his surroundings. He was experiencing both a strange kind of anti-anti-Semitism
from his Jewish neighbors and a more traditional version of that historical ill
from his Christian classmates, and he was living apart from his parents,
bouncing back and forth between his grandmother's in the Village and his
Jewish friend David Giovannitti's apartment on Central Park West. Without
a family home, he felt divided and uncertain about who he was, wandering
the streets alone, visiting the Museum of Modern Art almost every day and
the opera many nights.

In part to compensate for his loneliness, he began going to ever more
movies, indirectly discovering in them the extent of his love for music. In
addition to the Bach he'd heard in *The Phantom of the Opera*, he became
aware of Stravinsky via Disney's classic *Fantasia* and, not long after that, Ligeti
while viewing *2001: A Space Odyssey*. When *The Good, the Bad, and the Ugly*
introduced him to Ennio Morricone, he was, as he says, "blown away."
Already composing short pieces for piano, he began playing in a surf band
and worshipping Captain Beefheart, the Doors, and Frank Zappa—the
"weird shit," as he described it in a *New Yorker* profile detailing his early musical development.

By the time he left New York to study music at Webster College, a small
liberal arts school in St. Louis, he was more than primed to explore the fringes
of the music world. Furthering his interest in avant-garde classical and jazz,
he became especially interested in the Black Artists Group, a local collective
of African American experimentalists in theater, poetry, dance, visual arts,
film, and music. With jazz composers like Sun Ra and classical composers like
Christian Wolff both inspiring him, Zorn set about creating the "game pieces"
(largely improvised works for multiple performers) and free-form squawk
fests that brought him a small degree of attention upon his return to the city
at the height of the punk era.

For the most part, Zorn performed outside the formal club scene as part
of the growing "loft" movement sweeping the East Village and Soho. Yet he
also put in time at CBGB and the Kitchen, appearing onstage with others
such as Bill Laswell, Eugene Chadbourne, and Fred Frith. It was a divided
life, one that wavered between the Zen complexity of his classical "game
pieces" and the massive tumult that characterized his jazz-punk work. The
split was only partially bridged by his return to the beloved music of his
childhood, where he developed a growing reputation by reinterpreting clas-

sic soundtrack composers such as Morricone and cartoon-music-composer Carl Stalling in a series of critically well received if somewhat mainstream—at least for Zorn—records such as *Spillane* and *The Big Gundown*. Eventually, the split sent him fleeing from the neighborhoods where he'd felt so lonely as a teenager, all the way across the globe to Japan, where he lived intermittently for ten years, playing sax, becoming all the more deeply distanced from those around him, and ultimately stumbling upon a new style of music that came out like a scream.

*   *   *

When fans of Zorn's music recall their favorite early albums, they speak about their complexity, their rapid time changes, their incorporation of various musical themes from jazz to punk to film noir. Yet what they get back to first and foremost is their energy and intensity—in other words, their anger and violence.

Consider the following online review by someone identifying himself as Big Hairy Monster: "A slice of avant acid noise jazz . . . this recording will have you nearly in tears for its sheer beauty, and literally seconds later you will cringe in fear at its sheer ferocity. *Naked City* is beautiful, rich, challenging, and a recording of opposites . . . it is also brutal, harsh, and at times atonal. There is a dark beast that lurks here—it is the beastly side of this recording that scares the hell out of me."

So it should, for if anything defines Zorn during this period, it's his loneliness and consequent darkness. His music released the roiling tensions inside him. Like Jonathan Richman during the original Modern Lovers period, he vented the pain of being an outsider via his music. And like Richman, he did so after returning from a foreign country where he'd gone in search of something more spiritually satisfying, only to find himself bitterly disappointed.

"I don't think I'd ever felt more alienated anywhere than in Tokyo," Zorn says. "It's a strange city for anyone coming out of the West, but I think it was even more so for me considering my distance from my own background and the way that I was alienated from my own Jewishness." There's nothing like being abroad to remind you of who you are.

In Japan, Zorn came to learn that his Jewishness was a part of him whether he liked it or not; or rather, whether his parents chose to like it or not. The identification was not religious but something akin to "tribalism" for lack of a better word, a feeling of belonging to a certain people and place. Like being an American or a New Yorker—the latter of which he saw as intricately linked to his Jewishness.

Ultimately, Zorn realized that he had to get out of Japan, that he needed to get back to New York, and that he needed to explore what it meant to be Jewish. It was something that had been a part of him since childhood even if he'd ignored it. He felt that if he was ever going to find the security and calm that he sought, he was going to have to understand it and finally come to terms with it.

*   *   *

Back in New York in the early 1990s, Zorn began to associate with a group of musicians on a similar quest, though few of them realized it. Among them were Frank London, a trumpet-playing *macher* ("mover and shaker," to use Zorn's description) who in 1986 had joined the Plasmatics-referencing klezmer-punk band the Klezmatics; Anthony Coleman, a versatile keyboardist who would later found the Selfhaters, but at this point was still a participant in other avant-garde groups; and Joey Baron, a Jewish working-class drummer who taught himself to play by watching other musicians and drew on the rock, jazz, and television themes of his youth. Most important was Marc Ribot, a gifted guitarist in the tradition of Richard Hell and Lou Reed's accompanist Robert Quine, who, like Quine, was not only Jewish but also hard-edged in a punkish way, even though his approach was less staccato.

London, Coleman, and the others made numerous forays into Jewish music over the years, as did David Krakauer and Gary Lucas, the latter of whom composed an album of Jewish songs for children and a soundtrack for the silent film *The Golem*, and is now working on a song cycle exploring his grandparents' death in the infamous Polish massacre at Jebwadne. But it was Ribot (composer of "Yo, I Killed Your God") who was most engaged in the contemporary magnetism between Jewishness and punk, and it was Ribot who was most influential in bringing Zorn back to his Jewish roots, so indirectly helping to kick-start the new musical movement.

Born 1954 in Newark, New Jersey—home to many famous Jews, including Philip Roth, Jerome Kern, and Jason "Scott Greenspan" Alexander (better known as George Costanza)—Ribot had experienced a fairly typical Jewish childhood that included annual Yom Kippur trips to synagogue, twice-weekly bus rides to Hebrew school, and eventually a Bar Mitzvah. Like Lenny Kaye, he had always loved rock 'n' roll even if he found that he wasn't exactly being "chosen for it."

"My parents weren't really thrilled about me playing music," he says. "They would have preferred that I become a doctor. But I wasn't interested in that when I was teenager. I wanted to be Che Guevara."

With his typically middle-class Jewish family's grounding in both leftism and popular entertainment, Ribot ended up studying with an unusual teacher. After Ribot's aunt met his uncle at New York's left-leaning City College, she became a downtown-based songwriter and eventually befriended Frantz Casseus, the father of Haitian classical guitar. Since Ribot's parents felt that Casseus was part of their extended family, it was decided that Marc would study with him, even though he had no interest in that form of music.

Considering the later trajectory of Ribot's career, it seems that all turned out for the best. A rock musician who combined first blues and rock, then punk and klezmer, then finally rock and Caribbean music, Ribot is a classic synthesizer of various styles—he epitomizes the Jewish dynamic of give-and-take with the surrounding culture. Perhaps not too surprisingly, when he eventually headed for New York to pursue music, a certain Jewish bent guided him to the Lower East Side and what he calls a kind of ironic return to his roots. He says, "Those of us from suburban backgrounds who had moved (I nearly wrote 'returned') to the Lower East Side were acting out the reversal of a . . . dominant myth . . . in which these mean streets symbolized 'the painful immigrant beginnings' from which hard work, assimilation, and inevitable progress were going to save us . . . We were making time run backwards again, reversing manifest destiny, not even having the good taste to live on the Upper West Side let alone conquer the Great American West."

Arriving in 1978 when punk was just beginning to crest, Ribot directed his energies toward more traditionally black music, playing alternately with jazz organist Jack McDuff and soul/R&B legend Wilson Pickett. In this, Ribot believes he was like many others who later made up the downtown music scene. He discusses this idea in an unpublished essay he wrote on black music and its relation to Radical Jewish Culture, "Black Music, 1997": "The blues and its derivatives contain an encoded lesson in how to spiritually survive being hated by a powerful majority, the very same white Christian majority that 'tolerates' us."

And yet, Ribot goes on to say, this does not mean that Jewish musicians who found a richness in black music simply intended to adapt or "steal" it. Rather, he says, they did as earlier Jewish poets and musicians in Arab-dominated medieval Fez and Christian-dominated Renaissance-era Europe had. They enriched their art by incorporating and synthesizing outside influences, just as the majority culture did with their art in return.

Whether or not Ribot is correct in believing this was true for the other downtown musicians, there's no denying that it was true for him. A nice Jewish boy from Jersey who entered music—and American culture—via the backdoor of a fellow outsider group, he saw that he was speaking a related but still partially foreign musical language, and he realized that he would have to not so much modify it as synthesize it. Joining up with the Lounge Lizards in 1984, he helped transform that band from an ironic jazz parody to a hybrid of musical styles that was as punk as it was Monk (as in Thelonious). In doing so, he continued a process that he saw beginning with Lou Reed and the punks who followed him, one in which white musicians left off from singing in the "soulful" almost minstrel style of many 1960s rock performers, and instead adopted an often uninflected form of speech-song that ironically showed black music respect by no longer aping in. It wasn't that these punks were abandoning black music, he says, but rather translating it into something more endemic to their experience, something that the later post-punk downtown musicians could further incorporate by synthesizing African American blues-based musical forms with their own white-American-Jewish-etc. ones. It was the ultimate expression of the democratic impulse, he says, an embodiment of American diversity that ironically brought these Jewish musicians closer to their roots.

Ribot may not have been consciously thinking this at the time, but as it began to dawn on him, he embraced it. Never one to shy away from musical analysis or adaptation, he became one of the avant-garde's most sought after sidemen, adept at bringing out the half-understood new musical vocabulary emerging in established artists such as Tom Waits and Elvis Costello, who both found new voices and audiences through his magnificent guitar support. At the same time, he began transforming himself into a musician who openly addressed Jewish issues in unconventional formats, not only through his songs, which had titles like "Yo, I Killed Your God," but also through his ever evolving rock, punk, and jazz bands, which had names like the Rootless Cosmopolitans (Stalin's disparaging moniker for Jews), Shrek (a Yiddish word meaning "terror"), and Los Cubanos Postizos (the Prosthetic—or "fake"—Cubans).

* * *

It was in his work with Zorn—both musically and philosophically—that Ribot exerted his greatest influence. For if Joey Baron was the first to point out to Zorn that most of those in their musical circle were Jewish, it was Ribot who made Zorn consider the importance of this fact and how it related to his music. Ribot joined Zorn in pursuing an interest in Jewish-themed and klezmer-inflected music, and though he personally had no interest in klezmer, by accompanying Zorn as a guitarist he helped the leader of the avant-punk band Naked City to morph into the jazz-klezmer melodicist at the head of the overtly Jewish Masada. "I would have to say that Marc was instrumental in helping me realize what I had already come to feel inside without words," says Zorn.

What truly sparked the new music scene was the invitation to Zorn to curate a portion of Art Project, a 1992 Munich music festival. Considering which musicians to include, and remembering his conversations with Ribot, Zorn stumbled on the idea of making his segment a *Jewish* music festival. To what degree pure contrariness—staging a festival of Jewish music in the birthplace of the Nazi Party—played a part, Zorn can't (or won't?) say. But the choice is consistent with his career-long desire to create dissonance.

More important, though, Zorn decided to use the opportunity to define—or rather *undefine*—Jewish music. Far from limiting his festival within a festival to traditional folk stylings, such as klezmer or straight liturgical music as might be performed by a cantor, he posed the question whether Jewish music might be any music created by Jews or coming out of the Jewish experience, even the vicarious experience of this experience. In addition to actual Jews, Zorn included simpatico non-Jews—downtown New York musicians who played in Jewish bands or associated almost solely with Jewish musicians. It was Jewish New York music or New York Jewish music or perhaps just New York as a substitute for Jewish music. He called the festival Radical Jewish Culture. "I'd been reading a book that discussed the JDL, and as much as I deplored their practices and attitudes, there was something about that word *radical* that I liked. I'd been thinking of calling the festival 'New Jews' or 'New Jewish Music' and Ribot had suggested the ironically comic 'Loud and Obnoxious Music.' But then I heard that word and I had it—'Radical Jewish Culture.' That was it."

At the Radical Jewish Culture segment of the festival, Zorn and others such as Lou Reed, Gary Lucas, and Marc Ribot performed a variety of pieces. Some, like Frank London's, were overtly Jewish, while others, such as Reed's collaboration with bassist Greg Cohen, were tangentially so, if that. Zorn's own piece, *Kristallnacht*, was the most gripping, embodying as it did the history of Jewry in the Old World and beyond.

The success of the festival, and the rich vein of musical inspiration it had clearly tapped, pushed Zorn into pursuing radical Jewish music in earnest. He began organizing other shows back in New York, and before long he and Michael Dorf were using the Knitting Factory as a staging area, creating a kind of alternative radical Jewish CBGB.

In what Zorn calls "the classic tradition of Jews," dissension began to break out almost immediately. "You know the joke, you have two Jews, you have an argument. You have three, a debate. Four, a revolution—with splinter groups." First, some began taking the radical Jewish thing in a different direction, putting together talmudic study groups that undercut its original basis in music. Then others in various camps, such as traditional klezmer and folk music, began objecting to Zorn's definition of Jewish music, insisting it only include music that was specifically Jewish, not music that happened to be by Jews.

While some of the releases Zorn began putting out on his new label Tzadik (alternately defined by Zorn as "justice," "righteousness," and "holy man") could be seen as questionable in their relevance—his tributes to Burt Bacharach and Marc (Feld) Bolan, the Jewish leader of T. Rex, among them—Zorn's definition of Jewish music as that which reflects the Jewish experience, in some sense cannot be faulted. Since both Bacharach and Bolan were Jewish, the music they made was in some sense Jewish as well—if you defined Jewishness as reflective of a certain cultural experience.

"My basic idea," says Zorn, "of starting the Radical Jewish Culture movement, and the CD series, and the concerts that we've done, was not to make a claim on a variety of different music and say 'This belongs to us.' It's more celebrating what we do, and trying to show people that this music, this culture, can move into another century in a celebratory way. It doesn't always have to be crying about the Holocaust, or yelling and screaming. It doesn't have to be something underneath. We can be visible and still survive."

Ribot, however, was concerned about Zorn's seeming conflation of Jews (Bacharach and Bolan) and Jewish music (Tzadik's "Great Jewish Music" series). "So the Jewish early music specialist is making *Jewish* early music. The Jew who has studied Charlie Parker for fifty years is, in spite of what he thinks he's doing or what he wants to do, making *Jewish* jazz. Guess if you want to make just regular rock/jazz/classical or whatever, you better not hire any Jews, cause then it's unavoidably *Jewish* versions of these?" Similarly, Ribot believed that in subsequent Radical Jewish Culture festivals, too many musicians were artificially limiting "Jewish music" by defining it in ways that stereotyped Jews. Jewish artists from jazz, punk, and rock backgrounds were too often adopting klezmer-inflected styles out of misplaced nostalgia for a pre-Holocaust Old World that they saw themselves helping rebirth. Not only did this feed a "growing theology of Holocaust and redemption," it also created a false tradition by denying the reality of those Jews who had played klezmer. As Ribot points out, the klezmer musicians of the Old World incorporated a variety of styles, so that there was never such a thing as "true" Jewish music in the first place. Moreover, they were often criticized as hacks who substituted schmaltz for art; hence the derogatory expression "to klezmer something up." For New York musicians to refer to klezmer as *real* Jewish music was akin to the British royal family attempting to preserve the monarchy by instituting so-called historical rituals in the eighteenth century; or like the first modern Israeli government commissioning "folk songs" to give the country a sense of a tradition and national identity.

The great irony for the musicians who adopted klezmer stylings was that in hearkening back to a false tradition, they underplayed their own proficiency in the present. They caused Jewish music—not to mention their own Jewishness—to become a waxwork construction existing in a time warp that had little relation to the American landscape.

This was doubly ironic considering the degree to which American popular culture had been Jewish for decades, especially in music. As Ribot and many others have pointed out, everything from Brill Building pop to Broadway show tunes to the cartoon music of Bugs Bunny and Merrie Melodies

---

*Looney Tunes and Merrie Melodies soundtracks feature a "dizzying comic mix of classical music, Ellington jungle jazz, and Jewish klezmer," as *San Francisco Chronicle* writer Jesse Hamlin puts it. Similarly, their stories, like those of Fleischer Studios' Betty Boop cartoons, include Jewish jokes throughout. A striking instance of this takes place when the New Yoik-accented Betty goes to the Samoan Islands and is greeted by natives with a roaring "Shalom Aleichem!"

was inflected by Jewish culture.* John Zorn's music was inflected by those traditions, particularly by the classic cartoons that he regularly cited as among his earliest influences. Radical Jewish Culture had emerged as a rejection of artificial limits, like the DIY tag that became attached to so many punk bands, forcing them to fear becoming proficient at their instruments, it gave birth to a new musical style that took punk's false modesty and turned it on its self-hating, self-deprecating head.

Of course, not all bands fell prey to a faux-Jewish history. Ribot calls attention to the Klezmatics (whose name refers to both klezmer and Wendy O. Williams's Mohawk-wearing Plastmatics), Zorn's group Masada, and the ironically named Selfhaters as prime examples of bands that created provocative juxtapositions of punk, jazz, and klezmer. In particular, he cites a performance at New York's second Jewish Music Festival by guitarist David First in which the musician led his ensemble (sax, bass, keyboards, drums) in an extrapolation of the haftorah section from his Bar Mitzvah, improvising on it until it grew into a crescendo of Albert Ayler–like free jazz that brought out the affinities between that music and klezmer. When First and company showed the home movie from his Bar Mitzvah and played over it in a similarly rising fashion, Ribot says that it brought out not only the sonic but the philosophic interplay between the two cultures—the Jewish one in which First had been raised and the African American one from which he drew inspiration.

In short, the best new Jewish musicians melded the sounds, feelings, and attitudes of various cultures while underscoring their unique positions and perspectives in the world.

*   *   *

Where does that leave John Zorn, the man who started it all and continues to keep it alive today? Whether he was the actual instigator or merely the most aware, the avatar or the diviner of the zeitgeist, Zorn will forever be linked inextricably with new Jewish music. In addition to forming the first Jewish music festivals and later an avant-Jewish scene around the Knitting Factory and then Tonic, he also founded the Tzadik label to promote Jewish (and non-Jewish) work and has continued to do so through it ever since. The vast catalogue that Tzadik's Radical Jewish Culture imprint has created over the past ten years (more than one hundred releases in all) attests to the diversity of Jewish music—however you define it—in the downtown scene. Alongside artists such as Marc Ribot and Elliott Sharp stand others such as Steven Bernstein (*Diaspora Blues*) and Pharaoh's Daughter (*Out of the Reeds*), not to mention Rabbinical School Dropouts (*Cosmic Tree*) and Charming Hostess (*Sarajevo Blues*). What these have in common beyond their Jewishness is open to interpretation—though Zorn will venture a few possibilities, such as a shared sense of exile, irony, and otherness. Zorn appears to underscore these traits as intrinsically Jewish by including on Tzadik certain artists not born into the faith, but transplanted to New York, such as Dion McGregor (whose spoken descriptions of his dreams appear on the label's Lunatic Fringe imprint) and Ikue Mori (whose ambient film music is collected on *B/Side*). In this scene, Zorn seems to be subscribing to Lenny Bruce's famous dictum that if you're Catholic but live in New York, you're Jewish. He could just as well be saying that the artists on his label share the characteristics of kids from Brooklyn, the Lower East Side, and the Bronx. All of these Lenny Bruce–style New Yorkers who came up through the ranks of punk are as Jewish as any Jew because they're New Yorkers. Jew York and New York are synonymous, one and the same. It's *Yiddishkeit* City. A heeb-infested Hymietown. A place for punks and punkers with *shpilkes* or heebie-jeebies.

EPILOGUE

One of Us

Whatever became of Jew York punk? Did it just putter off like a beloved old *bubbe*, burning out—or at least deeply freckling—under the Miami sun?

To some extent, yes. Pop movements change quickly both in time and space. As punk basically left the city to infiltrate England and then other urban outposts both in DC and on the West Coast, it changed in form—so much so that it alienated the original punks. As we've already seen, English punk brought in class anger, mob rule, and genuine appreciation of fascist ideology (at least for significant segments of the audience), while the West Coast version turned into a testosterone-driven, thrash-oriented hardcore scene that was at the very least non-Jewish and in many respects equally anti-Semitic. Consider the experience of Steven Blush, author of *American Hardcore*, a Jewish New Yorker who followed punk to San Francisco when he was eighteen to find a world unlike any he'd known.

"I was shocked out of the rock scene [there]," Blush says. "At one point I was going to move to San Francisco. . . . But I heard 'kike' and those words coming out from hipsters so many times after a few drinks. I heard it so many fucking times."

Blush's experience was echoed by others in cities across the country. Photographer Lisa Law, long a fixture on the LA rock scene, was referred to indirectly in a song by X ("Los Angeles") that recounted how fellow scenester Farrah Faucet-Minor told Law she was fleeing town to get away from Jews like her ("she started to hate the niggers and Jews . . . she had to get out, get out").

In Boston, which had its own scene soon after New York, former Brooklyn Heights resident Eve Schlapik was going through an almost identical experience. "It was shocking for me to come to Boston and be seen as 'special' because I was from New York," Schlapik says. "I don't look classically Jewish, so I heard things. 'How do you like working with all those Jews?' I'd never heard anything like that before. Or the N-word. Roy Mental started up with it at a Real Kids gig, and I gave him a lecture on the history of rock. 'That music you love playing was created by black Americans, you idiot.'"

As both Schlapik and Blush stress, the shock of hearing these things was all the greater because they had grown up in New York. "You took being Jewish for granted there," says Schlapik. "No one made comments, maybe in part because so many people were Jewish." More importantly, they thought Jewish. New York Jewish punk attitude doesn't travel well.

With both England and the West Coast becoming all but *Judenrein*, perhaps it is not surprising that New York punk went off in a more overtly Jewish direction at the Knitting Factory. In doing so it lost the ear of the remainder of the country, which became increasingly attuned to hip-hop and black urban concerns. African Americans, the most oppressed minority in the country, had taken the forefront—the new Jews.

*   *   *

Of course, as Jewish punk became Jewish jazz and klezmer, and pop music became dominated by black hip-hop and its various offshoots (trip-hop, booty bass, metal rap, etc.), interesting developments took place in the liminal space between the two. The interstices separating America's outsider others, blacks and Jews, filled with a hybrid that combined the best of old-school punk and newer-school rap to create a unique form of personal protest.

In this realm were Jewish hip-hop producer Rick Rubin, Manhattan-born and LA-raised Jewish hip-hop promoter/manager Lyor Cohen, half-Jewish trip-hop explorer Beck Hansen, and above all, New York's own Beastie Boys. The Beastie Boys and their early producer Rick Rubin were an all-Jewish force that embraced the possibilities in rap long before most of their fellow "whites" seemed willing—or able—to do so. Sharing a love of the "authentic" New York with the mostly Jewish folk purists who, earlier, had searched for a "real" (or *echt*) America, the three Jewish members of the Beastie Boys voiced the discontent of bad-boy rebels though they came from the heights of upper-middle-class New York.

Their producer, Rick Rubin, was a Long Island native and surgeon's son. Michael Diamond was the Upper West Side offspring of an art dealer. Adam Yauch was the son of an architect and school administrator. Adam Horovitz was the only child of playwright Israel Horovitz. All of them felt somehow divorced from their origins even if they were privileged materially. Though they didn't see this at the time—and largely don't to this day—the classic New York Jewish punk rock dynamic is clearly visible on their latest album, *To the Five Boroughs* (2004).

This New York–centric love letter features recurrent Jewish references (most prominently to hallah) and a song that could function as the official Rap-Jew-Punk anthem, "Right Right Now Now" ("I'm a funky-ass Jew and I'm on my way / and yes I got to say fuck the KKK"). Moreover, it makes explicit what was already implied on earlier albums, such as *Paul's Boutique* (1989), which featured the song "Shadrach" and its chorus: "We're just three emcees and we're on the go / Shadrach, Meshach, Abednego." As any good yeshiva student listening to the Beasties would know, Shadrach, Meshach, and Abednego were three Jews who, according to the Bible, resisted the Babylonian king Nebuchadnezzar's injunction that they bow down to his golden statue when sacred music was played. As punishment they were thrown into a furnace, where, Holocaust-like, they were expected to burn alive. Instead, God defended them so that they danced in the flames. Nebuchadnezzar, wisely realizing he shouldn't fuck with Yahweh, set them free.

Former *Spin* and *Vibe* magazine editor Alan Light—who has just published what many consider to be the first major biography of the band, *The Skills to Pay the Bills: The Story of the Beastie Boys*—says, "The song also set them apart from the rest of the rap community, which insisted that three white boys couldn't really understand the music. The 'white boys' could just as well have been substituted with 'Jew boys' in many instances. But, despite the pressure, the Beasties stayed true to themselves and didn't bow down to another's definition of music, and as a result they ended up being set free to lead the way into new territory." In addition to three Jews from the Torah, "Shadrach" also featured that other holy Jew of New York, the one pictured on the cover of that modern-day Bible referred to in the line, "I'm madder than *MAD*'s Alfred E. Neuman."

In their smartass humor, their love of cosmopolitan pastiche (they largely popularized sampling), their promotion of liberal politics, and their desire to shock, undermine, and disrupt, the Beasties seem as firmly rooted in the Lenny Bruce Jewish punk tradition as any of the bands who played CBGB in its heyday. Even Yauch's later commitment to Buddhism strikes a deeply Jewish chord. Since at least the time of Allen Ginsberg, Jews have figured prominently among American practitioners of Buddhism. The informal term for this group is Jewdhists.

* * *

Of course, "Jewish" punk's influence in popular music did not stop with the Beastie Boys. Everything from Riot Grrrl to New Punk reflects a continued Jewish presence in rock, though it may seem increasingly unconscious or dilute. The indie movement of the 1990s, for instance, with its *post*-post-punk embrace of lo-fi informality informed by the Kill Rock Stars approach of punk, grunge, and riot grrrl, was led by Jewish children of the middle class who questioned authority and officially sanctioned notions of what rock could be. Whether it was Ira Kaplan of Yo La Tengo or David Berman of the Silver Jews, the impulse seemed to derive from an intellectual tradition that emphasized inquiry above all. Berman, an award-winning poet as well as rocker, describing both the Silver Jews and his good friend and frequent musical collaborator, ex-Pavement leader Stephen Malkmus, says: "In his nature [Malkmus is] the most Jewish WASP I've ever known, he's an honorary Jew. What I mean by that is that he is smart, funny, critical, and cheap. And it's been very important—[the musical collaboration] wouldn't have worked with a stock Christian."

One has to wonder where Malkmus came up with the wonderful Pavement line, "What about the voice of Geddy Lee, how did it get so high?" It seems to reference an almost private Jewish joke that would be understood by few in the audience; Gary, or "Geddy," Lee was the famous Jewish heavy metal figure who gained his moniker through his *zeyde*'s heavily accented inability to pronounce his real name.

Likewise, any movement that would give a prominent position to a band named the Silver Jews is already deeply attuned to Jewish culture. As Berman says, referring to the so-called Cool Jew movement that began just after the 1990s, "What's new is the increase in Protestants using Jewish manners and consciousness patterns. This newness creates the artificial effect of Jewishness seeming cool." Berman should know, for he himself is a kind of returnee to Jewish consciousness, having decided in 2004 to "convert" to an Orthodox version of Judaism so as to understand "how to be a Jew from the start."

As he wrote to his grandparents in a letter explaining his decision, "I look around the synagogue and know that there are people good and bad in here but that none force their (spiritual) views on others, that they count your good acts and not your beliefs as a measure of your character, [that their] tradition demands questioning, allows doubt, places learning above all other human activity . . . that well-to-do Jews have always voted against their economic self-interest to favor policies of fairness and justice, and that these bloodlines have endured four thousand years of constant bullshit hassling. I want to have fortitude like that, fairness, heart, independence of heart, and above all strength like that. I look around the synagogue and say I want what these people have."

Berman's embrace of religious Judaism may set him slightly apart from the indie rock pack, but the way he defines that embrace puts him right back in the center of it. Inquiry over acceptance, action over faith, and tolerance over conversion could just as well describe the culture surrounding indie rock. Moreover, his conversion signifies a general shift in American consciousness. Berman is but one of many Jewish rockers—and youth in general—who have come to see their culture as more significant in their art and lives than they ever imagined. Whether they are activists like Jennifer Bleyer, who hopes to reawaken interest in the Jewish-American radical political tradition, or editors like Josh Neuman, whose *Heeb* magazine (originally started by Bleyer) continues to spread the Cool Jew movement even as you read this, the renewed focus on Jewishness is obvious. It is equally obvious in the rise of hasidic reggae star Matisyahu and in the battles over semantics between the Rock and Roll Hall of Fame and its online cousin, the *Jewish* Rock and Roll of Fame. Their creators flaunt their Jewishness in ways that would have shocked and perhaps even embarrassed their grandparents.

What is it that drives them? What goads them to explore this last taboo, this last bit of shame, this secret identity with which the punks themselves so provocatively played? Ironically, it's the resurgence of the punks' cherished music. Bands such as the Strokes and the Yeah Yeah Yeahs, with lesser-knowns such as Mensch and the Monk Eastmans (named after an infamous Jewish gangster), are making New York in the new millennium a major breeding ground for rock bands for the first time since the punk explosion settled into new wave dust. Is it a coincidence that many of the major punk figures also disappeared during the period in which these bands have emerged, chief among them being the sanctified figurehead of the original outcast-among-outcasts, the Kafkaesque Jew-freak known as Joey Ramone? Probably not.

Jewish (and Jewesque) CBGB-era punks addressed taboo Jewish subjects such as Nazis, shiksas, and degenerates, and their figurative children (young enough to be their actual children) have done it again. When they regroup in places like CBGB to honor and build on the first punks' achievements, the very notion of Jewishness itself is suddenly out in the open. It is no longer referred to in code, no longer hidden like the crazy aunt in the attic. Now, Jewishness itself is often the subject, and the Jewishness of punk, too. So the consciousness of the consciousness at last becomes conscious. Mensch leader Seth Abrams, explaining his excitement at being involved in the first Joey Ramone Songwriting Contest, says, "It's so cool to be a Jewish kid from the suburbs who grew up listening to Joey and take part in something like this. It's like he made it all possible. When I sing, 'Don't want to be a schnook with a bone / Want to be a rockin' Jew like Joey Ramone,' it's not only true—it's liberating that I can even say it. And I think we have Joey to thank for that."

Or to put it in the words of Joey himself, as he welcomed us all onstage to join in with him, "Gabba gabba, we accept you, we accept you, one of us."

AFTERWORD

Seeing God

I'm leaning against the back of the sofa, my feet propped up, bathed in blue-silver TV light after a day of working on this book. I'm letting go, feeling good, relaxing with a glass of vodka. I can hear the ice tinkling as I raise my drink, the cool-hot going down, the expansive mood setting in.

The episode of *Curb Your Enthusiasm* ends, its Dick Van Dyke on Rye musical shtick bouncing by, and a commercial comes on making me reach for the remote. I'm about to see what's on the surgery channel, or at least what I call the surgery channel, the one they call TLC (not Tender Loving Care, but The Learning Channel, as in the channel where we *leaaaarn*). Maybe they have one of those bizarre medical anomalies on display, like "Woman with One Pound Tumor" or "Brain Surgery: Fit Induced" (the latter featured a woman who was fully conscious during her surgery, reading from flash cards as they explored beneath her skull to see where her problem lay, her voice calmly stating, "That's a red wheelbarrow, that's a brown fireplace, that's a yellow Tonka toy" before suddenly breaking down into "Thatzza Blamblubka Go oh oh, woh woh wawawa" as the doctor, just the mildest bit surprised, and pleased, said for the benefit of the camera, "Oh, I think I just induced a seizure").

Then I hear something that makes me stop.

"They're piling in the backseat / they're generating steam heat . . . Hey! Ho! Let's go! . . ."

As I sit there with the remote still in my hand, leaning forward, the controls frozen as if floating in space, it takes me a moment to realize what is going on. There on the TV are two SUVs, manfully rumbling over rocks and crevices like the horses of cowboys, the scene redolent of Superbowl studliness, suburban commercial power, the wonders of machinery, all that your money can buy; and there, in the background, is that most identifiable of punk national anthems, the one that calls to mind not just Joey and CB's and Nazis, but pogoing and drinking and pill popping, going out and getting wild and getting loud. Has my radio somehow crossed lines with my television? Have my two appliances gone crazy through interbreeding, like some sort of tune transmitted over a teenager's braces? A sound substituted for a color in an aphasiac's psychedelic circuitry? A message in the air itself signaling the apocalypse?

No, I realize, the remote still frozen by my face, no, I say aloud, it's really there, that's really the song, those are really the Ramones playing out over a Nissan Pathfinder commercial.

By the time I've come to appreciate what has just happened, the commercial's over and I'm back in front of the TV, back in the darkened room with my glass of vodka, back there sitting on the sofa in my late-night house. But something has changed.

The Ramones are here with me, like something that has entered the room, something that has come into the house to visit. Yet, they're different from before. It's as if they've come to plop down and watch TV along with me, not while smoking a joint and laughing sarcastically, but after eating dinner with my family, discussing stocks and housing prices, sharing a casserole.

The Ramones are now a commercial, and I'm now in a suburban home, and surgery is going on on the surgery channel. What to make of this? What to make of this world? What to make of these things? What to do?

I sit there, uncertain, uncertain how to feel or think.

Then I start to laugh.

I laugh out loud.

I laugh a hoarse laugh that sounds like a cough.

The Ramones are here. In my room. My all-too-suburban living room. My entertainment center. My TV.

They're here over a truck commercial, a stupid commercial, the kind of commercial I usually can't stand to look at. And yet, they've made me sit up and listen, they've made me stop in the midst of my daze, they've made me freeze in place and smile in awe.

They've still got it. They still can do it. They still have the power. And now they rule the airwaves. Finally.

More power to them if they got there by doing it over a Nissan commercial. We're a happy family, we're a happy family. And the Ramones have finally won.

SOURCE NOTES

In the following list, I cite sources on a chapter-by-chapter basis, followed by a list of materials that I used for reference throughout the book. "AI" indicates material from author interviews. "WC" indicates Web citations for information specific to the chapter.

1 | The Protocols of the Elders of Punk

AI: Snooky Bellomo, Richard Blum, Kitty Bruce, Paul Buhle, Tommy Erdelyi, Gyda Gash, Lenny Kaye, Tuli Kupgerberg, Andy Shernoff, James Sliman, Chris Stein, Lee Wolfberg.

Bilski, Emily D., and Emily Braun, eds. *Jewish Women and Their Salons: The Power of Conversation.* New York: Jewish Museum. New Haven: Yale University Press, 2005.

Birmingham, Stephen. *"Our Crowd": The Great Jewish Families of New York.* New York: Dell, 1967.

———. *The Grandees: America's Sephardic Elite.* New York: HarperCollins, 1971.

———. *"The Rest of Us": The Rise of America's Eastern European Jews.* New York: Berkley, 1985.

Bruce, Lenny. *How to Talk Dirty and Influence People: An Autobiography.* New York: Fireside, 1992.

Buhle, Paul. *From the Lower East Side to Hollywood: Jews in American Popular Culture.* New York: Verso, 2004.

Cohen, Rich. *Tough Jews: Fathers, Sons, and Gangster Dreams.* New York: Vintage Books, 1999.

Gaines, Donna. *Misfit's Manifesto: The Spiritual Journey of a Rock & Roll Heart: A Memoir.* New York: Random House, 2003.

Goldman, Albert. *Ladies and Gentlemen, Lenny Bruce!!* New York: Random House, 1974.

Gramaglia, Michael, and Jim Fields, co-producers and codirectors. *End of the Century: The Story of the Ramones.* Documentary. Chinagraph, 2004.

Hoberman, J., and Jeffrey Shandler. *Entertaining America: Jews, Movies, and Broadcasting.* New York: Jewish Museum, and Princeton, NJ: Princeton University Press, 2003.

Kite, B. "The Jerriad: A Clown Painting (Part One: Nutty Around the Edges)." *The Believer,* October 2003.

———. "The Jerriad: A Clown Painting (Part Two: Caught in the Act)." *The Believer,* November 2003.

Mailer, Norman. "The White Negro: Superficial Reflections on the Hipster." *Dissent,* 1956. Also in *Advertisements for Myself.* New York: Putnam's, 1959.

Simmons, Sylvie. *Serge Gainsbourg: A Fistful of Gitanes.* Cambridge, MA: Da Capo Press, 2002.

Staub, Michael E., ed. *The Jewish 1960s: An American Sourcebook.* Waltham, MA: Brandeis University Press, 2004.

Weide, Robert B., producer, writer, and director. *Lenny Bruce: Swear to Tell the Truth.* Documentary. Whyaduck, 1998.

2 | The Punk *Zeyde*

AI: Victor Bockris, Ira Cohen, Michael Dorf, Danny Fields, Nat Finkelstein, Joe Harvard, Jeff Marshall, Lynne Tillman.

WC: http://www.robertchristgau.com/xg/rock/reed-96.php

Bellow, Saul. *Humboldt's Gift.* New York: Penguin Books, 1996.

Bockris, Victor. *Transformer: The Lou Reed Story.* New York: Simon & Schuster, 1994.

——— and John Cale. *What's Welsh for Zen? The Autobiography of John Cale.* New York: Bloomsbury, 2000.

——— and Gerard Malanga. *Up-Tight: The Velvet Underground Story.* New York: Cooper Square Press, Reprint Edition, 2003.

Christgau, Robert. "Professional Pervert." *Village Voice,* March 19, 1996.

Epstein, Lawrence. *The Haunted Smile: The Story of Jewish Comedians in America.* New York: Public Affairs, 2001.

Harvard, Joe. *Velvet Underground's The Velvet Underground and Nico.* New York: Continuum, 2004.

Heylin, Clinton. *All Yesterday's Parties: The Velvet Underground in Print: 1966–1971.* Cambridge, MA: Da Capo Press, 2005.

McNeil, Legs, and Gillian McCain, eds. *Please Kill Me: The Uncensored Oral History of Punk.* New York: Penguin Books, 1997.

Mitchell, Tim. *Sedition and Alchemy: A Biography of John Cale.* London: Peter Owen, 2003.

Ruskin, Yvonne Sewall. *High on Rebellion: Inside the Underground and Max's Kansas City.* New York: Thunder's Mouth Press, 1998.

Schwartz, Delmore. *In Dreams Begin Responsibilities and Other Stories.* New York: New Directions, 1978.

Somma, Robert, ed. *No One Waved Good-bye. A Casualty Report on Rock and Roll.* New York: Outerbridge & Dienstfrey, 1971. (Includes an essay by Lou Reed, "Fallen Knights & Fallen Ladies," discussing the death of Brian Epstein.)

Witt, Richard. *Nico: The Life and Lies of an Icon.* London: Virgin Books, 1993.

3 | A Nice Jewish Boy

AI: Marc Bell, Thomas Erdelyi, Danny Fields, Linda Stein, Everett True, Arturo Vega.

Bessman, Jim. *Ramones: An American Band.* New York: St. Martin's Press, 1993.

Gabler, Neal. *An Empire of Their Own: How the Jews Invented Hollywood.* New York: Crown, 1988.

True, Everett. *Hey Ho Let's Go: The Story of the Ramones.* London: Omnibus Press, 2002.

4 | Suicide Is Painful

AI: Clinton Heylin, Lydia Lunch, David Nobakht, Martin Rev, Chris Stein, Alan Vega.

Heylin, Clinton. *From the Velvets to the Voidoids: A Pre-Punk History for a Post-Punk World.* New York: Penguin, 1993.

Nobakht, David. *Suicide: No Compromise.* London: SAF, 2005.

5 | I'm Straight!

AI: Victor Bockris, Asa Brebner, Ernie Brooks, John Felice, Jerry Harrison, Joe Harvard, Tim Mitchell.

Brooks, Ernie. Liner notes to the Modern Lovers' *Precise Modern Lovers Order: Live in Berkeley and Boston.* Rounder, 1994.

Miller, Arthur. *Death of a Salesman.* New York: Viking, 1949.

Mitchell, Tim. *There's Something About Jonathan: Jonathan Richman and the Modern Lovers.* London: Peter Owen, 1999.

Richman, Jonathan. Quoted in liner notes to *Twenty-three Great Recordings by Jonathan Richman and the Modern Lovers.* Castle, 1993.

6 | The Ten Nuggets

AI: Roberta Bayley, Victor Bockris, Richard Hell, Lenny Kaye, Howie Klein, Mickey Leigh (Mitchell Hyman), Richard Meltzer, Chris Stein, Mark Suall.

Bangs, Lester. *Psychotic Reactions and Carburetor Dung: The Work of a Legendary Critic: Rock 'n' Roll as Literature and Literature as Rock 'n' Roll.* New York: Anchor, 1988.

Bockris, Victor, and Roberta Bayley. *Patti Smith: An Unauthorized Biography.* New York: Simon & Schuster, 1999.

DeRogatis, Jim. *Let It Blurt: The Life and Times of Lester Bangs, America's Greatest Rock Critic.* New York: Broadway, 2000.

Johnstone, Nick. *Patti Smith: A Biography.* London: Omnibus Press, 1997.

Kaye, Lenny. *Nuggets: Original Artyfacts from the First Psychedelic Era (1965–1968).* Elektra, 1972. [The original double album was re-released on CD with three additional CDs' worth of material by Rhino Records in 1999 under the same name. The liner notes for both were used here.]

Meltzer, Richard. *A Whore Like the Rest of Us: The Music Writings of Richard Meltzer.* Cambridge, MA: Da Capo Press, 2000.

Pearlman, Sandy. Liner notes for the thirtieth anniversary re-release of Patti Smith's *Horses.* Arista, 2005.

7 | The Fiddler on the Bowery

AI: Daniel Brown, Seyom Brown, deerfrance, Annie Golden, Hilly Kristal, Genya Ravan.

WC: www.cbgb.com, www.scc.rutgers.edu/njh/Homesteads/jersey.htm

Buhle, Paul. *From the Lower East Side to Hollywood: Jews in American Popular Culture.* New York: Verso, 2004.

Brazis, Tamar, ed. *CBGB & OMFUG: Thirty Years from the Home of Underground Rock.* New York: Harry N. Abrams, 2005.

Kozak, Roman. *This Ain't No Disco: The Story of CBGB.* Boston: Faber & Faber, 1988.

8 | Juidos 'n' Decaf Italians

AI: Snooky Bellomo, Richard Blum, Bebe Buell, Scott Kempner, Richard Meltzer, J. P. Patterson, Camilla Saly, Andy Shernoff, Susan Wegzyn.

WC: www.thedictators.com/neworder.html, www.thedictators.com, www.furious.com/perfect/meltzer.html

Antonia, Nina. *The New York Dolls: Too Much Too Soon.* London: Omnibus Press, 2003.

Goldstein, Richard. *Goldstein's Greatest Hits: A Book Mostly About Rock 'n' roll.* New York: Tower, 1970.

Gross, Jason. Interview with Richard Meltzer. *Perfect Sounds Forever,* August 2000 (http://www.furious.com/perfect/meltzer.html).

Holmstrom, John, and Mark Rosenthal. "The Dictators Story." *PUNK,* 1977 (http://www.thedictators.com/punkmag.html).

Linna, Miriam. "The Dictators—Science Gone Out the Window." *New Order* (Issue Two), 1977 (http://www.thedictators.com/neworder.html).

Meltzer, Richard. *The Aesthetics of Rock.* Cambridge, MA: Da Capo Press, 1987.

Popoff, Martin. *Blue Öyster Cult: Secrets Revealed!* Simi Valley, CA: Metal Blade Records, 2004.

Price, Richard. *The Wanderers.* New York: Houghton Mifflin, 1974.

———. *Bloodbrothers.* New York: Houghton Mifflin, 1976.

9 | A Jewish American Band

AI: Marc Bell (Marky Ramone), Tomas Erdelyi (Tommy Ramone), Danny Fields, Mitchell Hyman (Mickey Leigh), Gary Kurfirst, Ida Langsam, Charlotte Lesher, Monte Melnick, Steve Miller, Kevin Patrick, Daniel Rey, George Seminara, Andy Shernoff, Everett True, Arturo Vega.

WC: www.ramones.com

Bessman, Jim. *The Ramones: An American Band.* New York: St. Martin's Press, 1993.

Gilman, Sander L. *Franz Kafka: The Jewish Patient.* London: Routledge, 1995.

Kafka, Franz. *Kafka's Diaries.* New York: Schocken Books, 1988. Entry for January 8, 1914.

Melnick, Monte A., and Frank Meyer. *On the Road with the Ramones.* London: Sanctuary, 2003.

Piccarella, John. "Interview: Tommy and Marky Ramone." *Perfect Sound Forever*, February 2005 (http://cc.msnscache.com/cache.aspx?q=2952139810221&lan g=en-US&mkt=en-US&FORM=CVRE).

True, Everett. *Hey Ho Let's Go: The Story of the Ramones.* London: Omnibus Press, 2002.

10 | *Der Übermensch!!!*

AI: Will Eisner, Neil Gaiman, John Holmstrom, Jonathan Lethem.

Chabon, Michael. *The Amazing Adventures of Kavalier and Clay.* New York: Picador, 2001.

Charles, Steve. "Rites of Violence: From King David to David Mamet: An Interview with *Men of Blood* Author Warren Rosenberg." *Wabash Magazine*, Winter 1999 (http://www.wabash.edu/magazine/1999/winter/features/ritesofviolence.htm).

Eisner, Will. *A Contract with God and Other Tenement Stories.* New York: Baronet Books, 1978.

———. "The Graphic Novel as Art." Keynote Address at The Graphic Novel: A 20th Anniversary Conference on an Emerging Literary and Artistic Medium. University of Massachusetts, Amherst, 1996.

Gross, Terry. Interview with Gene Simmons. *Fresh Air*. National Public Radio, February 4, 2002 (http://www.maniahill.com/funny/Gene_Simmons_Terry_Gross_Fresh_Air_02_04_2002.htm).

Howe, Irving, ed. *A Treasury of Yiddish Stories*. New York: Viking, 1954.

Lethem, Jonathan. *The Fortress of Solitude*. New York: Vintage, 2004.

Rosenberg, Warren. *Legacy of Rage: Jewish Masculinity, Violence, and Culture*. Amherst: University of Massachusetts Press, 2001.

Simmons, Gene. *KISS and Make-up*. New York: Three Rivers Press, 2001.

11 | A Jewish Hell

AI: Roberta Bayley, Richard Hell, Ivan Julian, Richard Meltzer, Leif E. Sorensen, Marvin Taylor.

WC: www.richardhell.com, http://dlib.nyu.edu:8083/falesead/servlet/SaxonServlet?source=hell.xml&style=saxon01f2002.xsl (Hell Papers at NYU)

Bockris, Victor. "Susan Sontag Meets Richard Hell." In *Beat Punks*. New York: Da Capo Press, 2000.

Hell, Richard, Papers. Fales Library and Special Collections, Elmer Holmes Bobst Library, New York University.

———, ed. *GENESIS : GRASP # 5/6*. New York: Genesis : Grasp Press, 1971.

———, and the Voidoids. *Blank Generation*. Sire, 1977.

———. *ARTIFACT: Notebooks from Hell, 1974–1980*. New York: Hanuman, 1992.

———. *The Voidoid*. Hove, UK: Codex, 1996.

———. *Raw Periphery #1*. San Jose, CA: Slave Labor Graphics, 1997.

———. *Go Now*. New York: Scribner, 1997.

———. *WEATHER*. New York: CUZ Editions, 1998.

———. *Hot and Cold: Essays poems lyrics notebooks pictures fiction*. New York: PowerHouse, 2001.

Stern, Theresa [Richard Hell and Tom Verlain, pseud.]. *Wanna Go Out?* New York: Dot Books, 1973.

12 | The Shiksa Goddess

AI: Tish and Snooky Bellomo, Elda Gentile, Richard Gottehrer, Debbie Harry, Gary Lachman (Valentine), Chris Stein.

WC: http://www.livedaily.com/artists/discography/album/R%20%20%20549916.html

Bockris, Victor. *Beat Punks*. New York: Da Capo Press, 2000.

Brazier, David. "Craig Leon: On Blondie." *Pogues in Print*, 1989 (http://www.pogues.com/Print/JJones/CLeon.html).

Epstein, Lawrence. *The Haunted Smile: The Story of Jewish Comedians in America*. New York: Public Affairs, 2001.

Harry, Debbie, Chris Stein, and Victor Bockris. *Making Tracks: The Rise of Blondie.* New York: Da Capo Press, 1998.

Hoover, Elizabeth. "The House That Pop Built." *American Heritage Entertainment,* November 7, 2005.

Lachman, Gary (Valentine). *New York Rocker: My Life in the Blank Generation.* Oxford: Sidgwick & Jackson, 2002.

Metz, Allan. *Blondie, From Punk to the Present.* Springfield, MO: Musical Legacy Publications, 2002.

13 | Hotsy-Totsy Nazi *Schatze*

AI: Thomas Erdelyi, Neil Gaiman, Gyda Gash, Debbie Harry, Richard Meltzer, Glenn O'Brien, Martin Popoff, Genya Ravan, Peter Robbins, Camilla Saly, Frank Secich, Andy Shernoff, Sylvie Simmons, Chris Stein.

WC: http://www.richardhell.com/cgi-bin/forum/showmessage.asp?messageID=7492, http://www.deepleafproductions.com/wilsonlibrary/texts/krassner-lenny.html

Dylan, Bob, "With God on Our Side." *The Times They Are A-Changin'.* Columbia, 1963.

Gainsbourg, Serge. *Rock Around the Bunker.* Universal/Polygram, 1975.

Hell, Richard. Talk on Jewish-American novelist Nathaniel West at Teachers & Writers Collaborative, December 7, 2005. Available on CD from Roy Scuggs at Richard Hell Web site.

Simmons, Sylvie. *Serge Gainsbourg: A Fistful of Gitanes.* Cambridge, MA: Da Capo Press, 2002.

Sontag, Susan. "Notes on 'Camp.'" *Partisan Review,* 1964. Also in *Against Interpretation and Other Essays.* New York: Farrar, Straus & Giroux, 1966.

14 | The New JAPS (Jewish American Punks)

AI: Mariah Aguiar, Judith Antonelli, Scott Beibin, Tish and Snooky Bellomo, Jennifer Bleyer, Albert Bouchard, deerfrance, Deborah Frost, Annie Golden, Debbie Harry, Nomy Lamm, Lydia Lunch, Richard Meltzer, Molly Neuman, Mariah Raha, Genya Ravan, Rina, Peter Robbins, Lynne Tillman, Holly Vincent, Allison Wolfe.

WC: http://en.wikipedia.org/wiki/SidandNancy

Antonelli, Judith. "Pornographic Ideology at Heart of Anti-Semitism." *Jewish Advocate,* February 20, 1986. 11– continued on 23.

———. "Analyst Decries Pornographic Images in Israeli Mass Media." *Jewish Advocate,* April 2, 1987. 1.

Bilski, Emily D., and Emily Braun, eds. *Jewish Women and Their Salons: The Power of Conversation.* New York: Jewish Museum, and New Haven: Yale University Press, 2005.

Dworkin, Andre. "Israel: Whose Country Is It Anyway?" *Ms.* 1, no. 2 (September/October 1990).

Epstein, Lawrence. *The Haunted Smile: The Story of Jewish Comedians in America.* New York: Public Affairs, 2001.

Gaines, Donna. *Misfit's Manifesto: The Spiritual Journey of a Rock & Roll Heart: A Memoir.* New York: Random House, 2003.

Juno, Andrea, ed. *Angry Women in Rock*, vol. 1. New York: Juno Books, 1996.

——— and V. Vale, eds. *Angry Women*. San Francisco: Re/Search Publications, 1991.

Raha, Maria. *Cinderella's Big Score: Women of the Punk and Indie Underground.* Emeryville, CA: Seal Press, 2005.

Ravan, Genya. *Lollipop Lounge: Memoirs of a Rock and Roll Refugee.* New York: Watson-Guptill, 2004.

Rossi, Melissa. *Courtney Love: Queen of Noise.* New York: Pocket Books, 1996.

Ruttenberg, Danya. *Yentl's Revenge: The Next Wave of Jewish Feminism.* Seattle: Seal Press, 2001.

Sessums, Kevin. "Love Child." *Vanity Fair*, June 1995.

15 | Write Yiddish, Cast British

AI: Vivien Goldman, Don Letts, Malcolm McLaren, Phil Strongman.

WC: www.amazon.com/gp/product/0688180035/qid=1140020734/sr=1-2/ref=sr_1_2/103-5676108-7196636?s=books&v=glance&n=283155 and www.mtholyoke.edu/courses/rschwart/hist255/bohem/ttrilby.html

Alvarez, A. "A Double Bind." *New York Review of Books* 51, no. 20 (December 16, 2004).

Antonia, Nina. *The New York Dolls: Too Much Too Soon.* London: Omnibus Press, 2003.

Bromberg, Craig. *The Wicked Ways of Malcolm McLaren.* New York: Harper & Row, 1989.

The Clash. "Rock the Casbah." *Combat Rock.* Epic, 1982.

Geller, Deborah. *The Brian Epstein Story.* London: Faber & Faber, 1999.

Lydon, John, with Keith Zimmerman and Kent Zimmerman. *Rotten: No Irish, No Blacks, No Dogs.* New York: St. Martin's Press, 1994.

Savage, Jon. *England's Dreaming: Anarchy, Sex Pistols, Punk Rock, and Beyond.* New York: St. Martin's Press, 1993.

Siouxsie and the Banshees. "Love in a Void." Polydor, 1979. (Appeared on *Once Upon a Time: The Singles*, 1980, but was never officially released with its original offensive line, "Too many Jews for my liking.")

Smith, Patti. "Rock 'n' Roll Nigger." *Easter.* Arista, 1978.

Spark, Muriel. *The Girls of Slender Means.* New York: Avon Books, 1963.

———. *Mandelbaum's Gate.* New York: Avon Books, 1965.

Spungen, Deborah. *And I Don't Want to Live This Life*. New York: Random House, 1983.

16 | A Post-Punk History of a Pre-Cool Jew World

AI: Scott Beibin, David Berman, Steven Blush, David Chevan, Anthony Coleman, Michael Dorf, Vivien Goldman, Lisa Law, Alan Light, Gary Lucas, Lydia Lunch, Marc Ribot, Eve Schlapik, Lynne Tillman, Russell Wolinsky, John Zorn.

WC: http://www.progressiveears.com/asp/reviews.asp?albumID=2216&bhcp=1

Blush, Steven. *American Hardcore*. Los Angeles: Feral House, 2001.

Buhle, Paul. *From the Lower East Side to Hollywood: Jews in American Popular Culture*. New York: Verso, 2004.

Kaplan, Fred. "Horn of Plenty—The Composer Who Knows No Boundaries." *New Yorker*, June 14, 1999. 74–84.

Ribot, Marc. "Black Music 1997," "The Representation of Jewish Identity in Downtown Music," and "The Way We Weren't." Unpublished essays.

Pavement. "Stereo." *Brighten the Corners*. Matador, 1999.

General Reference

Berrarde, Scott R. *Stars of David: Rock 'n' Roll's Jewish Stories*. Hanover, NH: Brandeis University Press, 2003.

Billig, Michael. *Rock 'n' Roll Jews*. Syracuse, NY: Syracuse University Press, 2001.

Gimarc, George. *Punk Diary: 1970–1979*. New York: St. Martin's Press, 1994.

Lunch, Lydia. *Paradoxia: A Predator's Diary*. New York: Creation Books, 1997.

Moore, Deborah, Dash. *GI Jews: How World War II Changed a Generation*. Cambridge, MA: Belknap Press, 2004.

O'Dair, Barbara, ed. *Trouble Girls: The Rolling Stone Book of Women in Rock*. New York: Random House, 1997.

Oseary, Guy. *Jews Who Rock*. New York: St. Martin's Press, 2001.

Sloman, Larry "Ratso." *On the Road with Bob Dylan*. New York: Three Rivers Press, 1978.

Spector, Ronnie, with Vince Waldron. *Be My Baby: How I Survived Mascara, Miniskirts, and Madness; or, My Life as a Fabulous Ronette*. New York: New American Library, 2004.

Spitz, Marc, and Brendan Mullen. *We Got the Neutron Bomb: The Untold Story of L.A. Punk*. New York: Three Rivers Press, 2001.

Tabb, George. *Playing Right Field: A Jew Grows in Greenwich*. Brooklyn: Soft Skull Press, 2004.

INDEX